Jean Daniélou's
Doxological Humanism

Jean Daniélou's Doxological Humanism

Trinitarian Contemplation and Humanity's True Vocation

Marc C. Nicholas

James Clarke & Co

James Clarke & Co
P.O. Box 60
Cambridge
CB1 2NT
United Kingdom

www.jamesclarke.co
publishing@jamesclarke.co

ISBN: 978 0 227 17404 3

British Library Cataloguing in Publication Data
A record is available from the British Library

First published by James Clarke & Co, 2013

Copyright © Marc C. Nicholas, 2012

Published by arrangement
with Pickwick Publications

All rights reserved. No part of this edition may be reproduced, stored electronically or in any retrieval system, or transmitted in any form or by any means, electronic, mechanical, photocopying, recording, or otherwise, without prior written permission from the Publisher (permissions@jamesclarke.co).

Contents

ONE   The Split between Theology and Spirituality   1

TWO   History and Prayer   10

THREE   Prayer, Trinity, and Mission   45

FOUR   Prayer and the Spiritual Life   93

FIVE   The Crisis of Interiority and the Truly Human City   124

SIX   Daniélou's Doxological Humanism   146

Bibliography   163

ONE

The Split between Theology and Spirituality

Hans Urs von Balthasar begins his important essay "Theology and Sanctity" with the observation that "in the whole of Catholic theology there is hardly anything that is less noticed, yet more deserving of notice, than the fact that, since the great period of Scholasticism, there have been few theologians who were saints."[1] In this remark is summed up the history of the divide between theology and spirituality that reached its acme with the Neo-Scholasticism of the nineteenth and twentieth centuries. Though this neo-Scholasticism waned after the middle of the twentieth century, it seems to be attempting to extend its influence again at the turn of the twentieth century.[2] Von Balthasar's entire theological project centered on the deconstruction of such a dichotomy. In the essay, he notes the pre-Scholastic naiveté concerning such a divide, the perpetuation of the divergence until the middle of the twentieth century, and the attempt to overcome the split that was commensurate with the overthrow of Neo-Scholastic theology prior to Vatican II.

Pre-Scholastic Theology and Spirituality

When one looks at the great personages of the early church, one is struck by the fact that most of them were both pastors and theologians. Their lives were models of the unity of the Christian life and the elucidation of

---

1. Von Balthasar, "Theology and Sanctity," 181.
2. Candler, "New Scholasticism," forthcoming.

Christian truth: a testament to a complete understanding of truth that "consist[ed] precisely in this living exposition of theory in practice and of knowledge carried into action."[3] Von Balthasar notes the New Testament teaching concerning the office of teachers and pastors. Both Ephesians 4:11 and I Corinthians 12:29 attest to the distinctiveness of the roles of pastor and teacher. However, one need not maintain the possibility of distinct roles to the detriment of seeing both offices in a single individual. Not all pastors are teachers, and not all teachers are pastors, but one should not be surprised to see the two offices coincident in a single individual since they are so closely related by Paul in his epistles. Therefore, it should be no surprise to see that the greatest Christians of the early centuries of the Church are both pastors and teachers: Irenaeus, Gregory of Nyssa, Athanasius, Chrysostom, and many others.[4] This unity of spirituality and truth is seen in a number of Johannine passages. The author of I John maintains: "Whoever says, "I know him," but does not keep his commandments is a liar, and the truth is not in him" (I Jn 2:4); and, later on in the letter, "Whoever is without love does not know God" (I Jn 4:8). "There is simply no real truth" von Balthasar contends, "which does not have to be incarnated in an act or in some action, so that the incarnation of Christ is the criterion of all real truth . . ., and 'walking in the truth' is the way the believer possesses the truth."[5] Indeed the New Testament and the early Fathers consistently exhibit a complete naiveté concerning such a divide. Instead, the writers of the New Testament and the early Fathers were "complete personalities," who were unable to envisage the separation of theology and spirituality. Even a cursory perusal of New Testament and Patristic sources would indicate the fact. Von Balthasar notes that it "would not only be idle but contrary to the very conception of the Fathers to attempt to divide their works into those dealing with doctrine and those dealing with the Christian life (spirituality)."[6] Perhaps Origen is the clearest indication of this fact. Origen left the Church an enormous amount of literature. Though it has been attempted by some modern interpreters, to divide his works into the speculative, polemical, spiritual, and hermeneutical would be artificial and

---

3. Ibid.

4. Von Balthasar notes that even those who were not both pastors and teachers in the monastic and mystical traditions "bring out still more clearly the union of doctrine and life." Ibid., 182.

5. Ibid., 181–82.

6. Ibid., 183.

detrimental to Origen's thought and to one's understanding of the work he bequeathed to the Church. Though some of his works may have been more or less practical or speculative or pastoral, each of his works has the primary aim of "expounding the word of God, which is as much a word of life as a word of truth."[7]

Von Balthasar maintains that this original unity was maintained for centuries. He contends that it was not until scholastic methodology gained prominence that such a division was made possible: "The early medieval thinkers in the West, under the aegis of Augustine, did not depart from this basic concept. Anselm, himself abbot, bishop and doctor of the Church, knew no other canon of truth than the unity of knowledge and life. The same may be said of Bede, Bernard and Peter Damian. But as theology increasingly took on a 'scholastic' form, and Aristotelianism burst in like an elemental force, the naïve unity hitherto accepted was gravely shaken."[8]

The Rise of Scholastic Theology

The rise of the Scholastic method within theological discourse radically transformed the way theology was envisioned from its bases and method to its purpose and sources. This change had a far-reaching effect on theology which would contribute to theology's own self-understanding. Whereas theology was initially more of a meditation on and exposition of God's self-disclosure in the Word, in the new style of theological discourse practiced by the schoolmen, theology increasingly became the methodical parsing of abstract truth which was dissociated from the concrete realities of an embodied Christianity. It must be noted that medieval Scholasticism made enormous contributions to the development of the Church's own self-understanding. Thinkers such as Thomas, Bonaventure and Albert were able to maintain a balance between theology and spirituality. However, it appears that it took such singular minds to keep the method from overtaking the aim.

Von Balthasar maintained that the progress attained by scholasticism primarily lay in the philosophical realm. Though of great importance, this method placed theology alongside philosophy as a coordinating system (sometimes as a competing system) for the exposition of truth.

---

7. Ibid.
8. Ibid., 184.

Von Balthasar writes of the advances of philosophical methodology of scholasticism:

> The booty in this case, however, was primarily philosophical, and only indirectly theological. Philosophy began to emerge as a special discipline alongside theology, with its own concept of philosophical truth, which was perfectly correct in its own sphere, and could lay no claim to superior content of revealed truth. *Adequatio intellectus ad rem* [conformity of the mind to reality]: this definition envisaged, primarily, only the theoretical side of truth. The intimate connection was seen, and indeed emphasized, between the true and the good as the transcendental properties of the one being, but it was looked at more from the human standpoint, in the mutual presupposition of intellect and will . . . , than in their objective mutual inclusion, or real identity. Philosophy, as a doctrine of natural being and excluding revelation, could not know that the highest mode of interpreting that philosophical definition of truth must be a trinitarian one.[9]

The scholastic method, left in inadequate hands, would provide disastrous results. The problem was that most practitioners were not equipped to maintain the balance between method and the integrity of theology and spirituality.

M. D. Chenu gives Abelard as a prime example of a practitioner of the scholastic method who was unable to balance the method and theology as practiced prior to Scholasticism. "In the west, the classic case of this failing is that of Abelard. This champion of dialectic was the first whose genius promulgated the laws of conceptual thinking in their application to theological knowledge. He is called, not without cause, the founder of scholastic theology. But in the intoxication of his discovery he could not maintain the proper spiritual attitude towards the awful silence of the mystery."[10] Chenu consistently commends individuals such as Abelard for the substantial contribution they were able to make, while at the same time chastising them for their inability to retain the proper spiritual balance. "It is in prayer and

---

9. Ibid., 185.

10. Chenu, *La Théologie est-elle une Science?*, 41; ET: *Is Theology a Science?*, 40. "Les cas classique e cette défaillance, en Occident. Est celui d'Abélard. Le chevalier de la dialectique, qui le premier eut le genie d'énoncer les lois du language conceptual dans l'elaboration du savoir théologique, et qu'on appelle à cause de cela, non sans raison, le fondateur de la théologie scholastique, ne sut pas, dans l'ivresse de se découverte , conserver a juste sensibilité spirituelle au respect, au silence du mystère." All subsequent English translations of this text will be Armytage's translation unless noted otherwise.

devotion, and in the profoundest sense of the devotion, that theology, the understanding of the Word of God, is born and lives. 'This sacred science,' reads the office of Albert the Great, 'is acquired through prayer and devotion rather than through study'—words not to be taken as an epigram but as a structural necessity. A theology that could be true without being devout would be a sort of monster."[11]

Furthermore, the Aristotelianism of the thirteenth century also opened up the space for the development of the concept of natural science, which would in turn give birth to a general secularism. Within this arena, the greatest of the practitioners of Scholasticism were able to transpose the concepts and methodology of Aristotelianism and the secular sciences into the field of Christian theology. This transposition had the effect of raising the method of the secular sciences to the "plane of the sacred, and so to import to [them] a real Christian ethos."[12] As a result, post-scholastic theology became a rational exposition of traditional theology (Von Balthasar uses the terms "biblical theology"), turning theology on its head. As the work of theology proceeded after scholasticism, the rational framework that had been attached to theology became more rigid with each succeeding generation. As a result of this process, the philosophical bases of theology usurped the position of tradition and scripture and became the arbiter of the faith, exercising authority over the entire theological process.[13]

The Effects of the Split between Theology and Spirituality

Von Balthasar concisely sums up the main effect of the split between theology and spirituality opened by the over-reliance on scholastic method. The period following the advent of scholastic theology "saw the disappearance of the 'complete' theologian . . . , the theologian who is also a saint. In fact, spiritual men were turned away from a theology which was overlaid and overloaded with secular philosophy—with the result that alongside dogmatic theology, meaning always the central science which consists in the

---

11. Ibid., 41–42. "C'est dans la prière, dans l'adoration, dans la devotion, au sens profond du mot, que naît et cit la théologie, l'intelligence de la Parole de Dieu. «Cette science sacrée, est-il dit dans l'office du maître Albert le Grand, s'acquiert par l'oraison et la devotion plus que par l'étude». Ne prenons pas cela comme une bon parole, mais comme une exigence structural. Une théologie qui pourrait être vraie sans être pieuse, serait en quelque sorte monstrueuse."

12. Von Balthasar, "Theology and Sanctity," 186.

13. Ibid.

exposition of revealed truth, there came into being a new science of the 'Christian life,' one derived from the mysticism of the Middle Ages and achieving independence in the *devotio moderna*."[14] The culpability need not fall solely on the introduction of scholastic method and the subsequent exacerbation by the neo-scholasticism of later centuries. Von Balthasar clearly notes that the "saints" were as culpable for the division as any other. While scholasticism pushed the practitioners of the spiritual life to the side, the "spirituals" all too readily retreated from the schools to widen the gap between theology and spirituality to an even greater degree.[15] "The saints, intimidated by the conceptual entanglements drawn round the gospel truth, no longer dare to collaborate in the necessary work of the exposition of doctrine, or think themselves qualified to do so. They leave dogma to the prosaic work of the School, and become—lyrical poets."[16]

This situation ends in a number of exacerbating results. There developed among the spirituals a concern to describe and delineate the affective states of ascetical and mystical theology.[17] Though this phenomenon can be seen earlier—particularly in the Spanish mysticism of the sixteenth century—it is in the nineteenth and twentieth centuries which demonstrate the most concrete instantiation of this fact. In the manuals of such thinkers as Adolphe Tanquerey, the Jesuit Joseph de Guibert and the immensely important Dominican Reginald Garrigou-Lagarange, an elaborate "technology of the self"—to use Mark McIntosh's language—fused the scholastic manualistic style with an extreme concern with delineating the progress of the soul to perfection through the stages of ascetical theology and mystical theology.[18]

---

14. Ibid., 187.

15. Ibid., 188–93.

16. Ibid., 192.

17. The terms ascetical theology and mystical theology came to have very specific and distinct meanings. *Ascetical theology* concerned the "form and progress of the Christian life up to the beginnings of passive contemplation," whereas, *mystical theology* "analyzed further stages up to mystical union." Sheldrake, *Spirituality & History*, 52.

18. McIntosh, *Mystical Theology*, 8. The fusion of the concern for affective mysticism and neo-scholastic method is laid out in Sheldrake, *Spirituality and History*, 52–55.

Prospects for Reintegration

In Mark McIntosh's contribution to Blackwell's "Challenges in Contemporary Theology" series, he, like von Balthasar, notes that theology, when it separates itself from mystical experience (or as McIntosh and Bernard McGinn prefer, "mystical consciousness), it "becomes ever more methodically refined but unable to know or to speak of the very mysteries at the heart of Christianity."[19] Likewise, mysticism, when it isolates itself from speculative theology, "becomes rootless, easily hijacked by individualistic consumerism." But, unlike William Johnston, who holds little hope for the reintegration of theology and spirituality (believing that theologians remain "unregenerate"), McIntosh believes that there are identifiable avenues in the study of theology and spirituality which may in fact lead to such a reintegration.[20]

Even more basic to the discussion than ways in which academic theology can reacquaint itself with spirituality, it appears that McIntosh's implicit, and more profound, solution to the problem of the split between theology and spirituality entails a view of the human person that disallows any division between one's articulation of Christianity and one's own lived "spiritual stance" concerning concrete events and situations. More important than whether or not one speaks of the encounter with God by means of "divine grounding language" or by means of "union language," more important than whether one describes the mystical encounter with God in terms of "mystical consciousness" or in terms of "mystical experience," McIntosh holds up the example of those individuals who exhibit an understanding of the encounter of divine presence by the manner in which they articulate that encounter and how they live their lives in light of their own understanding of the encounter with God. Here McIntosh gives the example of Edith Stein, who, on the night of her arrest by two German SS officers, demonstrated that her "theological understanding of what she saw as the self-sacrificing pattern of divine life grew increasingly more incarnate in her own spiritual stance. She repeatedly articulated her belief that a spirituality of compassion and responsibility for others enabled one to contribute in some limited personal way to the unlimited self-giving that she understood to be constitutive of God's existence—a self-giving embodied for her in the history of Jesus."[21]

19. McIntosh, *Mystical Theology*, 10.
20. Johnston, *Inner Eye of Love*, 195–96.
21. McIntosh, *Mystical Theology*, 4.

This picture of an individual who embodies the unity of the spiritual and theological indicates in a clear manner that the split between spirituality and theology is only entirely mitigated by integrated personalities. For Edith Stein, McIntosh tells us, "her work as an interpreter of major theologians such as Pseudo-Dionysius the Areopagite, Thomas Aquinas, and John of the Cross was all of a piece with her spirituality."[22] It is in such personalities that we are able to identify a "pattern for the re-weaving of spirituality and theology," a pattern found in "complete personalities"—to use von Balthasar's parlance—who are examples of an integrated anthropology.

McIntosh rightly points out that at its very roots the split between theology and spirituality seems to be a bifurcation of the individual person and represents a defective view of the human person—what would be described in theological short-hand as a defective anthropology. The answer to the gap between the disciplines is not bridged through methodological or academic orientation, but rather is achieved by realizing who we are. In a brief essay for *L'Osservatore Romano*, Jean Daniélou notes that investigation into the arena of who we are as human beings typically falls short because it fails to assess the human person in its entirety. The material sciences fail in their account of the *humanum*—as do the psychological sciences—in that they fail to see what is human in its totality and in turn omit what is most essential to humanity. Therefore, Daniélou reflects, "We must ask ourselves what these . . . types of inquiry lack. What they lack is, essentially, that they do not lead to the [essential] dimension of man at the core of his existence: the relationship with a God by whom he was begotten and for whom he was created."[23] Indeed, Daniélou maintains that "the idea that there is in our life two poles which are opposed—a human pole and a divine pole—by no means corresponds to the true Biblical conception of humanity."[24] The human person must be seen in its entirety which entails accounting for that which makes humanity truly human. This essential quality of the human person is found in humanity's participation in divine life without which humanity is a mutilated form of its true identity. As Daniélou notes, "There is in the relationship with God a relationship that constitutes the very being of man."[25]

---

22. McIntosh, *Mystical Theology*, 3.
23. Daniélou, "Man in Search of Himself," 10.
24. Daniélou, "La Vérité de l'Homme," 4.
25. Daniélou, "Man in Search of Himself," 10.

Conclusion

Daniélou believes that a proper understanding of humanity must entail an assessment of it as a unity. To propose that the material aspect of humanity and the spiritual aspect of humanity can be partitioned from each other is to "fall victim to the most detestable form of idealism which separates spiritual existence from its material and sociological substratum. *It is our profound belief that man is a unity; that is to say, that there is a fundamental connection between the problems of the body and those of the soul.*"[26] Thus, any true humanism is an integral humanism which views humanity in its totality.

Secondly, an essential aspect of this unified view of the human person is its doxological nature. For Daniélou, "prayer is an absolutely universal human vocation."[27] Therefore, he concludes, prayer is in itself "a fundamental part of all humanism."[28] To fulfill a basic quality of one's fullest expression of his humanity is to participate in the adoration, worship and contemplation involved in the life of prayer.

---

26. Daniélou, *L'Oraison Problème Politique*, 27; ET: *Prayer as Political Problem*, 27. "Le méconnaître serait pécher par cet idéalism que nous détestons par-dessus tout, car il sépare l'existence spirituelle de son substrat matériel et sociologique. Or nous croyons profondément que l'homme est un, c'est-à-dire qu'il y a une relation fondamentale entre les problémes du corps et ceux de l'âme." All subsequent English translations of this text will be Kirwan's translation unless noted otherwise. See also Daniélou, "L'Oraison comme problème politique," 62–73.

27. Ibid., 28–29. "L'oraison est . . . en élément constitutif de la vie humaine."

28. Ibid., 24. "Prière est . . . un dimension fondamentale de tout humanisme."

TWO

History and Prayer

ONE MIGHT WONDER WHY an exposition of Daniélou's ideas concerning prayer should begin with his theology of history. Indeed, most books on prayer have little to say about history and many times elide it altogether.[1] Contrariwise, Daniélou makes it a point to consider history in *Contemplation: Croissance de l'Eglise* with roughly a quarter of the small volume occupying itself with the relationship of prayer and history.[2] Prior to a full exposition of Daniélou's understanding of history, it is important to note how he relates the two areas in *Contemplation*.

Daniélou notes that to enter into prayer is—among many things—to rediscover God through a wonderment at the *magnalia Dei* ("wonders of God"), through one's recognition of one's own relationship to God as one of his children and a coheir with Christ, and finally as an entering into God's guiding of the story of history. It is this last point that is of importance to us here. Daniélou writes, "prayer is an entering into the ways of God an acceptance of the divine plan that God carries out in the world. It means becoming aware of the God who is coming, and not simply of the God who is. If we were only aware of the God who is, we might have the feeling that prayer withdraws us from the movement of life, and that there is an opposition between the contemplative life and the movement of history. But this is quite false. The God who is, is also the God who is coming, and the entire world is the accomplishment of the plan that comes from God and

---

1. It is important to note that a major critique of late neo-scholasticism by *ressourcement* thinkers is that it had no historical sense.
2. Daniélou, *Contemplation: Croissance de L'Eglise*.

is moving toward God."[3] This passage contains some important elements of Daniélou's theology of history which will be more fully discussed later but should be noted here. The vocabulary of *venir* and *être* points to the concept of advent (*adventus/venir*; coming-advent) which plays a vital role in Daniélou's coordination of prayer and history and to which he devoted an entire study.[4] Related to the idea of advent is that of a divine plan which God is executing through the events of human history. History is not a series of singular, unrelated events. Daniélou's typological reading of history does not allow for such a radical individualization of the events that make up history. Instead, "advent . . . appears as a pedagogy of the faith. Faith does not consist in the belief that God exists, but that God intervenes in history. This is what seems unreasonable to humans: that at the heart of the framework of ordinary events, in the midst of the determinism of physics and the chains of sociological facts, there are irruptions of God—a properly divine activity—in which God creates, visits, and saves."[5] And, indeed, Daniélou contends, this concern for history is seen in the paradigmatic prayer of the *Our Father*. Daniélou notes, "In the *Our Father* we pray for the fulfillment of God's plan for all humanity; we enter in a certain way into God's own intentions when we ask that his will be done."[6]

---

3. Ibid., 17–18. "Prier, c'est enfin entrer dans les voies de Dieu, dans l'acceptation de dessein divin qui s'accomplit dans le monde; c'est être sensible au Dieu qui vient et pas simplement au Dieu qui est. Si nous n'étions sensible qu'au Dieu qui est, nous pourrions avoir le sentiment que la prière nous retire du mouvement de la vie, et qu'il y a une opposition entre la vie contemplative et le movement de l'histoire. Ce seriat très faux, car le monde entier est l'accomplissement d'un dessein qui vient de Dieu et qui va vers Dieu." ET: *Prayer: The Mission of the Church*. All subsequent English translations of this text will be Schindler's unless noted otherwise.

4. Daniélou, *Le Mystère de l'Avent*; ET: *Advent* and *The Advent of Salvation*. All subsequent English translations of this text will be Sheed's unless noted otherwise.

5. Daniélou, *Contemplation*, 56–57 "L'Avent apparaît ainsi comme une pédagogie de la foi. La foi ne consiste pas à croire que Dieu existe, mais que Dieu intervient dans l'histoire. Et c'est cela qui apparaît invraisemblable à l'homme. Qu'au cœur de la trame des événements ordinaires, au milieu des déterminismes des faits physiques, de l'enchaînement des faits sociologiques, il y ait des irruptions de Dieu, des actions proprement divines, où Dieu crée, visite, sauve."

6. Ibid., 42. "Dans le *Notre Père* nous demandons le réussite du dessein de Dieu en tous les hommes; nous entrons en quelque sorte dans l'intention meme de Dieu quand nous demandons que son œuvre soit accomplice."

History in Twentieth-Century Catholicism

There is a certain sense in which there was a great deal of accord concerning history within twentieth century Catholic theology. Paul Henry notes that "despite their disagreements," those concerned with the idea of history within the context of Christian theology were "unanimous in their admission that Christianity alone has given and can give meaning to history, and that outside Judeo-Christian revelation or Islam (which is to some degree a Christian heresy) there is no philosophy of history."[7] This accord is commensurate with an understanding of the historical nature of Christianity as a "biblical revelation, which is not a metaphysic but essentially a history."[8] However, the "unanimous" accord must be said to end there, as a great deal of controversy arose around the relationship of history and doctrine.

Of the major thrusts of the renewal in twentieth century Catholicism, foremost within this context, was the sense that "theology should take seriously the concrete historicity of the Church's life and faith."[9] This mandate was thought to be a factor in the revitalization of the Church's increasingly desiccated spirituality. Proponents of renewal under the rubric of *nouvelle théologie* contended that "a theology grounded in historical understanding [would bear] the fruit of authentic spirituality."[10] This spiritual deficit and lack of historical sensibility no doubt was at least in part due to the education of theologians through the neo-scholastic manuals of the nineteenth and twentieth centuries (often pejoratively labeled "Denzinger theology"). Aidan Nichols notes that while this sort of theological formation gave the seminarians of the time a more robust grasp of the faith than their successors, "the drawback was that so crystalline an intellectual structure . . . could not easily be turned into a preaching and catechesis that moved souls."[11] While some Dominicans charged that the *nouvelle théologie* was infected with a historical relativism reminiscent of early twentieth century

---

7. Henry, "Christian Philosophy of History," 421. Daniélou writes, "Il n'est pas nécessaire d'être judéo-chrétien pour croire en l'existence d'un Dieu. Ceci se retrouve dans toutes les religions et constitue la religion comme telle. Mais il est nécessaire d'être judéo-chrétien pour croire dans l'intervention de Dieu, dans l'histoire humaine." *Approches du Christ*, 83.

8. Henry, "Christian Philosophy of History," 425.

9. Mayeski, "Quaestio Disputata: Catholic Theology and the History of Exegesis," 142.

10. Ibid., 149.

11. Nichols, *Catholic Thought Since the Enlightenment*, 131.

History and Prayer

Catholic modernism, the Jesuits of Lyons-Fourvière rejoined that "a certain Scholastic theology possesses the contrary vice in its own thorough insensitivity to history."[12] As de Lubac bitingly retorted to the charge, "si les mauvais jours du modernism sont, grace à Dieu, maintenant loin de nous, les mauvais jours de l'intégrisme ne fussent sur le point de revinir" (If the evil days of Modernism are now, thank God, far from us, the evil days of integralism may be coming back).[13]

In response to the overly abstracted theses of Denzinger theology, there arose, in Germany and Austria, what is today called the Innsbrück school. Rather than heaping thesis upon thesis concerning every imaginable topic, the Innsbrück school represented a "slimline theology" which demonstrated that not all Catholic doctrine carried equal weight.[14] While no less intellectually respectable, the Innsbrück school prioritized its core presentation of the gospel in order to lighten the overly cumbersome apol-

---

12. Nichols, "Thomism and the Nouvelle Théologie," 10.

13. *La Théologie et ses sources*, 95; quoted in Fouilloux, "Dialogue théologique?, 174 and quoted in Nichols, "Thomism and the Nouvelle Théologie," 10. See also "Integralism" and Modernism," in *Sacramentum Mundi*, v. 3, 151–52; v. 4, 99–104. For a distinction between *integralism* and *integrism*, see Milbank, *Theology and Social Theory*, 206–7. Milbank writes, "One's starting point should be the seemingly obscure claim made by the most important of the Latin American 'liberation theologians' . . . that the new theology of grace espoused by the second Vatican Council is what has made liberation theology possible: such, indeed, that liberation theology alone, is to be considered the authentic outworking of post-conciliar Catholic thought. What is alluded to here is the embracing by the council of what one can term the 'integralist revolution.' This means the view that in the concrete, historical humanity there is no such thing as a state of 'pure nature': rather, every person has always already been worked upon by divine grace, with the consequence that one cannot analytically separate 'natural' and 'supernatural' contributions to this integral unity.

"The liberation theologians contend, quite cogently, that the social and political implications of this 'integralism' were not properly realized by the council. Although this was precisely because the council was rightly concerned to repudiate earlier 'integrist' politics. The 'integrist' viewpoint has insisted upon a clerical and hierarchic dominance over all the affairs of secular life, founded upon a 'totalizing' theology which presents a complete system, whose details cannot be questioned without compromising the whole. (This difference between 'integralism' and 'intergrism' should be carefully noted)."

Speaking of Yves Congar's *Vraie et fausse réforme dans l'Église*, Fergus Kerr remarks that "this sectarian tendency to maximize whatever is settled by authority slips into condemning all openness, research, and questioning of received ideas. A Catholic's orthodoxy becomes measurable by the degree of hatred that he shows for those he suspects of heterodoxy. The problem with *intégrisme* is . . . that it has too little confidence in the truth, insufficient love of the truth." *Twentieth-Century Catholic Theologians*, 41.

14. Nichols, *Catholic Thought since the Enlightenment*, 130–33.

ogetic thrust of the manuals.[15] Contrary to manual theology, the Innsbrück school emphasized the traditional theological center of Catholicism in the doctrines of the incarnation and salvation through the person of Christ. While the Innsbrück school had effectively reoriented Catholic thought to a degree, its force was cut short because the "inhibitions on Church activity imposed by the National Socialists overtook Austrian Catholicism with the *Anschluss* of 1938."[16] Even so, while the Innsbrück school somewhat effectively undermined the abstract, dehistoricized propositions of high neo-scholasticism, it did not provide cogent answers to the relationship between dogma and history raised in the previous century in the modernist controversy. It fell to *la nouvelle théologie* to answer this demand.

Much of the debate over history and theology is encapsulated in the episode between Dominicans of Saint-Maximin and Toulouse and the Jesuits of Lyons, especially Daniélou, de Lubac, Bouillard, and others. In the early 1940's, two important series were begun under the guidance of Daniélou and his confreres, *Sources Chretiénnes* and *Théologie*, which immediately came under the suspicion of the prominent Dominicans Marie-Michel Labourdette and, more importantly, Reginald Garrigou-Lagrange.[17] Daniélou gives the purpose for beginning *Sources Chretiénnes* succinctly: "For the latter [the earlier work of Hemmer and Lejay], it was entirely a matter of publishing historical documents, the testimonial artifacts of the faith of the ancients. The new idea is that there is more to ask the Fathers. On this view, the Fathers are not only the veritable witnesses of a bygone state

---

15. The Innsbrück school of theology was a group of theologians who "were decidedly missionary or 'kerygmatic' in orientation. [They] looked for a truly evangelical theology which would identify the central core of the gospel, God in Christ with his good new, and relate all else to that. At Innsbrück a school of kerygmatic theology arose concerned to produce an articulation of the original proclamation in compelling language." Nichols, *Shape of Catholic Theology*, 336–37. Representative of this group is the well-known catecheticist and liturgist Josef Jungmann. Jungmann sought to draw on Scripture and the Liturgy in order to "suggest what was really paramount in Christian faith, the one thing necessary that might get lost in too abundant a plethora of doctrines," Nicholas, *Catholic Thought since the Enlightenment*, 132. See Pierce and Downey, *Source and Summit* for a select but useful bibliography.

16. Nichols, *Catholic Thought since the Enlightenment*, 133.

17. The most recent work on Garrigou-Lagrange is Peddicord, *Sacred Monster of Thomism*, which seeks to present "a more balanced account of his personality and his achievements" (Candler, "The New Scholasticism," forthcoming). For his part, Candler believes that this attempt at a reassessment marks an attempted "resuscitation of [the] errors" committed by Garrigou-Lagrange and his associates. See also Jürgen Mettepenningen, *Nouvelle Théologie New Theology*, 15–29.

History and Prayer

of affairs, they yet provide the most enduring and 'contemporary' nourishment for men of our own day. Indeed, we find in the Fathers categories of thought congenial to the questions being posed in the intellectual dialogues of contemporary thought, categories which scholastic theology unwittingly lost."[18] *Théologie* was chartered with the two-fold aim of a return to the

18. Daniélou, "Les Orientations Présentes de la Pensée Religieuse", 10. "Pour cette dernière, il s'agissait avant tout de publier des documents historiques, témoins de la foi des anciens. La nouvelle pense qu'il y a plus à deander aux Pères. Ils ne sont seulement témoins véritable d'un état de chose révolu; ils sont encore la nourriture la plus actuelle pour des hommes d'aujourd'hui, parce que nous y retrouvons précisément un certain nombre de catégories qui sont celles de la pensée contemporaine et que la théologie scolastique avait perdues." Translated by Peter M. Candler Jr. and Aaron Riches, "Current Trends in Religious Thought," *Communio* (forthcoming), fn. 24. Labourdette notes that this same sentiment is echoed in the introduction to Daniélou's *La Vie Moïse*, "La Théologie et ses sources," 25 n. 1. John Courtney Murray surmises the aim of *Sources Chrétiennes*: "And we know, too, that in the patristic climate of opinion the uninitiated rather tends to gasp for breath. It is to this problem and its solution that the recently inaugurated series of patristic texts . . . directly addresses itself, with altogether remarkable success" (Murray, "Current Theology: *Sources Chrétiennes*," 251; which provides reviews of the first 19 volumes of *Sources Chrétiennes*). "Though familiarity with the cultural and religious milieu and facility of encounter with the Fathers was certainly a goal of de Lubac and Daniélou, it seems that Labourdette had understood the more subtle and underlying aim of the series. It is rather the choice of texts which indicated the theological agenda which lay at the heart of the series. The inaugural volume, Gregory of Nyssa's *Vie de Moïse*, indicated the trajectory of the series. Instead of an Aquinas or a Bonaventure, Gregory of Nyssa established a mystical rather than a scholastic penchant (and concordantly a Greek rather than a Latin tone)." As A. N. Williams notes, "the broader purposes of the series of which it was the inaugural volume (*Théologie*), and the agenda of the first volumes of *Sources chrétiennes* series launched earlier by Daniélou and de Lubac; in all of these, Labourdette claimed to see a devaluation of Thomism. Although the all-sufficiency and unsurpassability of Thomism is no longer an issue, the debate over Bouillard's work and *Sources Chrétiennes* devolved on the underlying questions of the exhaustability of older theology and the relation of epochs of the Christian theological past to one another, and these remain pertinent. . . . If the theology of one era can simply render earlier ones obsolete, and if definitive readings of any theology can be . . . already arrived at, then there is scant reason to continue studying any of them: not only they, but also their contemporary significance, have already been plumbed.

"The most immediate challenge of the *nouvelle théologie* was simply that it stirred up interest in the Christian past by making the rich array of older theology available, notably through the inauguration of *Sources chrétiennes*. One significance of the latter was the way in which its editorial decisions constituted a tacit rejection of certain scholarly orthodoxies. By including texts of lesser-known medievals . . . , or by rejecting the decisions of earlier editors, *Sources chrétiennes* queried the regnant wisdom about which authors were worth attending and how they should be interpreted. Moreover, in publishing both patristic and medieval texts side by side, the scope of the series implicitly queried the notion of a vast and fundamental divide between the theological landscape of the Fathers

sources of Christian theology and to search those sources for truth which informed current Christian life.[19] In 1946, Labourdette published an investigation into the underlying suppositions of the two series in the *Revue Thomiste*, of which he was the editor at the time. His review constituted an attack on the "neo-patristic" revival under the rubric of these two series. The article, entitled "La théologie et ses sources," summarized the aim of the two series:

> There is a parallelism between the two collections, a community of spirit, about which we are not without serious reservations, we will say, but which manifests a positive and constructive design in itself more important than the defects which sully it: that of a theology more conscious at the same time of the richness of its sources, of the multiplicity of its historical expressions, of the circumstances of its evolution and of the closest, most contemporary, human realities. With this design, we grant our full accord and our entire sympathy.[20]

The article also maintained that the thrust of the two series was a devaluation and questioning of the "unsurpassability of Thomism."[21] While Labourdette "had no objection to people making more readily available the writings of the Greek Fathers" nor did he "think it reprehensible that, as with *Théologie*, Catholic scholars should investigate the history of Christian doctrine," he did "[express] grave reservations about the two series and called for a pacific but far-reaching debate on the nature and task of

---

and that of the Scholastics." Williams, "Future of the Past: The Contemporary Significance of the *Nouvelle Théologie*," 350.

19. "Puiser la doctrine chrétienne à ses sources, trouver en elle la vérité de notre vie," Henri de Lubac, *Mémoire sur l'occasion des mes écrits*, 29; ET: *At the Service of the Church: Henri de Lubac on the Circumstances that Occasioned His Writings*, 31: "to go to the sources of Christian doctrine, to find in it the truth of our life." Quoted in Williams, "Future of the Past," 353. De Lubac does not provide the context of his quotation of Bouillard.

20. Labourdette, "La théologie et ses sources," 26–27. "Il y a dans le parallélisme des deux collections, une communauté d'esprit, sur lequel nous ne sommes pas sans graves réserves, nous le dirons, mais qui manifeste un dessein positif et constructif, en lui-même plus important que les défauts qui l'entachent: celui d'une théologie plus consciente à la fois de la richesse de ses sources, de la multiplicité de ses expressions historiques, des circonstances de son évolution et des réalités humaines les plus proches, les plus contemporaines. Avec ce dessein nous disons notre plein accord et notre entière sympathie." (Translation mine.)

21. A. N. Williams, "Future of the Past: The Contemporary Significance of the *Nouvelle Théologie*," 350.

History and Prayer

Catholic theology in their light."[22] For his part, Labourdette maintained that the "two series were tainted . . . by both a historical relativism which treats truth as truth for this or that historical period, and an experiential relativism where a subjectivism of inner experience could undermine . . . the objective value of the truths of faith."[23]

Labourdette certainly had in mind Bouillard's *Conversion et Grâce chez S. Thomas d'Aquin*, in which Bouillard famously wrote, "Une théologie qui ne serait pas actuelle serait une théologie fausse" (A theology which is not "up-to-date" would be a false theology).[24] Bouillard's study of Thomas is primarily a study of the *initium fidei* ("the approach to faith").[25] "By demonstrating both Aquinas's reliance on Aristotelian philosophy and the changes in his own understanding of the *initium fidei*—the movement in the human person which precedes faith—Bouillard drew a convincing conclusion about the contingency of dogmatic formulae."[26] It is not difficult to imagine the reaction of contemporary scholastics as the claim amounted to an attempt to undermine the privileged place held by Thomism of the twentieth century. The challenge was even more alarming to theologians such as Labourdette and Garrigou-Lagrange because it used Thomas himself to undermine the prevailing Thomism of the day. In *Conversion et Grâce*, Bouillard essentially historicized dogma and demonstrated that theology is in a certain sense contingent. Labourdette and others read this sensitivity to historicity as a radical relativization of dogma. Bouillard writes of the theology of the manuals: "It is the inevitable defect of the manuals to let

22. Nichols, "Thomism and the Nouvelle Théologie," 3; *Catholic Thought since the Enlightenment*, 135; Labourdette, "La théologie et ses sources," 26–27: "Il y a dans le parallélisme des deux collections, une communauté d'esprit, sur lequel nous ne sommes pas sans graves réserves."

23. Labourdette, "La théologie et ses sources," 29–30. Nichols, *Catholic Thought since the Enlightenment*, 135; "Thomism and the Nouvelle Théologie," 3–4. A. N. Williams contends that Labourdette had good reason to question the aims of the two series. "Labourdette raised these issues of potential relativism in his 1946 article, 'La Théologie et ses sources.' Significantly, he did not accuse any of the thinkers he engaged with having fallen into this trap, but merely asked how it was to be avoided. The question was fair, given that the thinkers associated with the movement were more successful in suggesting avenues for exploration than in spelling out how one would avoid problems of either idiosyncratic innovation or calcifying repristination." "Future of the Past: The Contemporary Significance of the *Nouvelle Théologie*," 359n24.

24. Bouillard, *Conversion et Grâce chez S. Thomas d'Aquin*, 219.

25. Scully, "Henri Bouillard and the 'Nouvelle Théologie,'" 77. See also Scully, *Grace and Human Freedom in the Theology of Henri Bouillard*.

26. Ibid. See Bouillard, *Conversion et Grâce chez S. Thomas d'Aquin*, 214–16.

Jean Danielou's Doxological Humanism

theology be seen as science of everything with immutable concepts, timeless problems and definitive arguments, as a science given all at once which one discovers simply by turning the pages of a book."[27] Against this absolutely fixed notion of doctrine, Bouillard maintained that while there are invariants in dogma, these invariants are expressed in a variety of manners and theological systems.[28] For example, Eileen Scully points out, if one were to examine the theologies of grace from the perspectives of Augustine and Aquinas, one would see certain invariants (e.g., the gratuity of justification) while at the same time observing "a difference of conceptual framework and a tendency to address different questions."[29] What neo-scholasticism attempted was to concretize both the invariants and the framework by which the invariants were expressed, which led to an absence of historical understanding. For Bouillard, "there exists a relationship of mutuality between the invariant affirmation and its contingent expression. Not only do the various contingent expressions all point to the one invariant, but the absolute invariant demands its own development in historical forms. There must necessarily be an analogy between Christian truth and history. The task of the theologian is, therefore, to avoid any identification of the invariant with one or even several of its contingent forms."[30] Thus Bouillard

---

27. Bouillard, *Conversion et Grâce chez S. Thomas d'Aquin*, 211. "C'est le défaut presque inévitable des manuels, de laisser voir la théologie comme une science toute faite, aux notions immuables, aux problèmes intemporel, aux arguments définitifs,—comme une science donnée tout d'un coup, qu'on découvre en tournant simplement les pages de son livre." Translation mine. See also Scully, "Henri Bouillard and the 'Nouvelle Théologie,'" 81.

28. Bouillard, *Conversion et Grâce chez S. Thomas d'Aquin*, 211–24.

29. Scully, "Henri Bouillard and the 'Nouvelle Théologie,'" 81.

30. Ibid., 82. Bouillard maintains, "Nous opposons cet ensemble d'invariants à ce qu'il y a de contingent dans les conceptions theologiques. Il est essential de comprendre que ces invariants ne subsistent pas à côté et indépendamment des conceptions contingentes." Compare Daniélou's statements about the relative importance of particular instantiations of Christianity. "Le christianisme ne s'identifie définitivement à aucune des formes particulières de culture où il s'incarne. De même que le péché du judaïsme est un refus de mourir pour ressusciter, un refus de croissance, ainsi, en un certain sens, en est-il de ceux qui veulent maintenir rigidement le christianisme dans ses incarnations passes et dans les formes où s'est incrusté par des habitudes séculaires. Chacun doit, perpétuellement, mourir un lui ai vieil homme pour renaître à l'homme nouveau, et l'emploi des ces mots par saint Paul n'est pas sans signification. Ainsi en est-il en quelque sorte du christianisme. Il doit s'incarner dans les civilizations et former des chrétientés. Mais ces chrétientés seront toujours caduques et transitoires. Il faudra que l'Église, après les avoir revêtues, les rejette comme de vieux vêtements [Christianity is not finally identified with any of the types of culture in which it us successively embodied. Just as the distinctive

writes, "Thus, history expresses at the same time the relativity of concepts, of the schemas which shape theology, and the permanent affirmation which dominates them. It makes known the temporal condition of theology and, at the same time, offers with regard to the faith the absolute affirmation of the divine Word which became flesh."[31]

In 1944 Bouillard was dismissed from his teaching post in Lyon—thought to be associated with those condemned as modernists—and was prohibited from teaching until 1965. While Bouillard was able cogently to rebut the charges against him by maintaining that contingency does not imply error (the charge of relativism) and that absolute truth can be grasped through contingent systems (the charge of modernism), for one reason or another his adversaries could not be swayed.

But, while Bouillard's study of Thomas certainly garnered its share of attention, of those mentioned in Labourdette's essay, Daniélou was the primary target, insofar as "it seems likely that Labourdette regarded Daniélou's short study ['Les orientations présentes de la pensée religieuse'] as the key to the hidden agenda of the two series."[32] In the essay Daniélou calls for a three-fold reinvigoration of Catholic theology. First, he sought the *ressourcement*[33] of Catholic theology. D'Ambrosio notes that the theologians of *ressourcement* held to a paradox: "in order to go forward in theology, one first had to go backward. Étienne Gilson says it succinctly, 'If theological progress is sometimes necessary, it is never possible unless you go back

---

error of Judaism has been the refusal to die and rise again, or a failure to grow up, so it is, in a measure, with those who would petrify Christianity in its former shapes, preserving the incrustations of social custom that belong to past ages. Each of us is under the obligation to 'die daily' and to be born again a 'new man': St Paul meant what he said, and his language has an application to Christianity itself, which must necessarily adopt the forms of human societies, becoming incarnate as the appropriate Christendom of its time—but each successive Christendom will be only provisional, and transitory; garments to be put away when they are worn out]." Daniélou, *Essai sur le Mystère de l'Histoire*; ET, *The Lord of History: Reflections on the Inner Meaning of History*, 25–26. All subsequent English translations of this text will be from Abercrombie's translation unless noted otherwise

31. Bouillard, *Conversion et Grâce chez S. Thomas d'Aquin*, 221. "L'histoire manifeste donc à la fois la relativité des notions, des schèmes où théologie prend corps, et l'affirmation permanente qui les domine. Elle fait connaître la condition temporelle de la théologie et, en même temps, offre aux regards de la foi l'affirmation absolue, la Parole divine qui s'y est incarnée." Translation mine.

32. Nichols, "Thomism and the Nouvelle Théologie," 4. Daniélou, "Les orientations prèsentes de la pensée religieuse," 5–21.

33. This label I find much more apt than *nouvelle théologie* because of the pejorative sense intended by its original use.

Jean Danielou's Doxological Humanism

to the beginning and start over.' What was necessary, then, was a 'return to the sources' of tradition. The theological revolution which the Church so desperately needed had to begin with, in the words of Péguy, 'a new and deeper sounding of ancient, inexhaustible, and common resources.'[34] *Ressourcement* entailed more than a naïve reappropriation of patristic and medieval sources; it also meant a reinvigoration of Christian life through biblical, patristic and liturgical renewals informed and inspired by patristic and medieval thought.[35] Daniélou writes:

> The most significant mark of contemporary religious thought is the fact of its resumed contact with the essential sources: the Bible, the Church Fathers, and the liturgy. To be sure, in theory this contact was never lost. But since the thirteenth century, theology, which up until then consisted primarily in commentary upon Scripture, has come to be constituted as an autonomous science. In its own time this autonomy was an element of progress. But a growing rupture ensued between exegesis and theology (each a discipline developing according to its own method), resulting in the progressive desiccation of theology itself. Hence, Protestantism manifests, among other things, a radical return to the Bible, in repudiation of a purely scholastic theology.[36]

Second, Daniélou maintained that this *ressourcement* was not solely achieved through a re-appropriation of the Greek Fathers. In light of the contemporary philosophies of the time—for Daniélou Marxism and Existentialism—he sought to incorporate the categories of *historicité* and *subjectivité* into in order to *vivifier par son contact avec les courants de la*

---

34. D'Ambrosio, "*Ressourcement* Theology, *Aggiornomento*, and the Hermeneutics of Tradition," 537. Quoting É. Gilson, review of *Augustine et théologie modern* and *LeMystère du surnaturel*, by H. de Lubac, in *La Croix* (18–19 July 1965) 4; quoted by Gilson, *Letters of Étienne Gilson to Henri de Lubac*, 179.

35. For the biblical, patristic and liturgical movements, see Nichols, *Catholic Thought since the Enlightenment*, 115–19, 120–23, 107–10 respectively.

36. Daniélou, "Les orientations prèsentes de la pensée religieuse," 7–8. "Un premier trait marquant de la pensée religieuse contemporaine est le contact repris avec les sources essentielles que sont la Bible, les Peres de l'Église, la liturgie. Certes, ce contact en théorie n'avait jamais été perdu. Mais depuis le treizième siècle, la théologie, qui jusque-lá avait été essentiellement commentaire de la Bible, s'est constituée en science autonome. Autonomie qui fut en son temps facteur progress. Mais il en est résulté une rupture progressive entre l'exégèse et la théologie . . . et un dessèchement progressif de la théologie. Le protestisme manifeste entre autres choses un violent retour à la Bible, en désaveu d'une théologie purement scolastique."

pensée contemporaine.[37] Third, Daniélou notes that a renewed theology must retain a meaningful contact with life.

> What men of today, living in the world, demand of theology is that it give them an account of the meaning of life. It is no longer possible, as it once was, to dissociate theology and spirituality. The first used to be fixed high upon speculative and atemporal plane; the second all too often consisted solely of practical counsels divorced from the vision of man that justified such counsel. A defining trait of current renewal in religious thought is the concerted effort to reunite theology and *ascesis*, as they were once united during the time of the Fathers of the Church, in order to complete the one with the other.[38]

The faithful now demanded that theology retain its original organic unity with spirituality and, even more, that it be a spiritual theology which was relevant to their contemporary needs.

It is important to note—and here may be the reason why the Dominicans reacted so vociferously in their condemnation of Daniélou's program—that Thomism of the neo-scholastic incarnation would have little to do with this *ressourcement* project. As Aidan Nichols notes, "Though he never mentions St. Thomas by name, Daniélou gives the distinct impression that Scholastic theology will not have much of a role in all of this. Such theology is, he intimates, an obsolete stage in the development of Christian thought. It is now time to move on—and perhaps more than time, for he speaks of Scholasticism as an increasingly rationalistic and desiccated theology, detached in an abusive sense from spirituality, and above all peculiarly unsuited by its own genius to what contemporary sensibility requires."[39]

---

37. Ibid., 14, 17.

38. Ibid., 17. "Ce que des hommes d'aujourd'hui, vivant dans le monde, demanderont donc à la théologie, c'est de leur expliquer le sens de leur vie. Il n'est plus possible de dissocier, comme on l'a trop fait autrefois, théologie et spiritualité. La première se plaçait sur un plan spéculative et intemporel; la second était trop souvent faite uniquement de conseils pratiques séparés de la vision de l'homme qui la justifait. C'est un trait marquant de la pensée actuelle que l'effort pour joindre à nouveau, comme ells l'etaient du tèmps des Pères de l'Église, la théologie et l'ascèse, afin qu'elles se complètent l'une par l'autre."

39. Nichols, "Thomism and the Nouvelle Théologie," 5. Indeed, Nichols contends that Daniélou's project "had as a subsidiary purpose the marginalization of Scholasticism in this new context" (6).

A Theology of History

When moving to Daniélou's overall theology of history, is it important to remember that concepts such as *historicité* must give way to much more fundamental theological terms as *oikonomia*. Whereas, for Daniélou, *historicité* broadly indicates an historical awareness which was missing in theology, *oikonomia* indicates God's "economy" or "order."[40] This economy consists in the divine plan whereby God educates humanity. This is the order of the *magnalia Dei*—the great works of God—recorded in the Scripture of the Old and New Testaments in the time of the Jewish people, in the time of Christ, and in the time of the Church.[41] These mighty works of God constitute sacred history "where the individual inserts himself into the web of an economy which goes beyond him and which constitutes an objective plan."[42]

Sacred and Profane History

For Daniélou, any discussion of Christianity and history must account for the relationship between sacred and profane history.[43] By "profane history" Daniélou does not mean "academic history," which he considers a "pretence" and "self-deception,"[44] but simply "the whole period of this world's existence."[45] Sacred history, on the other hand, entails both life before the history of humanity—which includes God's preexistence and creative

---

40. For Daniélou's understanding of the terms "historicity" and "economy," see *Essai sur le Mystère de l'Histoire*, 12–14.

41. Daniélou pulls the phrase *magnalia Dei* from Acts 2.11: "both Jews and Proselytes, Cretans and Arabians—we hear them telling in our own tongues the mighty works of God" (Iudaei quoque et Proselyti Cretes et Arabes audiuimus eos loquentes nostris linguis magnalia Dei).

42. Daniélou, "Conception of History in the Christian Tradition," 172.

43. See Daniélou, *Essai sur le Mystère de l'Histoire*, 29–38; "Conception of History in the Christian Tradition," 175–79.

44. Daniélou, "Christianity and History," 182. Also, "Que «l'histoire académique» ne puisse se suffire à elle-même, qu'une interprétation soit nécessaire, la chose est évidente et M. Butterfield en est bien d'accord [Butterfield is quite clear that 'academic history' is not self-sufficient; plainly, as he appreciated, there must be an interpretation. It is the merest hypocrisy to pretend to be writing 'pure' history]." *Essai sur le Mystère de l'Histoire*, 95. See also Butterfield, *Christianity and History*.

45. Daniélou, *Essai sur le Mystère de l'Histoire*, 32. "L'histoire profane . . . remplit la totalité du siècle présent."

History and Prayer

work prior to the creation of humanity—and life after the conclusion of this world's history, that is the life of the world to come. Profane history treats Christianity as one of any number of passing progressive stages and Christianity is to that extent transient even as one Christianity gives way to another.[46] The other penchant is to view Christianity as completely transcendent of the historical process.[47]

In response to these two tendencies, Daniélou maintains that one must grasp a two-fold relationship between history and Christianity: 1) Christianity falls within history and 2) history falls within Christianity. The first position holds that Christianity "emerged at a given point in the sequence of historical eventuation. It provides a constituent part of the fabric of recorded facts. To this extent, it belongs to the historian's province to describe its appearance in the chronicle of documented reality."[48] The second position holds that "all secular history is included in sacred history, as a part, a prolegomenon, a preparatory introduction. Profane history covers the whole period of this world's existence, but Christianity is essentially the next world itself, present here and now in a mystery. The fundamental reality of Christianity is 'to come,' not just in a relation to a particular moment of time, but in relation to all historical time, past, present and future. It is indeed *novissimus*, the last thing: with Christianity, the end is already achieved. But in the mystery of the being and working of the Christian

---

46. Daniélou, *Essai sur le Mystère de l'Histoire*, 29. This is clear in the Marxist account of history in regard to Christianity. See "Histoire marxiste et histoire sacramentaire," 99–110; ET: "Marxist History and Sacred History," 503–13. All subsequent English translations of this text will be Corbett's unless noted otherwise.

47. Daniélou, *Essai sur le Mystère de l'Histoire*, 30. "A l'extrême oppose, d'autres penseurs, soucieux d'affirmer la transcendence du Christianisme, en font une réalité étrangère à l'histoire; mais il apparaît alors comme une évasion hors du mouvement historique, indifférent à l'effort humain. Nous revenons à la gnose et à la condamnation de la creation et du monde de la nature. Cette conception pessimiste de l'histoire, nous l'avons déjà dit, est contraire au christianisme [There is a school of thought so anxiously committed to safeguard the transcendence of Christianity as to divorce it altogether from the historical process; but this is escapism, a flight from reality, a withdrawal from human struggle. It is a return to the Gnostic denial of natural values, a condemnation of creaturely existence. We have seen how this pessimistic concept of history is incompatible with the Christian position]."

48. Ibid., 30. "Il apparaît à un moment donnée dans le développment des événements historiques. Il fait partie de la trame de l'histoire totale. En ce sens, il est objet de connaissance pour l'historien qui le décrit en tant qu'il affleure sans la série des faits historiques observables."

Jean Danielou's Doxological Humanism

Church, this thing which is beyond history exists now in historical fact."[49] The first aspect of this two-fold relationship is important because it represents a real incarnation of Christianity into the realm of human events. "As Christ himself belonged to one nation, one culture, one period of time, so the Church is embodied in successive cultural forms—which are themselves no less transitory than the very civilizations they represent."[50] At the same time, Christianity must remain to some extent detached in order to avoid equation with any particular instantiation of itself. "For detachment is just as much a matter of duty as integration. Christianity is not finally identified with any of the types of culture in which it is successively embodied."[51]

In holding these two positions in tension, one is able to avoid the two errors of *integrism* and *modernism*. *Integrism*, according to Daniélou, is the "conservative attachment to inadequate categories and conceptions wrongly identified with imperishable truth. This archaizing tendency takes various forms, according to the particular stage of history chosen to represent the ideal of Christianity—it may be a nostalgic hankering after the Primitive Church of the first centuries or a more or less romantic medievalism, or a desperate attachment to the vanishing outline of *bourgeois* Christendom."[52] Here one can detect echoes of Bouillard's ideas of doctrinal invariants and contingent systems. *Modernism*, on the other hand, is the attitude "whereby the necessary process of adaptation is allowed to endanger the essential

---

49. Ibid. "Mais, par ailleurs, l'histoire est dans le christianisme; l'histoire profane rentre dans l'histoire sainte, car c'est elle à son tour qui est une partie dans un tout où elle constitue une préparation. Cette préparation remplit la totalité du siècle présent. Mais le christianisme est précisément le siècle future, déjà présent en mystère. En ce sens, dans sa réalité profonde, il est un au-delà non seulement d'un moment, mais de la totalité de l'histoire. Il est vraiment «novissimus», le dernier; avec lui la «fin» est déjà là. Mais, et c'est tout le mystère de l'Église, cet au-delà de l'histoire est déjà present et coexiste avec elle."

50. Ibid. "Comme le Christ a été l'homme d'un pays, d'une civilisation, d'une époque déterminée, ainsi en est-il de l'Église. Elle s'incarne dans les civilisations successive. Et ces incarnations participant de la caducité qui est celle de ces civilisations."

51. Ibid., 32. "Car, à côté de ces incarnations, il y a un égal devoir de dégagement. Le christianisme ne s'identifie défintivement à aucune des formes particulières de culture où il s'incarne."

52. Ibid., 32–33. For the heresy of archaism, see Turner, *Pattern of Christian Truth*, 132–48. "Orthodoxy must always steer a difficult course between the Scylla of archaism and the Charybdis of innovation. Its upholders need to be delivered both from the facile assurance that they are wiser than their fathers and from a blind refusal to accept new truth and to grapple with new tasks" (132). In other places Daniélou refers to this phenomenon as the error of anachronism instead of archaism: *Essai sur le Mystère de l'Histoire*, 13.

structure of the *depositum fidei*, discarding the substance along with its ephemeral accidents."[53]

Given these concerns, Daniélou maintains that secular history is entirely encompassed by sacred history—sacred history being a whole cosmic history and profane history being a smaller, limited subdivision.[54] Cullmann argues that this has been the point of view of the Christian thinker from primitive times.[55] In line with many of the Fathers of the Church, Daniélou argues that "the history of salvation embraces not only the history of [humanity], but the whole of cosmic history." It is because of the expansiveness and authorship of sacred history that it encompasses secular history. In his *Proof of the Apostolic Preaching*, Irenaeus gives record of sacred history in a manner that highlights this aspect.[56] He narrates sacred history beginning with the creation of humanity by God (*Dem. Apost.* 11) to the resurrection of Christ and all believers with and through him (*Dem. Apost.* 42). With the creation and the resurrection—which extends this history into the world to come—Irenaeus includes all human history within sacred history. Because of this understanding of human history, Irenaeus is able to write,

> And because He is Himself the Word of God Almighty, who in His invisible form pervades us universally in the whole world, and encompasses both its length and breadth and height and depth—for by God's Word everything is disposed and administered—the Son of God was also crucified in these, imprinted in the form of a cross on the universe; for He had necessarily, in becoming visible, to bring to light the universality of His cross, in order to show openly through His visible form that activity of His: that it is He who makes bright the height, that is, what is in heaven, and holds the deep, which is in the bowels of the earth, and stretches forth and extends length from East to West, navigating also the Northern parts and the breadth of the South, and calling in all the dispersed from all sides to the knowledge of the Father.[57]

---

53. Daniélou, *Essai sur le Mystère de l'Histoire*, 32. "Mais il y a un autre danger, qui est celui du modernism et qui consiste à évacuer l'essentiel avec le caduc et à pousser l'adaptation jusqu'à sacrifier le depot de la foi."

54. Ibid., 33.

55. Cullmann, *Christus und die Zeit*; FT: *Christ et le temps*; ET: *Christ and Time*, 20–21.

56. Irenaeus, *Demonstration of the Apostolic Preaching*, 11–42.

57. Ibid., 34. See Quasten, *Patrology*, volume 1, 287–313.

Daniélou is in accord with this view when he summarizes the content and expansiveness of sacred history:

> As against [the] empirical interpretation of historical facts, we find in the ancient world a vision of history such as the Bible gives us. It does not dispense with the laws regulating an empirical study of facts, but presupposes a belief in supernatural events, the *magnalia Dei*, which constitute sacred history. This visionary history encompasses all time, beginning with the creation of the world, viewed as a historical event, and going on to interpret the history of primitive man theologically. It treats God's special choice of Israel and the vicissitudes of that covenant. It reaches its summit in the Incarnation and Resurrection of the Word. It continues invisibly in the Church, viewed as a supernatural body. And finally it sets a limit to history in the Parousia of Christ, which again lies within the sphere of Faith.[58]

What Daniélou is proposing is a view of history which is cosmic in scope. The divine nature of this history is derived from the fact that it exceeds the limits of human history and entails the activity of the creative God prior to the creation of humanity and the activity of the redemptive God in the life of the world to come.

The Central Event of History

Daniélou's theology of history is centered on the incarnation, and its correlates (resurrection, ascension, etc.), as a new event which stands at the center of all history as both the beginning and the end of all things. Daniélou notes the first problem facing a Christian conception of history was that of the Incarnation. The decisive nature of the Incarnation "radically changes human existence, and . . . sets down a qualitative frontier between the Before and the After. But nothing was more foreign to ancient thought than this importance given to a single event."[59] Furthermore, he notes, "with the Resurrection of Christ the decisive event of history was accomplished and no possible event will ever possess as much importance as this."[60] For many

---

58. Daniélou, "Has History a Meaning?," 42.
59. Daniélou, "Conception of History in the Christian Tradition," 171.
60. Daniélou, "New Testament and the Theology of History," 27. (It appears that this article was originally written in English.) Daniélou notes that it is the great merit of Oscar Cullmann to make this point: see Culluman, *Christ and Time*, 121–30.

History and Prayer

ancients this was the scandal of Christianity. This is the primary claim made by Celsus in his criticism of Christianity's novelty. According to Daniélou, ancient thought held that "that which is real is capable of repeating itself. A single event, in its particularity, is something insignificant. The idea that such an event could introduce a new decisive factor is basically foreign to it."[61] Despite his scathing critiques of Celsus, Origen acquiesced on this point and attempted to elide the "novelty" of Christianity.

> The Christians were at first disconcerted by these criticisms [of novelty] and that, before being aware of the originality of their message, they began by trying to wipe out this element. Thus, for Origen, the spiritual creation has existed in its perfection from the beginning and no doubt is coeternal with the Logos. But this creation has fallen. The role of the Incarnation is therefore to re-establish that which had already existed previously. The events of history introduce nothing new. It would have been better if nothing had ever occurred, and if everything had remained in the original state of immobility. Likewise, for Eusebius, Christ did not bring a new message, but he merely came to re-establish in its purity the religion of primitive humanity . . . Thus we continually come back to the Greek idea that perfection is what has always existed.[62]

---

61. Daniélou, "Conception of History in the Christian Tradition," 171.

62. Ibid., 171–72. When Daniélou contends that some lines of Greek thought contended "that perfection is what has always existed," I believe he specifically has Philo of Alexandria and Origen in mind. See Daniélou, "Conception of History in the Christian Tradition," 171–72 for Origen and *Philon d'Alexandrie*, 168–72 for Philo. This passage echoes a paragraph in "Les Orientations présentes de la pensée religieuse": "C'est en effet une exigence irrépressible de la foi chrétienne que l'histoire ait un sens, que le temps ne soit pas ce reflet de l'éternité qu'il est pour la platonisme, mais une croissance où la succession même soit un progrès au sens fort terme, c'est-à-dire acquisition de valeur. Et, à cet égard, il faut se défier de cette déformation du christianisme par la gnose, telle qu'on la trouve jusque chez certains Pères de l'Église, où la Rédemption semble présentée comme n'ayant pour objet que de ramener l'homme à son état primtif, en sorte qu'il semble qu'il eût mieux valu que rien jamais ne se fût second siècle, saint Irénée dénonçait cette conception statique et affirmait, avec la bonté foncière de la création, la valeur religieuse de l'histoire [It is an essentially irrepressible demand of Christian faith that history have a meaning, that time be not merely a reflection of eternity (as it is in Platonism), but a development or even a progress in the strong sense of the word—that is, an acquisition of worth. And, in this respect, it is necessary to be on one's guard against the deformity of Christianity by *gnosis*, such as one finds in certain Fathers of the Church, where redemption is conceived as having no object but that of returning man to his primitive state. This view tends to suggest that man would have been better off had nothing ever happened to him, that it would have been better if he had simply remained fixed in his primitive stasis.

But for many of the Church Fathers, and for Daniélou, history is comprised of particular events which derive from this central *novitas*. Irenaeus clearly saw that the novelty of the Christian message should not be occluded. In *Against Heresies* he asks concerning the Incarnation, "What then did the Lord bring to us by His advent? Know that He brought all novelty, by bringing Himself who had been announced. For this very thing was proclaimed beforehand, that a novelty should come to renew and quicken mankind."[63] Indeed, other Christian theologians were soon to realize that the originality of a Christian vision of history need not be elided, but, on the contrary, constituted a decisive contribution.

Daniélou contends that prior to the development of a Christian view of history, whose originality was fully realized in Augustine's *City of God*, there were two primary conceptions of historical reality. First, there are those things that have neither beginning nor end. Second, there are those things which have a beginning and an end.[64] These two categories encompass the divine, incorruptible reality and mundane arena of the corruptible respectively. But, with Augustine, Christian theology becomes fully aware that "sacred history is made up of absolute beginnings which remain eternally thereafter a part of that history."[65] This constitutes a new category of historical eventuation: that which has a beginning yet no end. This is what the writer of the Epistle to the Hebrews has in mind when he tells his readers that Christ "did not enter by means of the blood of goats and calves; but he entered the Most High Place once for all (*ephapax*) by his own blood, having obtained eternal redemption" (Heb. 9:12). This new event is "unique and irrevocable," *ephapax*. Likewise, the Epistle to the Romans, using the same important Greek word, claims "The death [Christ] died, he died to sin once for all" (Rom. 6:10). "Here we are presented with an event which has introduced a definitive, qualitative change into time of a kind that precludes the possibility of ever returning to the former state of affairs."[66] For Daniélou, these unique beginnings consist of the "great creative decisions of God, which constitute sacred history": the creation of the world,

---

In the second century, Saint Irenaeus denounced this static conception and affirmed, through the fundamental goodness of creation, the religious value of history]." Daniélou, "Current Trends in Religion," *Communio* (forthcoming).

63. Irenaeus, *Adversus Haereses*, IV.34.1 (PG 7.1083C–1084A). See also Daniélou, "Saint Irénée et les origins de la theologie de l'histoire," 227–31.

64. Daniélou, "Conception of History in the Christian Tradition," 172.

65. Ibid.

66. Daniélou, "New Testament and the Theology of History," 26.

History and Prayer

the creation of humanity, the covenants with Noah and Abraham, and the establishment of the new covenant through Christ.[67] But, for Daniélou, it is not enough that singular historical events should have importance, there must be a continuity to those events as well. This is where Daniélou's well-known ideas concerning typology have bearing for it is through typology that history is given intelligibility.[68]

History and Typology

The interaction of Christian theology with the Greek world brought about the realization of the importance of single events. A second interaction, that with the Jews, would bring about another important aspect of history: the continuity between singular events. Not only do single events have importance, they are intimately related in a single economy: "For, in order that there should be history, it is not enough that events have importance; there must be as well a continuity in them."[69] It is this continuity in events perceived through a typological reading of scripture which comprises the events of sacramental history. Viewing history in this manner allows

---

67. Ibid. Commenting on the creation of the world, Augustine writes in the *City of God*, "it was created in time but will never perish in time—that it has, like number, a beginning but no end" (xi.4). In reference to the creation of humanity, he writes, "there happens in time a new thing which time shall not end" (xii.13). Concerning the covenant with Abraham, he maintains, "all things" related to the Abrahamic covenant "proclaim newness" (xvi.26). Lastly, concerning new but eternal things in general, he states, "we have solved . . . this very difficult question about the eternal God creating new things" (xii.21).

68. Daniélou contrasts this with an existential attitude toward history where individual events have importance; however, these events are so radically individualized that there is no purpose for the singular events. "Car pour qu'il y ait histoire, il ne suffit pas que les événements aient de l'importance, il faut encore qu'il y ait entre eux une continuité. C'est précisément ce qui fait la différence entre la conception de «l'historicité», telle que la représente la philosophie existentielle, et qui est seulement la décision présente de la liberté individuelle, et celle de l'histoire sainte où l'individu s'insère dans la trame d'une économie qui le dépasse et qui constitue un plan objectif [There is no such thing as history unless events, besides having some importance, can be shown in some way to be continuous. It is just this latter point which distinguishes the idea of 'historicity,' as understood by existentialists, meaning no more than the present decision of an individual free will, from the idea of sacred history, wherein the individual fits into a pattern of a larger and objectively planned arrangement of reality]." Daniélou, *Essai sur le Mystère de l'Histoire*, 12. See also Daniélou, "Existentialisme et Théologie de l'Histoire," 131–35; ET: "Existentialism and the Theology of History," 66–70.

69. Daniélou, "Conception of History in the Christian Tradition," 172.

Jean Danielou's Doxological Humanism

Daniélou to see history as a single progressive economy through which God accustoms humanity to His ways.

This second aspect of Daniélou's theology of history is a typological reading of sacred history.[70] For Daniélou, *typology* is, simply put, the "science of the similitudes between the two testaments."[71] But, typology is not a mere symbolism. Typology is distinguishable from other kinds of symbolism because of its "historicity."[72] For Daniélou, typology "denotes a relationship between various events belonging to sacred history. . . . This figurative sense of Scripture is grounded in the structural unity of God's design: the same divine characteristics are revealed in the successive strata of history. The typological interpretation of events does not in any way tend

---

70. For Daniélou's thought on typology see primarily *Bible et Liturgie* and *Sacremuntum Futuri: Études sur les Origines de la Typologie Biblique*; ET: *From Shadows to Reality*.

71. Daniélou's use of the term *typology* has been disputed by some. For instance, Andrew Louth writes, "Anyone who heard the late Cardinal Daniélou speak on the subject will not easily forget that for him there was a very sharp distinction to be drawn between allegory and typology, and allegory was a bad thing, typology a good thing. He held the heart of the difference to be that allegory is concerned with words, typology with events; allegory elides history, typology is rooted in history. There is doubtless something of a distinction here, but I would not want to follow Daniélou and express the difference by the words 'allegory' and 'typology.' For two reasons: first, because in defending allegory I am seeking to defend an aspect of the thought of the Fathers and early medieval theologians, and though I would argue that they do anticipate the distinction Daniélou and others indicate by the words 'allegory' and 'typology' . . . , they do not express it by these words. What Daniélou calls 'typology' they call 'allegory' (this is particularly true of the Latin tradition), and we are all set to misunderstand them if we restrict the reference of the term 'allegory' to something opposed to typology." *Discerning the Mystery*, 118. However, it seems that Daniélou is simply using the term in order to avoid certain misunderstandings associated with the use of the term *allegory*. He says as much when he writes, "we must make a rigorous distinction between such a typology—which is a historical symbolism—and the kind of allegorism practiced by Philo and adopted by certain doctors of the Church [I think Daniélou specifically has in mind here Theodore of Mopsuestia]. For the latter is really a reappearance of a cosmic symbolism without an historical basis." Daniélou, "New Testament and the Theology of History," 30. While noting that typology is the "science des correspondances entre les deux Testaments" [science of the similitudes between the two Testaments]—and we need not read more into it than exactly that—he admits that his usage of the term is somewhat dependent on the adoption of the term by most modern exegetes. See Jean Daniélou, *Bible et Liturgie*, 8; ET: *Bible and the Liturgy*. All subsequent English translations of this text will be from the English translation by University of Notre Dame Press unless noted otherwise.

72. Daniélou, *Essai sur le Mystère de l'Histoire*, 135–36.

to ignore or mask their individual existence and value, but affords a frame of reference for intelligible coordination."[73]

Daniélou's typological understanding of scripture and history contains multiple stages of progression.[74] Within this science of scripture, there is a "primary typology" that takes place entirely within the ambit of the Old Testament. Both the signification and the realization occur within the purview of the time of the Jewish people. "And here, we would do well to remind ourselves of its [typology's] foundation, for this is to be found in the Old Testament itself. At the time of the Captivity, the prophets announced to the people of Israel that in the future God would perform for their benefit deeds analogous to, and even greater than those He had performed in the past. So there would be a new Deluge, in which the sinful world would be annihilated, and a few men, a 'remnant,' would be preserved to inaugurate a new humanity; there would be a new Exodus in which, by His power, God would set mankind free from its bondage to idols; there would be a new paradise into which God would introduce the people He had redeemed."[75]

Following this, there exists a "secondary typology"—though not secondary in importance but in chronology—whereby it is exhibited that the figures of the Old Testament are fulfilled in the New Testament in the person of Christ. "With Jesus, in fact, these events of the end, of the fullness of time, are now accomplished. He is the new Adam with whom the time

73. Ibid. This also affords us the opportunity to rebut the claim by Dawson in *Christian Figural Reading and the Fashioning of Identity*—an expansion of "Figural Reading and the Fashioning of Christian Identity in Boyarin, Auerbach and Frei," 181–96—that Daniélou is a violent supersessionist willing to efface Jewish identity. Daniélou's claim—"the typological interpretation of events does not in any way tend to ignore or mask their individual existence and value"—should in itself indicate that his views on supersessionism are much more nuanced that Dawson is willing, or able, to see. Dawson asks if this reading of Daniélou is too uncharitable and I must conclude that it is. This reading might possibly arise on the basis of a limited reading of Daniélou's corpus and be responsible for a far too cursory assessment of Daniélou's stance.

74. "Il y a un sens christologique, un sens ecclésial, un sens mystique, un sens eschatologique [There will be a Christological sense, an ecclesiastical sense, mystical and eschatological senses]." Daniélou, *Essai sur le Mystère de l'Histoire*, 211.

75. Daniélou, *Bible et Liturgie*, 9. "Il est bon d'en rappeler le fondement. Son point de départ se trouve dans l'Ancien Testament lui-même. Les Prophètes en effet ont annoncé au people d'Israël, au temps de sa captivité, que Dieu accomplirait pour lui dans l'avenir des œuvres analogiques, et plus grandes encore, à celles qu'il avait accomplies dans le passé. Ainsi il y aura un nouveau Déluge qui anéantira le monde pécheur et où un reste sera préservé pour inaugurer une humanité nouvelle; il y aura un nouvel Exode où Dieu libérera par sa puissance l'humanité captive des idoles; il y aura un nouveau Paradis où Dieu introduira son people libéré."

Jean Danielou's Doxological Humanism

of the Paradise of the future has begun. In Him is already realized that destruction of the sinful world of which the Flood was the figure. In Him is accomplished the true Exodus which delivers the people of God from the tyranny of the demon. Typology was used in the preaching of the apostles as an argument to establish the truth of their message, by showing that Christ continues and goes beyond the Old Testament."[76] This constitutes the Christological face of typology.

A typological reading of scripture does not conclude with the life of Christ. There also exists a tertiary typology which is fundamentally a sacramental typology that is found in the New Testament.[77] "The Gospel of St. John shows us that the manna was a figure of the Eucharist; the first Epistle of St. Paul to the Corinthians that the crossing of the Red Sea was a figure of Baptism; the first Epistle of St. Peter that the Flood was also a figure of Baptism."[78] Importantly, these various stages in the study of the similitudes between the Testaments draw out the fact that a typological reading of scripture is a theological reading of sacred history and an understanding of the relationship between the particular events of that history. Concerning sacramental typology, Daniélou notes, "This means . . . that the sacraments carry on in our midst the *mirabilia*, the great works of God in the Old Testament and the New: for example, the Flood, the Passion and Baptism show us the same divine activity as carried out in three different eras of sacred history."[79] Finally, "In general, then, sacramental typology is

---

76. Ibid., 9–10. "En effet, avec Jésus, les événements de la fin, de la plénitude des temps, sont accomplis. Il est le Nouvel Adam avec qui les temps du Paradis future sont arrivés. En Lui est déjà réalisée la destruction du monde pécheur que figurait le déluge. En Lui est accompli l'Exode véritable, qui libère le peuple de Dieu de la tyrannie du démon. La prédication apostolique a utilisé typologie comme argument pour établir la vérité de son message, en montrant que le Christ continue et dépasse l'Ancien Testament."

77. It must be noted that Daniélou also writes of a fourth level of typological reading which one might refer to as eschatological typology to complement primary typology (or prophetic typology), secondary typology (or Christological typology) and tertiary typology (or ecclesiological/sacramental typology). The entire spectrum of a full typological reading can be seen in the typology of the Eucharist in the signification from paschal meal (primary), last supper (Christological), Eucharist (ecclesiological/sacramental) and the eschatological banquet. *Bible et Liturgie*, 194–219.

78. Daniélou, *Bible et Liturgie*, 10. "L'Évangile de Jean nous montre dans la manne une figure de l'Eucharistie, la *Première aux Corinthiens*, dans la traverse de la Mer Rogue, une figure du baptême, *la Première Épitre de Pierre*, dans le déluge, une autre figure du baptême."

79. Ibid. "Par là est signifié que les sacrements continuent au milieu de nous les *mirabilia*, les grandes œuvres de Dieu, dans l'Ancien et le Nouveau Testaments: Déluge,

History and Prayer

[a] form of typology of the theological analogy between the great moments of Sacred History."[80]

In *Bible et Liturgie*, Daniélou notes the primary sources of typology in the work of the Fathers. Though this sort of reading of texts is fundamental to most patristic exegesis as a whole, Daniélou believes that the fourth century provides at once a developed and ancient exposition of a sacramental typology.[81] The principal works for this discussion involve the *Mystagogical Catecheses* of Cyril of Jerusalem, the *De mysteriis* and *De sacramentis* of Ambrose of Milan,[82] the *Ecclesiastical Hierarchy* of Pseudo-Dionysius[83] and the *Catechetical Homilies* of Theodore of Mopsuestia.[84] The discussion of these figures within the context of an exposition of typology and history is important because of the inclusion of Theodore of Mopsuestia. Both Cyril and Ambrose—the Aeropagite exudes "certain special characteristics"— catechize through an explication of the figures of the Old Testament, the symbolism of the rites and a dogmatic explanation of the symbolism.[85] In essence, both Cyril and Ambrose relate the events of the past, i.e., the Old Testament and to some extent the New Testament, to their contemporary liturgical situation. This approach firmly places their catechesis within the realm of an explication of sacred history through a typological reading of scripture. Theodore, however, has a slightly different approach in his catechesis. While a certain caricature of Antiochene exegesis has it that writers

---

Passion, Baptême nous montrent les mêmes mœurs divines à trios époques de l'histoire sainte."

80. Ibid. "Typologie sacramentaire est [un] forme de la typologie général, de l'analogie théologique entre les grands moments de l'Histoire sainte."

81. "Le IVe siècle au contraire nous apporte des traits d'ensemble. Avec l'organisation du catéchuménat, l'usage se répand alors de donner aux nouveaux chrétiens une explication des sacrements qu'ils reçoivent. Or nous avons la chance de posséder quelques-unes de ces catéchèses sacramentaires données durant la semaine pascale. Elles seront pour nous la source la plus importante. [The fourth century gives us treatises on the whole subject. With the organization of the catechumenate, the custom spread of giving new Christians an explanation of the sacraments which they had received. We have the good fortune to possess some of these sacramental catecheses given during the Easter week, and they furnish us with the most important sources for our purpose.]" Ibid., 15–16. See also Daniélou, "La Catéchèse Eucharistique chez les Pères de l'Église," 33–72.

82. *De Mysteriis* (PL 16.405–26); *De sacra.* (P.L. 16, 435–482). See Angelo di Berardino, *Patrology*, volume 4, 144–80.

83. *De Ecclesiastica Hierarchia* (PG 3.369–584).

84. *Cat. hom.* See Quasten, *Patrology*, volume 3, 401–23.

85. Daniélou, *Bible et Liturgie*, 16–19.

such as Theodore were strict literalists, Theodore certainly makes use of typology but not to the degree that other exegetes do. However, his typological reading of scripture is different than either Cyril or Ambrose.

> The sacramental symbolism of Theodore presents several characteristic aspects. In his Introduction, Msgr. Devreesse mentions "typology" several times; but what actually strikes us, when we compare Theodore to St. Cyril of Jerusalem, and, even more, to St. Ambrose, is the almost complete absence of any typology borrowed from the Old Testament. There is only one exception. Although Theodore ignores the baptismal figures of the Deluge or of the Crossing the Red Sea, the theme of Adam appears several times, in particular in connection with the preparatory rites,—the examination, the exorcisms, etc.,—and the parallel between the situation of Adam in the garden and that of the catechumen in the baptistery dominates Theodore's presentation. But this is an exception, for his whole sacramental symbolism is founded on the parallel between the visible and the invisible liturgies. We are here in line with the symbolism of the *Epistle to the Hebrews*. We can certainly speak of typology, but we must make it clear that Theodore is concerned more with the relation of things visible to the invisible than with the relation of things past to things to come, which is the true bearing of the word.[86]

Daniélou does all this to emphasize the point that typology properly understood must remain a historical practice of relating the similitudes of one era to another. To limit typology, as Theodore does, to the relationship of visible and invisible realities is outside the pale of typology by virtue of its effacement of the historical nature of typology. Daniélou claims that Theodore's partial rejection of typological readings of scripture derives

---

86. Ibid., 20–21. "La symbolique sacramentaire de Théodore présente plusieurs aspects caractéristiques. Monseigneur Devresse, dans son Introduction, parle à plusieurs reprises de «typologie». En réalité ce qui frappe plutôt, si on compare Théodore à saint Cyrille de Jérusalem et surtout à saint Ambroise, c'est l'absence presque complète de toute typologie empruntée à l'Ancien Testament. Il y a toutefois une exception. Si Théodore ignore les figures baptismales du Déluge ou de la traverse de la Mer Rouge, le thème adamique apparaît à plusieurs reprises, en particulier à propos des rites préparatoires: examen, exorcismes, etc. Le parallélisme de la situation d'Adam au jardin et de celle du catéchumène dans le baptistère domine la représentation de Théodore. Mais ceci est une exception. L'ensemble de sa symbolique sacramentaire est fondé sur le parallélisme de la liturgie visible et de la liturgie invisible. Nous sommes dans la ligne de l'Épitre aux Hébreux. On peut bien parler de typologie, mais précisant qu'il s'agit davantage de la relation des choses visible aux choses invisibles, que des choses passes aux choses futures, ce qui serait le vrai sens du mot."

History and Prayer

from his refusal to admit that there was a relationship between different events within the economy of God's plan.[87] Daniélou's critique of Theodore hinges on the fact not of an absence of typology but of a deficient typology without a historical sense. For it is from a "characteristically Christian point of view of history as prophetic, that is to say a view in which the events and institutions of one epoch, of one 'aeon' foreshadow those of the following 'aeon,'" that one is able to apprehend the historical nature of typology which Theodore did not admit.[88]

Daniélou contends that typology is crucial for a historical understanding of the divine plan. "At the very heart of historic reality . . . there appears a new dimension in which the symbol finds its place. God's successive actions in history are bound together by their common characteristic of being creative interventions. But over and above this, in proportion as the divine plan develops it becomes clear that these interventions are connected with each other by a relationship of correspondence."[89] Many critics of spiritual hermeneutics in general, and allegory or typology specifically, have charged that such readings can easily be manipulated at the fancy of each individual interpreter. However, it is the historical nature of the divine plan which sets the boundaries for such interpretations. This "symbolism has its foundations in the unity of the plan of God. It is a divine consistency which manifests itself on the different levels of history."[90] The comprehension of these irruptions of God into history perceived through interconnection of biblical symbolism allows one to enter into the drama of the *magnalia Dei*.

---

87. "Et ceci nous amène à remarquer que le platonisme sacramentaire de Théodore est la conséquence même de son littéralisme exégétique. Dès lors qu'il se refuse à voir une correspondence entre réalités historiques, en rejetant la typologie, il est amène à interpréter la symbolique sacramentaire dans le sens vertical de la correspondance des choses visibles aux choses invisibles [And this leads us to remark that the sacramental platonism of Theodore is itself the consequence of the literal quality of his exegesis. Rejecting typology because he refused to see a relationship between historic realities, he was led to interpret sacramental symbolism in a vertical sense, as a relationship of visible things to invisible]." Ibid., 14.

88. Daniélou, "New Testament and the Theology of History," 28.

89. Ibid., 28–29.

90. Ibid., 29.

Jean Danielou's Doxological Humanism

History and the Divine Pedagogy

When one sees that all of history is a single economy of progress from shadows to reality, from figures to the referent, from sign to signified, it can be seen that each era is simply the next successive stage in the development of the divine plan. Irenaeus saw this scheme as explicable by the idea that sacred history is the means by which God teaches his children. It is through this divine pedagogy that God accomplishes the goal of accustoming his people to his ways in order to move them to more developed understandings of who he is. For Daniélou, the events of the Old Testament represent "that slow process of education in which the Word, present to the creature made in His own image even from the beginning, progressively familiarized man with divine things from the very time when he had scarcely left his animal condition. For before the mystery of the redemptive Passion was revealed to him, [humanity] needed to be taught the meaning of suffering; before the mystery of the Triune God was revealed, a humanity always inclined to polytheism has to be made familiar with the idea that God is One."[91]

The idea of the pedagogical nature of sacred history is indicated in the Letter to the Galatians. Paul writes that "before faith came, we were imprisoned and guarded under the law until faith would be revealed. Therefore the law was our disciplinarian until Christ came, so that we might be justified by faith. But now that faith has come, we are no longer subject to a disciplinarian" (Gal. 3:23–24).[92] Daniélou notes the pedagogical nature of sacred history when he says, "the goal of sacred history is to familiarize us with [the] divine ways."[93] Irenaeus succinctly shows the pedagogical nature of sacred history in *Against Heresies*, where he contends that God does nothing out of need. God did not create Adam because he lacked something, but in order that he might allow his superabundance to be received by another. "In the beginning, therefore, did God form Adam, not as if He stood in need of man, but that He might have [someone] upon whom to confer His benefits" (*Ad. haer.* IV.14.1). God did not require that the Jews practice their liturgy for his own benefit. "Thus, too, He imposed upon

---

91. Ibid., 28.

92. The operative terminology here is *paidagogos* which is translated with varying indications of the pedagogical aim of the word.

93. Daniélou, *Approches du Christ*, 207. "Le but de l'histoire sainte est de nous familiariser avec ces mœurs divines." ET: *Christ and Us*, trans. Walter Roberts. All subsequent English translations of this text will be Roberts' unless noted otherwise.

the [Jewish] people the construction of the tabernacle, the building of the temple, the election of the Levites, sacrifices also, and oblations, legal monitions, and all the other service of the law. He does Himself truly want none of these things, for He is always full of all good" (*Ad. haer.* IV. 14.3). Rather than his own benefit, God had the instruction of the Jewish people in mind.

> God formed man at the first, because of His munificence; but chose the patriarchs for the sake of their salvation; and prepared a people beforehand, teaching the headstrong to follow God; and raised up prophets upon earth, *accustoming man to bear his Spirit* [within him], and to hold communion with God: He Himself, indeed, having need of nothing, but granting communion with Himself to those who stood in need of it, and sketching out, like an architect, the plan of salvation to those that pleased Him. And He did Himself furnish guidance to those who beheld Him not in Egypt, while to those who became unruly in the desert He promulgated a law very suitable [to their condition]. Then, on the people who entered into the good land He bestowed a noble inheritance; and He killed the fatted calf for those converted to the Father, and presented them with the finest robe. Thus, *in a variety of ways, He adjusted the human race to an agreement with salvation* (emphasis added).[94]

This instruction, however, was not limited to the Jews and did not cease following the Incarnation.

The divine pedagogy is not limited to the time of the Old Testament. Sacred history remains the context within which the education of individuals takes place. "The real purpose of history is to achieve—through the mill of temporal vicissitudes—'the manufacture and education of human souls.' The real measure of history is not to be sought in the level of technical attainment, but in the more or less effective production of personalities, 'which represent the highest things we know in the mundane realm.'"[95] It is within this context that contemporary history must be viewed as well.

---

94. Irenaeus, *Adversus Haeresus*, IV.14.2 (PG 7.1011A–1011C). The Latin text of the italicized portions reads *assuescens hominem portare ejus Spiritum* and *multis modus componens humanum genus ad consonantiam salutis*, with *assuescens* and *componens* being the operative pedagogical terms. Each of these terms signifies the pedagogical aim of sacred history. See also Daniélou, *Approches du Christ*, 110–11.

95. Daniélou, *Essai sur le Mystère de l'Histoire*, 100. "Mais le vrai sens de l'histoire est à travers la diversité des vicissitudes extérieures d'être «the manufacture and education of human souls». Il faut juger une époque, non à ses résultats techniques, mais à son aptitude à susciter des personnalités «which represent the highest things we know in the mundane world»."

Current events must be seen in the context of their pedagogical value. As in the past, God continues to form his people within the context of historical events and the procession of sacred history until the end of human history and the advent of the world to come.

The Schema of Cosmic History

Cosmic history can be divided into five eras: the time of God's activity prior to the creation of humanity, the era of the Old Testament, the era of the New Testament, the era of the Church and the life of the world to come.[96] Prior to the creation of humanity, and therefore human history, God was active in a number of ways. The Creation accounts of Genesis clearly show that God was working creatively before the creation of humanity with the creation of the heavenly bodies, with the creation of flora and fauna, as well as the creation of the earth. But, the activity of God was not limited to the creation of an earthly reality. The Triune God was active in himself through Trinitarian relationality and thus constitutes a perpetual activity without beginning or end. It is after this self-substantial activity that God sought to spread the divine superabundance.

Upon creating the first man and woman, God began the long history of the people of God from Adam and Eve to Abraham and to Moses. It is here that Yahweh began the long education of a stiff-necked people. He began the process of accustoming his people to his ways. The action of God in human history first took the form of the education of the people of Israel; therefore, the institutions of Israel have a divine origin and inherent value. However, whereas the Jews believe that these institutions have value in themselves, the Fathers of the Church maintained that the institutions of Judaism functioned as signifiers which point to a progressive reality. God's accustoming of his people through a slow pedagogical process finds its fulfillment in the next stage of cosmic history.

The third stage in sacred history is constituted by the realities of the New Testament which the figures of the Old Testament anticipated. "The Old and New Testament enter into a single plan but represent two successive

---

96. Daniélou, "Le Sens Chretien de l'Histoire," 129; ET: "Christian View of History," 70. Subsequent references will be to the English translation in *The Month*. Given Daniélou's concerns to establish sacred history as a cosmic history, I have added the first and the last category which are implicit in Daniélou's thought but not specifically mentioned in this particular article.

History and Prayer

moments of it."[97] Like the events of the Old Testament, the events of the New Testament have a permanent value. For example, the birth, death and resurrection of Jesus certainly have a crucial value in the divine economy. Indeed, the figures of the Old Testament are realized in the events of the New Testament and find an absolute fulfillment in the person of Christ. Yet, the events of the New Testament also point beyond themselves.

The fourth period of sacred history moves into the time of the Church.[98] Daniélou contends, "The Church, present in our midst, visibly continues the institution whose visible foundation was laid by Christ during His earthly life. She is therefore the most obvious visible link with the Jesus of history. But at the same time the Church invisibly contains the divine acts of Christ in His Passion and Resurrection. She is not only a visible institution; she is the setting of the *magnalia Dei* in our midst."[99] And, later he maintains that "the Church as an institution is an essential aspect of sacred history."[100] At the same time, the Church can still be characterized as a shadow or a veil, and it constitutes the penultimate fulfillment of the figures of the Old Testament, which points to the final period of sacred history: heavenly existence. Of course, this schema is intimately bound up with Daniélou's typological understanding of history.

The final category reflects Daniélou's insistence that the tropes in the New Testament signify a fifth era in the schema of cosmic history, the Eighth Day—the life of the world to come.[101] One thing that differentiates the Christian view of history from a secular view of history is that the Christian view envisions an end to the history of this world. This is, simply put, the eschatological nature of Christianity, where the believing community looks for the end of this world and toward the world of the life to come.[102] As the Church professes at the end of the creed, "we look for the resurrection and the life of the world to come." Yet, while the Church looks

---

97. Daniélou, "Conception of History in the Christian Tradition," 173.

98. Daniélou, "We are Still Living in Sacred History," 12.

99. Daniélou, *Approches du Christ*, 180. "L'Église, présente au milieu de nous, continue visiblement l'institution dont le Christ a pose le fondement visible durant sa vie terrestre. Elle est ainsi le lien visible le plus évident avec le Jésus de l'histoire. Mais en même temps l'Église contient invisiblement les actions divines du Christ dans sa passion et sa résurrection. Elle n'est pas qu'une institution visible. Elle est le lieu des *magnalia Dei* au milieu de nous."

100. Ibid., 185. "L'Église comme institution est un aspect essential de l'histoire sainte."

101. See *Bible et Liturgie*, 355–87 for Daniélou's thoughts on the Eighth day.

102. Daniélou, "New Testament and the Theology of History," 27.

forward to the end of secular or profane history, she also recognizes that cosmic history continues in union with the Triune God.

This understanding of the end of human history is clearly illustrated in the idea of the Cosmic Week and the Eighth Day. In the *Epistle of Barnabas* the reader is given a picture of the end of history and the continuance of the people of God in the life to come. In the epistle, the writer reconceived the week of creation as a paradigm of human history with each day representing a thousand years. But, at the end of all the days of the cosmic week, the author contends that God will create an eighth day, i.e., the beginning of another world: "it is not the present Sabbaths that are acceptable to me, but the one that I have made; on the Sabbath, after I have set everything at rest, I will create the beginning of an eighth day, which is the beginning of another world."[103]

Sacraments as Historic Actions

Within the schema of sacramental history, it is important to ask the question: "Was sacred history concluded with the incarnation, death and resurrection of Christ?" Daniélou argues that sacred history continues to unfold—continuing the economies of the Old Testament and the New Testament—in the time of the Church. It is liturgical actions which extend the *mirabilia Dei* into the time of the Church: "One reason for taking the Sacraments as the co-ordinates of our point of view is the need to show the place they occupy in the history of salvation, being the continuation, into the ecclesiastical era, of the *mirabilia Dei* recorded in the Old and New Testaments. . . . [W]e now observe the full deployment of the historical process in the Church, the Sacraments being the decisive events of this period."[104] Daniélou says of this period, "Faith and the sacraments, by which the action of God breaks into our world of history, constitute its events and milestones."[105] During the time of the Church, Christians live

---

103. *Epistola Barnabae*, 15.8 (PG 2.772B). See Jeffords, *Reading the Apostolic Fathers: An Introduction*, 11–31 and Quasten, *Patrology*, vol. 1, 85–92.

104. Daniélou, *Essai sur le Mystère de l'Histoire*, 201–2. "Si nous prenons les sacrements comme centres de notre perspective, c'est parce que qu'il est important de montrer qu'ils représente un moment de l'histoire du salut, qu'ils sont dans le temps de l'Église, la continuation des *mirabilia Dei* dans l'Ancien et le Nouveau Testament. . . . Nous assistons à son déploiement dans l'Église, dont les sacrements représentent les événements essentiels."

105. Daniélou, "Le Sens Chretien de l'Histoire," 129. "Il y a donc une histoire sainte

in a tension between the Incarnation and the *parousia*. Christ has inaugurated the end; however, the end has yet to be fulfilled. During this time, the Church "reproduce[s] the sacerdotal actions of Christ by which all things have attained their end."[106]

Given the schema of sacramental history, it is important to concentrate on the current era in history: the era of the Church. It is vital to determine how the Church participates in sacred history. Daniélou maintains that this is done through the sacraments of the Church, that the "sacraments are the historical actions corresponding to the particular characteristics of the time which extends from the Ascension to the Last Judgment, that is to say, of the time in which we live."[107] The crucial event of sacred history has already been achieved in the life of Christ, and in a certain sense the end has already been achieved. "In one sense it can add nothing to time. Jesus Christ cannot be surpassed."[108] However, at the same time, though the victory is certain, "His glory has not yet been visibly manifested."[109] As the Gospel of Matthew reports Christ saying, "And this gospel of the kingdom will be preached in the whole world as a testimony to all nations and then the end will come" (Mt. 24:14; NAB). This brings into focus the missiological nature of the sacraments. No doubt the delay of the *parousia* is because of the needed extension of the Church throughout the entire world. "Christ is the Head, but his Body is still being formed."[110] This point is not missed by Daniélou when he writes, "the universal preaching of the Gospel is the prerequisite condition for Christ's return, as the Scriptures tell us. Now the sacraments are the essential instruments of that Mission which constitutes the reality of contemporary history, of which profane history is merely an external shell."[111]

---

présente dont les événements sont la foi et les sacrements, par lesquels l'action de Dieu fait irruption sans le temps." Elsewhere Daniélou notes, "Ces actions du Verbe [dans l'histoire] ont des formes diverses dans l'Église. Mais leur foyer est le milieu sacramentaire," *Approches du Christ*, 197.

106. Daniélou, "New Testament and the Theology of History," 31.

107. Daniélou, "Histoire Marxiste et Histoire Sacramentaire," 104. "Les sacrements sont les actions historiques qui correspondent aux caractères particuliers du temps qui va de l'Ascension à la Parousie, c'est-à-dire de celui que nous vivons."

108. Daniélou, "New Testament and the Theology of History," 31.

109. Ibid.

110. Daniélou. *Contemplation*, 102–3. "Le Christ est la Tête, mais actuellement se construit son Corps."

111. Daniélou, "Sacraments and Parousia," 401. See also Daniélou, "Histoire Marxiste

Jean Danielou's Doxological Humanism

It is here that one detects the missiological nature of the sacraments, which places the sacraments in the center of the work of the era of the Church. "These sacramentary actions are the great events of the existing world. Such actions are much nobler than the mighty achievements of philosophers or scientists, nobler than the great victories or great revolutions. The latter apparently cover the whole façade of history but they never reach the roots of real history. They are achievements in the intellectual and physical order. But the sacraments are the greatness of the order of charity."[112] Indeed, Daniélou argues that the solution to the problems of contemporary history is the sacramentary actions of Christ in the Church. As an alternative to other contemporary solutions to the problems of the world Daniélou proposes that the "right answer, as we understand the matter, should be sought from the other end, in the dedicated life of Christianity, especially through the sacraments: there is no reason why Christians should feel like refugees whenever they practise their religion; on the contrary, they are then in the vanguard of the historical process."[113] As is typical for Daniélou, he does not counterpose the spiritual life of the Church with the movements of the historical process. Indeed, he contends that "the real protagonists of . . . history are the saints."[114] All the more, he locates the spiritual life of the Church at the center of historical activity. "The highest

---

et Histoire Sacramentaire," 105, "Entre l'Ascension et la Parousie, son contenu propre est la Mission, commence à la Pentecôte et qui se continuera jusqu'au Retour du Christ, puisque, nous dit l'Evangile, la condition de ce retour est l'évangélisation de tout l'univers [Between the Ascension and the Parousia its special function is missionary activity, begun at Pentecost and continuing until the return of Christ, since, the Gospel tells us, the condition of this return is the evangelization of the whole universe]"; "Conception of History in the Christian Tradition," 175, "If the return of Christ is delayed, it is indeed because his message must first be preached to the entire universe"; "New Testament and the Theology of History," 30, "But what has been acquired by it [the Redemption] as a right for all humanity must in fact be transmitted to all men. This is the New Testament mystery of the missions. Sacred history is the history of the present in which we live, in which the task is to extend to all nations what Jesus Christ brought to us"; *Contemplation*, 95, "What has been accomplished in Christ must be extended into the whole of humankind [Mais ce qui est accompli dans le Christ doit s'étendre à l'humanité tout entière]."

112. Ibid., 401–2.

113. Daniélou, *Essai sur le Mystère de l'Histoire*, 79. "Or nous disons que le vraie réponse est au contraire dans un christianisme intégralement vécu et en particulier dans la vie sacramentaire—et que c'est ainsi que les chrétiens ne vivront pas en quelque sorte, réfugiés dans leur christianisme, mais seront à l'avant-garde du veritable mouvement de l'histoire."

114. Daniélou, "Histoire Marxiste et Histoire Sacramentaire," 110. "De cette histoire, ce sont alors les saints qui sont les grands protagonists."

and deepest supernatural aspects of Christian life, and in particular the sacraments, furnish the best solution of contemporary problems. Thus it will appear that these eternal realities, far from being a side-issue, belong to the innermost structure of our world: practicing Christianity is not merely an optional arrangement to secure good relations with almighty God, but means of committing oneself utterly, and for good."[115]

Conclusion

Upon the release of *Essai sur le Mystère de l'Histoire*, *The Downside Review* published a review article by Eric John concerning Daniélou's thoughts on history.[116] John opines, "The title of the book is seriously misleading, it is not a treatise on the theology of history—an impossible theme. What could possibly be irrelevant, what could reasonably be left out? It is rather a collection of odd studies on the kind of topics people usually have in mind when they talk about history."[117] John goes on to characterize history as "the sum total of past human activity, which of course is to mean what it is impossible for humans to know. By far the greatest part of this activity was purely private to the agent concerned and not even accessible to his contemporaries, let alone to a later generation."[118] Granted, the author of the review asks his reader for permission "to praise and to carp at" Daniélou's work despite the embarrassment of riches in the book. Nonetheless, John's comments in the review are indicative of misunderstanding of Daniélou's thrust, that is, history involves the "mighty works of God," which are continued in the present life of the Church and the life of the Spirit granted by the believer's participation in that life and constitutes a *mystère* in a richly theological sense. Indeed, as has been noted earlier, Daniélou believed that the saints are the primary movers of history. He was fond of quoting Léon

---

115. Daniélou, *Essai sur le Mystère de l'Histoire*, 80. "C'est précisément dans les réalités les plus surnaturelles, les plus essentielles, les plus propres au christianisme, telles que les sacrements, que nous trouverons la réponse la plus profonde aux problèmes du monde présent. Toutes ces réalités ne nous apparaîtront plus alors comme un à-côté de notre vie, mais au contraire, comme en étant le cœur; elles ne seront plus comme une pratique dont on s'acquitte pour être en bonne conscience avec Dieu, mais un engagement total et réel."

116. John, "Daniélou on History," 2–15.

117. Ibid., 2.

118. Ibid., 2–3.

Jean Danielou's Doxological Humanism

Bloy's statement from *La Femme Pauvre*, "Il n'y a qu'une tristess, c'est de n'être pas des saints [There is only one misery, and that is not to be saints]."[119]

What John seemingly misunderstood about Daniélou's book on history is that Daniélou wholeheartedly believed that history was driven by the saints and the practices of holiness, poverty, zeal, and hope. John is somewhat dismissive of the chapters in *Essai sur le Mystère de l'Histoire* on Christian virtues as having nothing really to do with history. What do Christian virtues have to do with history which is "about public activity" and "what men have done that has altered the shape of their common life with their fellow-men?"[120] In stark contrast to this vision of history as mere events, Daniélou asserts that the movement of history is enacted by those who participate in the *magnolia Dei* through the spiritual life of the Church. "More important than the rise and fall of empires, the fame of victories, the discoveries of scientists and scholars, the masterpieces of art, are the Incarnation of the Word, his Resurrection, the Coming of the Holy Spirit, and the mission of the Apostles, the conversion and the sanctification of souls. *Saints are more important to it than are geniuses or heroes.*"[121]

It is through contemplation that the saints enter into the flow of history. It is through prayer that Christians participate in the irruption of God into the historical process. Theirs constitutes the true history of the world, the history of the holy acts of the people of God. The saints exercise their faith in God when they affirm that God does intervene in human history. Just as importantly, prayer is a means of exploring the working out of sacred history and an instrument for understanding its content and its meaning.

---

119. Bloy, *Le Femme Pauvre*; ET: *The Woman Who Was Poor*.

120. John, "Daniélou on History," 4.

121. Emphasis added. Daniélou, *L'Oraison Problème Politique*, 46. "Plus importantes que les montées ou les chutes des Empires, que l'éclat des victoires, que les inventions des savants, que les creations de l'art, sont l'Incarnation du Verbe, et sa Résurrection, l'effusion de l'Esprit et la mission des Apôtres, la conversion et la sanctification des cœurs. Les Saints lui important plus que les génies ou les héros."

THREE

Prayer, Trinity, and Mission

Comtemplation and the Trinity

IN 1968, DANIÉLOU PUBLISHED a small work titled *La Trinité et le Mystère de l'Existence*, which began with the observation that contemporary society is in desperate need of a reorientation toward contemplation in order that individuals might be able to realize their full stature as human beings made in the likeness of God.[1] This reorientation is necessary because though society seeks to make human fulfillment possible for the members of its society, without a place for contemplation and adoration it only affords its members partial fulfillment through material means. Daniélou contends that for individuals to achieve complete fulfillment contemporary society must provide a space where total human fulfillment is the aim. This milieu is the Church, where the solution to the crisis of the contemporary world, the contemplative posture, is practiced and both contemplation—with all its concomitant practices—and the extension of contemplation are sought. "With temporal engagement assuming an ever more important place in the life of Christians, there is an urgent need for a counterweight in the form of contemplative thinking. Behind all the changes of present day civilization, we can glimpse an obscure search for greater human fulfillment. But this fulfillment cannot be attained at the level of a purely material civilization, or even at the level of a fraternal human society. In the final analysis, it is the search for God that lies at the heart of today's crisis. We must therefore

---

1. Daniélou, *Trinité et le mystère de l'existence*, 7–8; ET: *God's Life in Us*. All subsequent English translations of this text will be Leggat's translation unless noted otherwise.

strive to make transcendence an integral part of our technical civilization; without it, a true humanism is inconceivable."[2] Daniélou maintains that contemporary society not only makes the contemplative stance difficult, it makes a concerted effort to minimize or eliminate it from public view as a personal and largely irrelevant aspect of human activity. However, he continues, for a city to be a truly human city there must be a space for adoration, contemplation, and prayer. Though societies, in most cases, seek the good of their individuals, they do so in an incomplete way. The aim of the political is the "temporal common good."[3] According to Daniélou, political entities seek the common good of their members by means of three objectives: "to make a world in which human relations can flourish in freedom, that is to say, a society in which man does not exploit man, from which racism of every sort is banished, where understanding is open and peace between nations becomes possible."[4] In his provocative little work *L'Oraison problème politique*, Daniélou contends that

> politics limited to these objectives would still not assure a complete temporal good. . . . [T]he true city is that 'in which [individuals] have their homes and God also has his. . . .' A city which does not possess churches as well as factories is not fit for [people]. It is inhuman. The task of politics is to assure to [people] a city in which it will be possible for them to fulfill themselves completely, to have full material, fraternal, and spiritual life. It is for this reason that we consider that, in so far as it expresses this personal fulfillment of man in a particular dimension, prayer is a political problem; for a city which would make prayer impossible would fail to fulfill its role as a city.[5]

---

2. Ibid., 9. "Il s'agit donc de render présent au milieu de la civilisation technique la dimension de la trancedance en dehors de laquelle il n'y a pas d'humanisme possible."

3. Daniélou, *L'Oraison Problème Politique*, 25; ET: *Prayer as Political Problem*. "J'entends ici par politique la sphère du bien commun temporel." All subsequent English translations of this text will be Kirwan's translation unless noted otherwise. See also Jean Daniélou, "L'Oraison comme problème politique," 62–73.

4. Ibid., 26. "La politique a aussi pour but de créer un monde dans lequel les relations entre les personnes puissant s'épnouir librement, c-est-à-dire une société dans laquelle il n'y ait pas d'exploitation de l'homme par l'homme, où les racismes soient bannis, qui tende à la transparence dans les rapports humains, où la paix entre les peoples soit possible."

5. Ibid., 26–27. "Mais si la poitique limitait à cela ses objectifs, elle n'assurerait pas un bien commun temporel total. Je pensé avec La Pira, selon une formule que j'ai souvent citée, que la vraie cité est celle «où les hommes ont leur maison et où Dieu a sa maison.» Une cité où il n'y a pas d'églises à côté des usines est une cité inhumaine. Or le rôle de la

Prayer, Trinity, and Mission

Yet, it is the case that the societies in which we find ourselves make contemplation difficult. Daniélou believes that there are three major hindrances to contemplation for the modern individual: the modern rhythm of life, lack of solitude, and general desacralization of society. Daniélou's first point will be admitted by most. In general—and particularly in Western societies—life proceeds at such a frantic pace, with every moment being planned and managed, that there is virtually no time for any contemplation whatsoever. Daniélou writes, "The first thing that strikes one is that our technological civilization brings about a change in the rhythm of human existence. There is a speeding up of tempo which makes it more difficult to find the minimum of freedom on which a minimum life of prayer depends. These are elementary problems, but none the less basic."[6] The speed of modern society and all its demands requires a monumental act of discipline by the one who has not removed himself completely from society. "Prayer is thus rendered almost impossible for most [individuals], unless they display a heroism and a strength of character of which . . . the majority of men are not capable. If it is only the shelter of a rule which makes possible the flowering of a life of prayer for professed religious, then the laity, without this shelter and with added obstacles, must indeed be in difficulties."[7]

The second obstacle to contemplation in the modern world is the hypersocialization of individuals to the point that there are few times where one is actually by oneself in solitude. With a lack of solitude, there is a concomitant lack of silence. With the absence of solitude and silence, it is increasingly difficult to be in the presence of God.[8] While one must avoid

---

politique est d'assurer une cité dans laquelle il soit possible à l'homme de se réaliser complétement, dans le plénitude de sa vie matérielle, fraternelle et spirituelle. C'est en quoi nous pensons qu'en tant qu'elle exprime cet épanouissement personnel d'une dimensión particulière de l'homme, l'oraison est un problème politique, dans la mesure où une cité qui la rendrait imposible trahirait son rôle de cité."

6. Ibid., 31. "Il est certain tout d'abord que la civilisation technique entraîne une modification du rythme de l'existence humaine, une accélération du temps qui rendent plus difficile à trouver le minimum d'espace dont a besoin un minimum de vie d'oraison. Ces problèmes sont élémentaires et pourtant fondamentaux."

7. Ibid. "La prière est ainsi rendue quasi impossible à la plupart des homes, en dehors d'un héroïsme, d'une force de volonté sont nous devons reconnaître que la majorité des hommes n'est pas capable. Si pour des religieux le cadre d'une règle rend seul possible l'épanouissement d'une vie d'oraison, qu'en sera-t-il des laïcs, dépourvus de ces appuis et affrontés au contraire à des obstacles?"

8. Bernard McGinn notes the need for solitude and silence in the context of mystical contemplation. McGinn observes that the mystical element of Christianity is "that part of belief or practice that concerns the preparation for, the consciousness of, and

47

the temptation of radical individualism; one must also avoid the other danger of becoming merely a "unit of collective existence."[9] Daniélou warns, "even as prayer has need of a certain minimum of time, so also it has a need of a certain minimum of solitude, a minimum of personal life [as contrasted to collective life]. In the actual conditions in which [people] have to live today, this is practically impossible. Urban life sucks people up into a relentlessly collective existence."[10] And more, Daniélou describes the modern individual as "an alienated creature, one who has lost the possibility of finding himself, who no longer knows who he is, who has to meet this never-ending barrage of demands from outside himself and who has ended by becoming depersonalized."[11] Without a modicum of silence and solitude, the modern individual is unable to develop his inner self making prayer and contemplation a mere external practice with little to no effect on the fulfillment of a flourishing, true humanity.

A third obstacle to contemplation is that of desacralization. The fact—if not the causes—of secularization is well known. It entails a partitioning of the sacred and the profane, severing the organic bond between the sacred realm and civic culture. "It is evident . . . that technological civilization and the phenomena it brings in its train (urbanization, for instance) break into and overthrow the old social cultures, separate profane culture from religious life, and destroy a certain balance between the social and

---

the reaction to what the mystics understand as the direct, immediate, and transformative encounter with the presence of God." Part of being open to the presence of God is allowing for extended periods of quiet and solitude within the context of the sacred. Bernard McGinn and Patricia Ferris McGinn, *Early Christian Mystics*, 10. This volume is a popular reworking of McGinn's multivolume work *The Presence of God: A History of Western Christian Mysticism* which contain the following volumes, *The Foundations of Mysticism: Origins to the Fifth Century* (1991), *The Growth of Mysticism: Gregory the Great through the Twelfth Century* (1994), *The Flowering of Mysticism: Men and Women in the New Mysticism*—1200–1350 (1998), and *The Harvest of Mysticism in Medieval Germany* (1300–1500) (2005).

9. Daniélou, *L'Oraison Problème Politique*, 32–33. "Il intéresse tout homme, menace de n'être plus qu'un élément d'une existence collective."

10. Ibid., 32. "De même que l'oraison a besoin d'un minimum de temps elle a besoin d'un minimum de solitude, d'un minimum de vie personnelle. Or il est certain que, dans le conditions concrètes de l'existence de l'homme d'aujourd'hui, ceci est à nouveau pratiquement impossible."

11. Ibid., 32. "L'homme d'aujourd'hui est un homme aliéné qui a perdu la possibilité de se retrouver lui-même, qui ne sait plus ce qu'il est, parce qu'il ne fait que répondre perpétuellement à des sollicitations du dehors, et qui finit, par conséquent, par être dépersonnalisé."

Prayer, Trinity, and Mission

the religious dimensions of life."[12] Without a provision within societies for the sacred—and this can be dramatically seen in the western Europe of the twenty-first century—those societies are barely sustainable in the long term. Daniélou writes:

> We come always back to the same thought. If that dimension remains completely absent from that society, if we accept a complete dissociation of the sacred and profane worlds, we shall make access to prayer absolutely impossible to the mass of [humankind]. Only a few would be able to find God in a world organized without reference to him. Men move not only in their social environment, but in their cultural environment as well. It is through this cultural environment that they can have access to the realities of religion. A world which had built up its culture without reference to God, a humanism from which adoration was completely absent, would make the maintenance of positive religious point of view impossible for the great majority of [people].[13]

Desacralization has served as a major contributing factor toward the erosion of the contemplative stance and providing a society in which crisis of religion becomes more acute.

Monastic institutions are able to create a space for all of the aspects of the spiritual life which makes contemplation attainable (if still difficult). All of these things are present for religious in consecrated communities. Still, not all are able to create a space for contemplation in the way that religious do. Yet, Daniélou notes a further problem when he observes, "If monks feel the need to create an environment in which they will find prayer possible, if they think that prayer is not possible without certain conditions of silence, solitude, and rule, what are we to say of the mass of [humankind]? Should

---

12. Ibid., 33. "Or il est évident que l'irruption de la civilisation technique, avec les phénomènes qu'elle entraîne, l'urbanisation par exemple, bouleverse les anciennes structures sociales, sépare la culture profane de la vie religieuse, détruit un certain équilibre entre la dimension sociale de l'homme et sa dimension religieuse."

13. Ibid., 35. "Car—et nous revenons toujours à la même idée—, si cette dimension reste totalement étrangère à cette société, si nous acceptons une dissociation totale entre un monde profane et un monde sacré, nous rendons absolument impossible à la masse des home l'accès à l'oraison. Seuls alors quelques-uns pourraient trouver Dieu dans un monde tout entier constitué en dehors de lui. Non seulement les homes beignet dans un milieu social, mais ils beignet aussi dans un milieu culturel. C'est à travers ce milieu culturel qu'ils peuvent avoir accès aux réalités religieuse. Un monde où la culture se constituerait totalement en dehors de Dieu, un humanisme dont l'adoration serait totalement absente, rendrait pratiquement impossible à la majorité des homes le maintien d'une certain attitude religieuse."

prayer be the privilege of a small spiritual aristocracy, and should the bulk of the Christian people be excluded from it?"[14] The problem is especially acute for the laity because they are unable to rely on the conditions that monastic communities are able to secure for themselves. Thus the modern individual finds himself in the midst of a crisis which disables him from achieving the fullness of his humanity as a creature of God.

In an attempt to provide the laity with a template for the contemplative posture within the context of modern, technological culture, Daniélou writes his small work *La Trinité et le mystère de l'existence*. As a preface to his meditations concerning Trinitarian existence, Daniélou informs his reader of the aim of this small work. He first notes the crises of contemporary life.[15] He then notes that the only real solution—which to some would seem to be more of an escape than a solution—to the crisis is contemplation. "This little book is designed to meet this need. The meditations aim at direct expression of a spirituality for men and women of action who wish to be dedicated to God. They are addressed to all Christians concerned with the place of prayer in a world in which prayer appears to many to be superfluous, in which everything leads away from prayer. I hope they show that prayer is not a luxury for the privileged few, but a vital need for everyone."[16] It is important to take note of a couple of things at this point. When Daniélou provides a solution for contemporary society "for men and women of action," he proposes contemplation. This may seem to be contradictory to some who do not see the active nature of contemplation. It is important to remember that Daniélou highlights the fact that there is no contradiction between the apostolate and contemplation. The false dichotomization of

---

14. Ibid., 28. "Si les moines sentent la nécessité de se donner des conditionnements pour rendre l'oraison possible, s'ils pensent qu'en dehors de certaines conditions de silence, de solitude, de rythme de vie, l'oraison est impossible, alors qu'en est-il de la masse des homes? L'oraison ne deviendrait-elle pas le privilège d'une petite aristocratie de spirituels, et la totalité de peuple chrétien ne s'en trouverait-elle pas exclue?"

15. Daniélou's corpus is replete with the theme of this crisis. For example, see "Y a-t-il une Crise de la Vie Religieuse?," 1029–31; "In Connection with the Crisis of Religious Life," 53–58; and *La Crise Actuelle d'Intelligence*; ET: *The Crisis in Intelligence*, 75–111.

16. Daniélou, *La Trinité et le Mystère de l'Existence*, 8. "C'est à ce but que veut répondre ce petit livre, qui sera le premier d'une série. Les méditations qui le constituent sont celles d'une retraite qui a été donnée à l'Institut Saint-Jean-Baptiste. Elles cherchent donc directement à exprimer la spiritualité de vies consacrées à Dieu sou une forme contemplative au milieu du monde. Mais elles s'adressent aussi à tous les chrétiens pour qui se pose le problème de l'espace de la prière dans un monde où tout en détourne. Et la prière n'est pas le luxe de quelques privilégiés, mais un besoin vital de tous."

Prayer, Trinity, and Mission

Mary and Martha holds no sway in Daniélou's mind. This is verified by statements such as: "It is essentially through the battles of the spiritual life, through the battles of sanctity, that we contribute to the salvation of the world."[17] Secondly, it is clear that this sort of solution to the problems of contemporary society will not resonate with the society that needs an infusion of contemplation. It is in this regard that Daniélou's often used notion of the "extension of adoration" coordinates with Trinitarian contemplation. This idea is succinctly noted when Daniélou writes, "Prayer is related to mission because it is to the extent that we have discovered who God is and how much a knowledge and love of God is constitutive of a comprehensive humanism and a full and complete existence that we suffer from, and are stuck by, situations in which God is not known or loved."[18] The total fulfillment of humanity must entail contemplation (particularly Trinitarian contemplation) and the extension of contemplation and adoration.

The Presence of the Holy Trinity

The conception of "presence" plays an important role in Daniélou's thought. He highlights the role of the presence of the Trinitarian God in the life of the believer in contemplation. Prayer, he maintains, "is a drawing near to the Holy Trinity dwelling in our souls. This is a fundamental supposition of Christian prayer; that is, it is no longer the prayer of a creature, but that of a child of God."[19] This presence of God in the soul of the Christian is thoroughly represented in the writings of the Old Testament. In the Old Testament, the presence of God was communicated to the people of God through His presence in the temple.[20] This presence is generally manifested

17. Daniélou, *Contemplation*, 156. "C'est essentiellement à travers les combats de la vie spirituelle, à travers les combats de la sainteté, que nous contribuons à sauver le monde." ET: *Prayer*. All subsequent English translations of this text will be Schindler's translation unless noted otherwise.

18. Ibid., 133–34. "La contemplation est liée à mission, parce que c'est dans la mesure où on a réalisé ceci qu'est Dieu et à quel point le fait de connaître et d'aimer Dieu est constitutif d'un humanisme total et d'une existence complète, qu'on souffre et qu'on est surprise de ce que Dieu ne soit pas connu et ne soit pas aimé."

19. Daniélou, *Contemplation*, 31. "La prière est une approche de la Sainte Trinité demeurant dans notre âme. C'est une donnée fondamentale de la prière chrétienne, c'est-à-dire non plus de la prière de l'homme en tant que créature, mais en tant que fils de Dieu."

20. Daniélou gives a short study of the presence of God in the Old Testament and in the person of Christ in *Le Signe du Temple; ou, de la Présence de Dieu*; ET: *The Presence of God*. All subsequent English translations of this text will be Robert's translation unless noted otherwise.

in three ways: 1) the presence of God in the universe[21], 2) the presence of God in the Jewish people and the temple of Jerusalem,[22] and 3) the presence of the Trinitarian God in the members of the body of Christ.[23]

Daniélou begins his small work with an explanation of how the Trinity is present to humanity. First and foremost, the Trinity is the principle and aim of the whole of reality. "In the Trinity, the ultimate depths of the real and the whole mystery of existence are revealed to us. The Trinity is the principle and the origin of Creation and Redemption. Ultimately all things are borne back to it in the mystery of worship and adoration. Above all else, it is what gives substance to all things: everything else flows from it or tends toward it."[24] It is in the light of the presence of the Holy Trinity that the Christian finds his true self. In recognizing the presence of the Trinity within all reality, one is able to move from the external world to the inner reality of all existence. "In the light of the Trinity, we discover our true selves. For the essential conversion is the one that leads us from the visible world with its external temptations to the invisible world which is at once supremely real, since it constitutes the ultimate basis of all reality, and supremely holy and admirable, since it is the source of all bliss and joy."[25] It is the understanding of the Trinity as the basis of all reality that constitutes the beginning of the contemplative conversion which is the solution to the crisis of civilization.

> Any progress in our lives, must embody this fundamental conversion of self to ultimate reality. This is what is involved: opening ourselves to the absolute reality of the Holy Trinity, discovering there the fullness of all things, seeking perfect contentment in it and finding in it our life's greatest treasure both now and for eternity. In this sense, contemplation is primarily a way of penetrating reality more deeply. Inversely, sin consists in not opening

21. Daniélou, *Le Signe du Temple*, 9–14.
22. Ibid., 15–19.
23. Ibid., 20–54. See also *Contemplation*, 32.
24. Daniélou, *La Trinité et le Mystère de l'Existence*, 11. "Dans la Trinité se dévoilent à nous les profondeurs dernières de réel, le mystère de l'existence. Elle est le principe et l'origine de la création et de la rédemption; par ailleurs toutes choses lui sont finalement rapportées dans le mystère de la louange et de l'adoration. Elle est, au-delà de tout, ce qui donne à tout sa consistance. Tout le reste en procède et y tend."
25. Ibid. "Dès lors la conversion essentielle est cette conversion qui nous fait passer du monde visible, qui nous sollicite de l'extérieur, à ce monde invisible qui est à la fois souverainement réel, puisqu'il constitue le fond dernier de toute réalité, et souverainement saint et admirable, puisqu'il est la source de toute béatitude et de tout joie."

Prayer, Trinity, and Mission

ourselves to what is truly real, in remaining in an outward and superficial world that stems from the life of the self. It is this basic contemplative conversion that we must undertake, striving to open ourselves to the sovereign reality of the Holy Trinity so that our hearts may be filled with its light, turning our souls toward it and leaving all else behind us.[26]

With this in mind, it is important to note how the life of the Trinity is manifested and revealed in the world.

The presence of the Holy Trinity is active throughout all of created reality. To begin with, Trinitarian action is first manifested in its work "in the world, in nature, in the cosmos." This is most strikingly manifested in the action of the Trinity in the creation of the world.[27] "Creation is presented as the work of the Holy Trinity. Through His Word and His Spirit, God calls forth, breathes life into, orders and guides the universe."[28] Though many interpretative stances—particularly in modern biblical studies—are inclined to dismiss a Trinitarian reading of creation, Daniélou robustly defends the presence of the Trinity at creation. The initial and primary evidence for the presence of the Trinity at creation comes from Scripture itself. No doubt, many interpreters would anticipate the use of the prologue to the gospel of John at this point. "In the beginning was the Word, and the Word was

---

26. Ibid., 11–12. "Tout progrès de notre vie, il y a cette conversion fondamentale, qui est ouverture à la réalité foncière des Personnes divines, découverte que c'est en elles que réside la plénitude de toutes chose, appel à nous suffire d'elles et à trouver en elles ce qui sera dans le temps et l'éternité le trésor de nos vies. C'est en cela que la contemplation est avant tout une certaine manière de pénétrer plus profondément dans la réalité. Et inversement, le péché consiste à ne pas s'ouvrir à ce qui est vraiment réel et à reste dans un monde extérieur et superficiel, qui relève de notre vie égoïste. C'est dans cette conversion contemplative fondamentale que nous devons entrer en essayant de nous ouvrir à cette réalité souveraine de la Sainte Trinité, de manière à ce que nos cœurs soient remplis de sa lumière, laissant là le reste et tournant nos âmes vers elle."

27. "Il y a une première chose qui en frappante à travers l'Ancien et le Nouveau Testament, c'est que les Personnes divines nous apparaissent à travers leur action dans le monde, dans la nature, dans le cosmos. Si nous prenons les premières expressions du Mystère de la Trinité dans l'Ancien Testament, nous voyons qu'elles sont en rapport avec le monde de la création. La création apparaît comme étant l'œuvre des Personnes divines. C'est Dieu qui par sa parole et par son Esprit suscite, vivifie, gouverne et conduit l'univers. Il y a là une première approche importante dans la mesure où elle met le mystère trinitaire en rapport avec la réalité même du monde matériel." Daniélou, "La Trinité dans l'Existence Humaine," 6.

28. Daniélou, *La Trinité et le Mystère de l'Existence*, 13. "La création apparaît comme étant l'œuvre des Personnes divines. C'est Dieu qui par sa Parole et par son Esprit suscite, vivifie, gouverne et conduit l'univers."

with God, and the Word was God. He was in the beginning with God. All things came to be through him, and without him nothing came to be" (John 1:1; NAB). Daniélou contends that in the prologue to the gospel of John, "we have a strikingly fore-shortened image, establishing an immediate link between Jesus of Nazareth, the Jesus whom John claims to have touched with his own hands and seen with his own eyes, and the life-giving Word Himself—that is to say, the divine power which calls all things into being."[29] At every moment, the entirety of existence is upheld by the presence of the Trinity.

A second passage emphasizes the dependency of creation on the Holy Trinity. Daniélou points to Psalm 33 where the Word is again present at the creation of the world. "By the Lord's Word the heavens were made, by the breath of His mouth all their host" (33:6; NAB). It is entirely possible that the author of the Gospel of John was familiar with this passage. In any case, this passage further draws attention to the role of the Word in creation. Daniélou contends that the "Word of God" has "the same meaning that the rest of the Bible gives it, that is, essentially a creative agency and not simply an intellectual concept."[30] Instead, the agency of the Word in creation is achieved by a unity between utterance and accomplishment.

To this point, Daniélou has only made note of the role of the Son in the creative action of the Trinity. But, the same activity can be applied to the Spirit. The first passage in Scripture that comes to mind when speaking of the creative activity of the Spirit is in the first verses of Genesis. "In the beginning when God created the heavens and the earth, the earth was a formless void and darkness covered the face of the deep, while a wind from God swept over the face of the waters" (Gen 1:1–2; NRSV). Daniélou provides the instructive image of "a bird beating its wings to kindle a spark of life" to illuminate the activity of the Spirit in creation.[31] He draws this image from a passage in Deuteronomy which gives the figure of an eagle beating its wing over its nest in order to provoke its young to flight. The *ruah* rouses the void to life "as an eagle incites its nestlings forth by hovering over its brood" (Deut 32:11; NAB). "The idea here is of *provoking* existence, of wresting

---

29. Ibid. "Il y a là un raccourci saisissant qui établit une relation immédiate entre Jésus de Nazareth, celui que Jean nous dit avoir touché de ses mains et vu de ses yeux et le Verbe créateur lui-même, c'est-à-dire la puissance divine par laquelle toutes choses ont été suscitées dans l'existence."

30. Ibid., 14. "La parole de Dieu a ici le sens que lui donne la Bible, c'est-à-dire essentiellement celui d'une efficience créatrice, et pas simplement un contenu intellectuel."

31. Ibid., 15.

Prayer, Trinity, and Mission

movement from inertia. In the same way the Spirit moved over the waters and called forth from primordial nothingness all the species and varieties of Creation."[32] Likewise, the words of the psalmist in Psalm 104 are used liturgically to remember the creation of the Church at Pentecost. However, Daniélou informs his reader that before the text was used to express the role of the Spirit in the institution of the Church, it previously indicated the activity of the Spirit in the Creation of the universe.[33] In the liturgical reading of Scripture one hears, "When you send forth your breath, they are created, and you renew the face of the earth" (Ps 104:30; NAB).[34] Given Daniélou's reading of Scripture—which is patently typological—it is clear to see that both the Son and the Spirit are agents in the creation and sustenance of the created order by which—in one way—the Trinity is present to all created reality. Importantly, Daniélou concludes his remarks on this subject by writing, "By this means a fundamental relationship is established from the very beginning of the Bible between the Trinity and the world of nature, between the Trinity and the cosmos, so that Redemption comes to mean a recapturing and renewal by the life-giving Trinity of this universe, which is its own because it has created it and can alone lead it to total fulfillment. . . . The origin of the material world lies exclusively in the action of the Holy Trinity. All of it, moreover, is destined to be recaptured and transfigured by the Holy Trinity."[35]

These thoughts emphasize the religious character of nature. Yet, contemporary thinking seeks to desacralize nature by emphasizing the scientific aspect of the cosmos. In providing a Trinitarian understanding of the natural world Daniélou provides "a primary and radical point of departure" from the

---

32. Ibid. "Le sens est de provoquer l'existence, de suscitat à partir de l'inertie le mouvement. C'est en quoi l'Esprit était porté sur les eaux et suscitait à partir du néant primordial toutes les espèces et toutes les variétés de la création."

33. Ibid., 15–16.

34. It is interesting that the idea of creation in Psalm 104 is liturgically associated with the creation of the Church at Pentecost. However, the passage retains its general sense of creation as well.

35. Daniélou, *La Trinité et le Mystère de l'Existence*, 15–16. "C'est par là que dès l'origine s'établit dans la Bible une relation fondamentale entre la Trinité et le monde de la nature, entre la Trinité et le cosmos, en sorte que la Rédemption sera la reprise et la ressaisie par la Trinité créatrice elle-même de cet univers qui est sien, parce qu'elle l'a créé, pour le conduire à la plénitude de son achèvement. . . . Le Monde matériel n'a son origine que dans l'action des Personnes divines, et d'autre part, il est tout entier appelé à être ressaisi et transfigure par les Personnes divines."

prevailing materialization of reality.[36] In further contradiction to this spirit, Daniélou aptly maintains that "this same universe in which science operates is also the mirror through which the Trinity reveals itself to us."[37]

In light of this discussion, it is important to note the ways in which the Trinity relates to creation. Daniélou draws attention to three ways in which Trinity relates to the cosmos. First, as has been noted in the preceding, the Trinity is the source of all existence. The Trinity is the origin of all things. The material universe "has a relationship with the Trinity in that it exists only through the Trinity, and that at every instant it is enunciated in the Word and called into being by the Spirit."[38] Second, the material world functions as an immense sign pointing all things back toward its origin. All of creation is a vast sacramental reality where everything is a *signum* pointing to the one true *res* to which these signs are ordered.[39] Third, Daniélou maintains that the natural order is "oriented toward the Trinity, in the sense that it suffers and groans with expectation as it waits for the sons of God to manifest themselves."[40] Daniélou is, of course, referring to the passage in Romans where Paul writes, "I consider that the sufferings of this present time are as nothing compared with the glory to be revealed for us. For creation awaits with eager expectation the revelation of the children of God; for creation was made subject to futility, not of its own accord but because of the one who subjected it, in hope that creation itself would be set free from slavery to corruption and share in the glorious freedom of the children of God. We know that all creation is groaning in labor pains even until now; and not only that, but we ourselves, who have the firstfruits of the Spirit, we also groan within ourselves as we wait for adoption, the redemption of our bodies" (Rom 8:18–23; NAB). Creation waits to "share in the glorious freedom of the children of God" which is Trinitarian life through adoption as co-heirs in Christ. Though the universe anticipates the fullness of Trinitarian existence in this passage, it is also clear that although humanity has not realized Trinitarian life in its fullest manifestation, humankind has been afforded the presence of the Trinity within the human

36. Ibid., 16–17. "La Trinité est un point de départ ... primairement et radicalement."

37. Ibid., 17. "C'est ce même univers sur lequel s'exerce la science et qui est le miroir à travers lequel la Trinité se manifeste à nous."

38. Ibid. "L'univers matériel ... a une relation à la Trinité dans le mesure où il ne subsiste que par elle et où, à chaque instant, il est proféré par le Parole et vivifié par l'Esprit."

39. See Augustine, *De doctrina Christiana*, I.2 (PL 34.19–20).

40. Daniélou, *La Trinité et le Mystère de l'Existence*, 18. "Cet univers est orienté vers la Trinité dans la mesure où il gémit en attendant la manifestation des fils de Dieu."

Prayer, Trinity, and Mission

soul. So the Church awaits the time when the reality of the Trinity within each individual will manifest itself completely in the external world.

At the same time, even though we live in a world "still dominated by death, suffering and striving, and which groans as it awaits a transfiguration," it is clear that "the world we live in is a world filled with the Trinity" if we can only train our eyes to see the presence of the Trinity.[41] From this point of view, one must realize God's gratuity in giving. The author of the epistle of James maintains, "all good giving and every perfect gift is from above, coming down from the Father of lights" (Jas 1:17; NAB). Daniélou contends that this is all the more clear when one understands the nature of poverty which sees all things coming from God. "In reality, all things are gifts from God. Between God and ourselves there is a perpetual movement of grace. This is the basis of the mystery of poverty, according to which we have nothing which belongs to us, but all things are wonderful gifts from God. And if we were already capable of seeing, we would recognize even more readily the mark of His presence and His love in all that is given to us."[42] However, the presence of God is not only perceived through the benefits that he lavishes on us. The presence of the Trinitarian God can also be seen in all "created beauty" which is a "reflection of the splendor of the Trinity, a radiation of its glory."[43] Furthermore, not only is God seen in his gifts and in the beauty of his creation but he is also present to the world in that he is the perpetual impetus behind all things. Or, as Daniélou puts it, "there is nothing to which God's action does not extend and in which God Himself is not present," following St. Paul's words "In him we live and move and have our being" (Acts 17:28; NAB).[44]

For Daniélou, Trinitarian life is the source and summit of all existence. Though this presence is obscured by a variety of phenomena, the Christian

---

41. Ibid., 19, 21. "Et en même temps il vit dans un monde qui est encore tout entier sous la loi de la mort, de la souffrance, de l'effort et qui gémit dans l'attente d'une transfiguration." "En réalité, le monde à l'intérieur duquel nous vivons est un monde qui est rempli de la Trinité."

42. Ibid., 22. "Toute choses en réalité sont des dons qui viennent de Dieu. Il y a entre Dieu et nous comme une perpétuelle circulation de grâces et donc d'action de grâces. C'est le fond même du mystère de la pauvreté, qui fait que nous n'avons rien qui soit à nous, mais que toutes choses sont des dons merveilleux de Dieu. Et si déjà nous savions voir, nous reconnaîtrions davantage ainsi, dans tout ce qui nous est donné, la marque de sa présence et de son amour."

43. Ibid. "Toute beauté créée est un reflet de la splendeur trinitaire."

44. Ibid, 23. "Il n'y a rien où ne s'étende l'action de Dieu et où Dieu lui-même ne soit présent."

is able to see through appearances in order to look into and participate in the life of the Trinity.

> In truth God is hidden everywhere, but He reveals Himself only to the heart which is capable of discovering Him and converting itself. For the presence of God is coextensive with the totality of beings. There is nothing His gaze does not penetrate. There is nothing in which His action is not felt. Thus we should strive to rediscover ourselves as beings immersed in the life and the light of the Trinity. We should realize—and this is already a form of contemplation—that all things at all times emanate from the Father of light through the Son and through the Spirit; we should therefore dwell in their presence and their radiance. To close ourselves to them is sin. In reality, we live in the brightest light. This light, the light of the Trinity, shines constantly. But it is we who do not let it enter our souls, because the entrance is blocked. Thus we must throw open the entrance to our souls and let the light penetrate them through and through, illuminating, uniting and transforming everything.[45]

The Trinity and the Soul

While the Trinity is present and to a certain degree accessible through the natural world, Daniélou emphasizes the need to approach the life of the Trinity through the sphere of interiority. Thus, he writes, "Another way to the life of the Trinity is through the experience of our own inner life, since the Trinity is the reality in which we are rooted in our innermost personal lives."[46] In developing the structure of the Trinitarian nature of our personal

---

45. Ibid., 24. "En réalité Dieu est caché partout, mais il ne se manifeste qu'au cœur qui sait le découvrir et qui se convertit. Car la présence de Dieu est coextensive à la totalité de l'être. Il n'y a rien où son regard ne pénètre. Il n'y a rien où son action ne soit efficace. Donc déjà nous devons nous redécouvrir comme immerges dans cette lumière et dans cette vie de la Trinité; nous devons réaliser, et c'est déjà un mode de contemplation, que toutes choses et à chaque instant émanent du Père des lumières par le Fils et par l'Esprit et donc vivre dans cette présence et dans cette irradiation. Nous y fermer, c'est le péché. En réalité, nous vivons en pleine lumière. La lumière brille toujours, cette lumière de la Trinité. Mais c'est nous qui ne la laissons pas pénétrer à l'intérieur de notre âme parce que les issues en sont fermées. Il faut donc ouvrir cette issue de notre âme, laisser cette lumière pénétrer partout, tout illumine, tout unifier et tout transformer."

46. Ibid., 27. "Un second aspect par lequel nous pouvons rejoindre la vie trinitaire est l'expérience de notre propre intériorité, dans la mesure où la Trinité est la réalité dans

Prayer, Trinity, and Mission

lives, Daniélou posits that there are three images helpful for developing our understanding of the Trinity. One can develop his understanding of the Trinity based on the visible world, on the communion between persons, or on the structure of the Spirit itself. Elaborating on this theme Daniélou contends, "One school, that of Saint Augustine, sees the mark of the Trinity in the life of the Spirit, which is at once memory, Word, and love. And Augustine is sure that since we define the second member of the Trinity as the Word . . . , and the third member as Love . . . , then we realize that there may be a certain analogy between the structure of our own spirit's life and the archetype of all spirits—that is, the life of the Trinity itself."[47] Based on these reflections, Daniélou maintains that we have our most profound access to Trinitarian life when we enter into the depths of our own souls.

To this point Daniélou again cites the authority of Augustine when he notes the Augustinian contention that there is "one who is in me, more myself than I am."[48] Daniélou believes that this Augustinian adage points to the Trinitarian basis of every being's personal and spiritual existence. "In the order of our personal life, in the order of our innermost being, we are at root immersed in the life of the Trinity."[49] This immersion in the Trinity is not in any way inherent to humanity in itself.[50] Instead, in going within oneself, one goes beyond oneself "into the self-created light which illumines all intelligence."[51] Daniélou looks further at Augustine for an explanation on what the return into the self reveals about Trinitarian existence. The

laquelle nous-même, dans notre existence personnelle la plus profonde, nous sommes en quelque sorte enracinés."

47. Ibid., 27–28. "Or il y a une ligne, celle de saint Augustin, qui voit le premier vestige de la Trinité dans la vie même de l'esprit, qui est à la foi mémoire, verbe et amour. Et il est sûr que dans la mesure où nous définissons la seconde Personne comme Parole . . ., et quand nous définissons la troisième Personne comme Amour . . ., à ce moment-là nous saisissons qu'il peut y avoir une certain analogie entre la structure même de la vie de notre esprit et ce qui est l'archétype de tout esprit, c'est-à-dire, la vie même de la Trinité."

48. The reference seems to be to Augustine's statement in *Confessions* 3.11, which is usually translated into English as "You were more inward to me than my most inward part" (Quelqu'un qui est en moi plus moi-même que moi).

49. Daniélou, *La Trinité et le Mystère de l'Existence*, 28. "Dans l'ordre même de notre vie personnelle, dans l'ordre de notre être le plus personnelle, nous baignons originellement dans cette vie trinitaire."

50. For Daniélou, there are certain religious practices that are common to all religions centered around certain rites and occasions. Trinitarian life, on the other hand, is a result of revelation and is not basic to humanity in general.

51. Ibid., 29. "Nous devons nous répandre au-delà de nous-mêmes dans cette lumière incréée qui éclair toute intelligence."

personal inward journey to the Trinity is clearly seen in the Augustinian phrase *in interior homine habitat veritas* ("for the truth dwells in the interior man").[52] This should not be taken as a bland Socratic exhortation to *nosce te ipsum*. Interiority has value only insofar as it reveals the Trinitarian nature of existence. To know oneself in an Augustinian fashion is to know oneself through an interaction with the life of the Trinity within the soul. For Daniélou, "The Trinity is not merely present outside ourselves, but—in a still deeper and more intimate way—inside ourselves, in the sanctuary of the heart. This is the other temple—no longer the temple of the world but the temple of the soul, created in the image of God, where the Trinity is present."[53] Daniélou maintains that it is through the journey of prayer that one most intimately finds oneself. But, even more, as one takes the path of interiority, one must not stop at the self. Instead, the interior individual must press on past the self and "reach that which is beyond us, that which is fixed whereas we are uncertain and shifting, that which is wholly good whereas we are a mixture of good and evil."[54]

It is at this point that one must realize existence only has meaning insofar as it participates in its source and origin. To the extent that the believer is able to draw upon that source and reinvigorate his inner life through contact with the presence of the Trinity within the soul contemplation and prayer are truly Christian in nature. This is the particularly Christian notion of prayer: that whatever methods or forms prayer takes, it must always have as its source and summit the eternal wellspring of the Holy Trinity. Furthermore, "this is why we are never ourselves except when we find ourselves in God. In a sense it is in Him that we live and have our being. It is when we are once again in Him that we find ourselves again. Only there do we discover the truth of what we are."[55]

52. Augustine, *De vera religione* 39 (PL 34.154).

53. Daniélou, *La Trinité et le Mystère de l'Existence*, 29. "Ce n'est pas simplement au-dehors de nous-mêmes que la Trinité est présente, mais d'une manière encore plus profonde et intime à l'intérieur e nous-mêmes, dans le sanctuaire de cœur. C'est là l'autre temple, non plus le temple du monde, mais le temple de l'âme créée à l'image de Dieu, où la Trinité est présente."

54. Ibid., 30. "Mais nous ne pouvons pas nous arrêter à nous-mêmes; au-delà de nous-mêmes nous atteignons ce qui est au-delà de nous, ce qui est stable, alors que nous sommes incertains, ce qui est entièrement bon alors que nous restons mêlés."

55. Ibid. "C'est pourquoi nous ne sommes jamais nous-mêmes que lorsque nous nous retrouvons en Dieu. C'est en quelque sort en lui que nous vivons et que nous sommes. C'est quand nous nous retrouvons en lui que nous nous retrouvons nous-mêmes. C'est là seulement que nous retrouvons la vérité de ce que nous sommes."

Prayer, Trinity, and Mission

At the same time, Daniélou confirms that not only does the Trinity dwell within us, but also we dwell within the sphere of the Trinity. These affirmations should not be seen as a contradiction in how one understands the relationship between the Trinity and the believer. On the contrary, Daniélou adamantly maintains that these two aspects of the dwelling and presence of the Trinity express different aspects of the same reality. "The outward and inward images are absolutely complimentary."[56] Furthermore, he notes, "We can say with equal truth that we live in the Trinity and the Trinity dwells in us, because the two things are like two faces to the same reality. But each of them is also the expression of that extraordinary intimacy and closeness to which the Holy Trinity beckons and calls us. This is why living fully means living truly in the life of the Trinity, opening ourselves to its action within us, letting the Holy Trinity touch, win over, and guide our hearts, fostering within ourselves the mystery which God wishes to accomplish by transmitting His life to us."[57]

It is by this indwelling of the Trinity that God establishes a new relationship with those who find the Trinity in the depths of their soul and in turn dwell in the sphere of the life of the Trinity. It is through this experience of Trinitarian interiority that the Christian becomes "caught up in the movement of the life of the Trinity."[58] All of those who are able to recognize and develop their baptismal graces through interiority are able to understand the presence of the Trinity within their own souls. Whatever the circumstances may be, the believer is able to descend into the "most secret depths" where one "can always enter the presence of the Trinity—provided he can leave behind him the successive stages of his spirit in order to sink himself, like a stone sinking to the bottom of the sea, into the abyss which is in us and which is God's abode."[59]

---

56. Ibid., 31. "Les images d'intérieur et d'extérieur sont absolument complémentaires."

57. Ibid. "On peut aussi bien dire que nous vivons dans la Trinité ou que c'est la Trinité qui demeure en nous, parce que les deux choses ne sont que comme les deux faces d'une même réalité , mais qui sont l'une et l'autre l'expression de cette extraordinaire intimité et proximité à laquelle les Personnes divines nous attirent et nous appellent. C'est pourquoi ici encore, pour nous, exister pleinement ce sera vivre vraiment de cette vie trinitaire, nous y ouvrir en quelque sorte pour la laisser agir en nous, laisser les Personnes divines toucher nos cœurs, les convertir et les instruire, laisser s'accomplir en nous ce mystère que Dieu veut y accomplir de la communication de sa vie."

58. Ibid., 32. "Cette recréation de notre être qu'opère l'habitation des Personnes divines en nous, établit entre elles et nous un type de relations nouvelle par lesquelles nous sommes comme entraînés dans le mouvement même de la vie trinitaire."

59. Ibid., 33. "Dans quelques circonstances que ce soit, de retrouver cette présence de

Unlike many other forms of interiority which are merely other means of self-discovery, Christian interiority seeks to get beyond the self where one can "plunge us into the abyss where the Trinity dwells, to unite us with the Trinity within us."[60] For Daniélou, this is the whole aim of Christian prayer and contemplation. One must descend into one's soul—pushing aside all the distractions and enticements of the external world—to find the source and paradigm for all of Christian existence through the practice of contemplation.

The Trinity in Itself

When speaking of the Trinity in Itself, Daniélou does not spend a great deal of time exploring the interrelation of the persons of the Trinity.[61] There is nothing speculative about the nature of his writing in this regard. Instead, when speaking of the Trinity, Daniélou prefers to limit himself to understanding how the individual can enter into the life of the Trinity. This is true partly because of the mysterious nature of the Trinity.

One would be hard pressed to think of one of the great spiritual writers in the Catholic faith who did not in some sense affirm that the Trinity is inscrutable. Furthermore, Daniélou contends that the believer's entrance into the life of the Trinity is in some way dependent on recognizing that the life of the Trinity is inaccessible to our intelligence. He notes, "When one speaks of the Holy Trinity, the first thing is to remember it is supremely mysterious and transcendent. It is always in a profound attitude of reverence, of adoration and of humility that we must recover the presence of the mystery of the unfathomable God. Indeed, the Holy Trinity is that of God which most evades the grasp of natural man. In his search, man can attain something of God by his intelligence, by his feelings. There is in this a

---

la Trinité, pour vu qu'elle dépasse les espaces successifs de la psychologie pour s'enfoncer, comme une pierre au fond de la mer, dans cet abîme qui est en nous et où Dieu demeure." See also *Contemplation*, 33.

60. Daniélou, *La Trinité et le Mystère de l'Existence*, 33. "L'oraison est de s'enfoncer dans cet abîme où la Trinité demeure, de venir rejoinder ainsi la Trinité qui est en nous."

61. That is not to say that he is unconcerned with Trinitarian theology. Daniélou was well-acquainted with the "new Christological thought" characteristic of the Dutch school and felt that the modern Trinitarian errors of the 1960's and 1970's were indeed very dangerous. See, "Cardinal Daniélou on Modern Errors on the Trinity," 3. For the Christological thought of the Dutch School see, Mark Schoof, *Aggiornomento: De doorbraak van een nieuwe katholieke theologie*; ET: *A Survey of Catholic Theology*, 131–43.

Prayer, Trinity, and Mission

certain manifestation of God. But what God is in the depths of his inner life is completely inaccessible to men."[62] All of one's initial notions are useless. These preconceived ideas must be thrown out in order to get to the reality of the triune God who reveals himself instead of being discovered. Along this line, Daniélou writes, "God alone can lead us into the mystery of God. The Trinity alone can lead us into the secret of its own mysterious life. We truly open ourselves to God when we cast aside all hope of penetrating His mystery through intelligence."[63] Instead, knowledge of the Trinity is contingent on humility and impotence. For Daniélou, this is clearly indicated in Scripture by Christ's exhortation to become as children. In the gospel of Matthew, Christ said, "I give praise to you, Father, Lord of heaven and earth, for although you have hidden these things from the wise and the learned you have revealed them to the childlike" (Matt 11:25; NAB). And, again in the gospel of Luke, "Amen, I say to you, whoever does not accept the kingdom of God like a child will not enter it" (Luke 18:17; NAB).

One might be tempted to think that such inscrutability is due to obscurity. To the contrary, the Holy Trinity is unknowable to the human intellect due to its intensity rather than obscurity. This is expressed well by the images chosen by such mystical thinkers as Gregory of Nyssa. Two of Gregory's most expressive images are that of darkness and of dizziness. These images demonstrate that the inscrutability of the Trinity is because of God's fullness of being and the inadequacy and limitedness of human apprehension rather than a gnoseological defect.

Daniélou notes that in many of the great spiritual writers of the Catholic tradition, the spiritual life is a movement from light to darkness.[64]

---

62. Daniélou, *La Trinité et le Mystère de l'Existence*, 42. "Quand on parle de la Sainte Trinité, la première chose est de se rappeler son caractère souverainement mystérieux et transcendant. C'est toujours dans une attitude profonde de révérence, d'adoration et d'humilité que nous devons nous remettre en présence du mystère insondable de Dieu. En effet, la Sainte Trinité est ce qui de Dieu échappe le plus aux prises de l'homme naturel. Dans sa recherché, l'homme peut atteindre quelque chose de Dieu par son intelligence, par son cœur. Il y a en ce sens une certain manifestation de Dieu. Mais ce qu'est Dieu dans le secret de sa vie intérieure est totalement inaccessible à l'homme" (translation mine).

63. Ibid., 43. "Seul Dieu peut nous introduire dans le mystère de Dieu. Seule la Trinité peut nous introduire dans la secret de sa vie mystérieuse. C'est d'abord en dépassant toute prétention de nos intelligences à pénétrer en quelque sorte par effraction dans ce mystère de Dieu, que nous nous ouvrons vraiment à lui."

64. Daniélou, "Introduction" to *From Glory to Glory*, 23. The themes of darkness and dizziness will be treated at greater length in chapter 4.

Jean Danielou's Doxological Humanism

Gregory of Nyssa depicts Moses' vision of God in this way: "Moses' vision of God began with light; afterwards God spoke to him in a cloud. But when Moses rose higher and became more perfect, he saw God in the darkness."[65] And, the Psalmist depicts God as being hidden in darkness: "He made darkness the cover about him" (Ps 18:12; NAB). For Daniélou, "intense divine light" is always "hemmed in with darkness" as a means of making the faithful seek it with their spiritual eyes.[66]

A second familiar image illustrates the believer's utter impotence in the face of the sheer mystery of God in His fullness. Dizziness is often used by the mystics to demonstrate the believer's disorientation at the brilliance of God's existence. "They speak of dizziness on the brink of a bottomless gulf, dizziness over which we have no control. They bring us as it were to the edge of a precipice, beyond which we have no hope of advancing through our own strength."[67] Daniélou particularly has in mind here a passage from Gregory of Nyssa's *Commentary on Ecclesiastes*:

> Imagine a sheer, steep crag, of reddish appearance below, extending into eternity; on top there is this ridge which looks down over a projecting rim into a bottomless chasm. Now imagine what a person would probably experience if he put his foot on the edge of this ridge which overlooks the chasm and found no solid footing in material things, in its quest for that which has no dimension and which exists for all eternity. For here there is nothing it can take hold of, neither place nor time, neither measure nor anything else; it does not allow our minds to approach. And thus the soul, slipping at every point from what cannot be grasped, becomes dizzy and perplexed and returns once again to what is connatural to it.[68]

Daniélou explains that the "symbol of vertigo express[es] the soul's anguish before the infinite majesty of God."[69]

---

65. Gregory of Nyssa, *Commentarius in Canticum Canticorum*, sermon 11 (PG 44.1000C).

66. Daniélou, *La Trinité et le Mystère de l'Existence*, 44. "En effet, cette intense lumière divine est comme environnée d'obscurité."

67. Ibid., 45. "Ils parlent de vertige, en présence d'un abîme insondable et sur lequel nous n'avons aucune prise. Ils nous jettent comme au bord d'une falaise, au-delà de laquelle nous ne pouvons absolument plus avancer par nos propres forces."

68. Gregory of Nyssa, *Expositio in Ecclesiasten Salomonis,* sermon 7(PG 44.729D–732D). Another passage also uses the same imagery, Gregory of Nyssa, *De beatitudinibus*, sermon 6 (PG 44.1264C).

69. Daniélou, "Introduction," 43.

Prayer, Trinity, and Mission

It is important to notice that in both cases the disorientation of the mystic is based not in defect but in the intensity and immensity of the reality of God. To that point, Daniélou contends, "God's unfathomable nature does not stem from the fact that there is no obscurity, no darkness within Him; . . . it stems from the fact that God is light in all its fullness, existence in all its fullness, life in all its fullness; it is linked to the very intensity of God's existence, to the very superabundance of His life. It is precisely because of this that He is inaccessible to us, for our means are too limited."[70] One must not derive from the fact that he cannot perceive the depth of God that somehow God is unintelligible.

The acknowledgement of the immensity of the divine presence and the human inability to comprehend it is of the utmost importance in the life of prayer. The believer's receptivity to the Spirit is contingent on an awareness of utter inability to find God for oneself. Daniélou attributes this fact to many of the saints' practice of beginning prayer with the *Veni Creator* which "expresses a consciousness of fundamental impotence."[71]

> Come, Holy Spirit, Creator blest,
> and in our souls take up Thy rest;
> come with Thy grace and heavenly aid
> to fill the hearts which Thou hast made.[72]

For Daniélou, the *veni creator spiritus* is an important entrée into the mode of prayer because when understood correctly and given a proper attitude, the hymn is steeped in the conviction that outside of the aid of the Creator Spirit the contemplative individual is utterly incapable of comprehending God.

Passing from the mysterious nature of the Trinity, Daniélou turns his attention to the personal aspect of the Trinity. Initially, God is inscrutable by virtue of his brilliance and the human incapacity to perceive that brilliance. But, it is through the acknowledgement of this fact that God leads

---

70. Daniélou, *La Trinité et le Mystère de l'Existence*, 45. "Cette incompréhensibilité de Dieu ne vient pas de ce qu'il y ait lui aucune opacité, aucune obscurité; elle vient au contraire de ce que Dieu est plénitude de lumière, plénitude d'existence, plénitude de vie; elle tient à l'intensité même de l'existence de Dieu, à la surabondance même de sa vie. C'est précisément à cause de cela qu'il est au-delà de notre portée, parce que nos forces sont trop limitées."

71. Ibid., 47. "Ceci est l'expression de cette prise de conscience d'une radical impuissance."

72. For an excellent article on this important hymn see Julian, "Veni Creator Spiritus," 1206–11.

the contemplative soul into communion with Himself. To acknowledge one's inability to understand God's fullness is the first act in removing the scales from one's eyes. "By this revelation of the Spirit, by the divine force which succors us in our impotence, the veil which hid the abyss of divinity from us is partly drawn aside. This is the very meaning of revelation, which might be more accurately translated as 'unveiling.' It means that this veil, the veil of our carnal blindness that hid the divine life from us, is drawn aside so that we may be led into the heavenly sanctuary that lies beyond all created things, . . . the sanctuary where the Trinity dwells."[73] By accepting one's finitude and impotence the life of the Trinity is opened up to the faithful. Though the life of God was at first obscured by "the crushing weight of glory, a glory dazzling to our gaze," now the triune God seeks to reveal himself as that reality which is most intensely real. It is here that Daniélou emphasizes the personal aspect of the Trinity. Once one is given access to the inner life of the Trinity it becomes clear that God is not an impersonal force but is in fact a someone with whom a personal relationship is possible. "Revelation . . . shows us that the mysterious abyss of the divine life has a face; it is not an impersonal reality, a philosophical absolute, it is a Someone."[74] Furthermore, "God is . . . Someone with whom we can enter into that person-to-person relationship which is love. He is a God to whom we can speak and a God who hears us. He is a God who . . . possesses the attributes that constitute personal life on the human plane, that turn a being into a person with whom we can have a relationship. It is then that we discover, in God's depths, what it is that allows us to communicate with Him, to enter a whole series of relationships with Him that constitute the very essence of truly Christian spiritual life."[75]

73. Daniélou, *La Trinité et le Mystère de l'Existence*, 48. "A travers cette révélation de l'Esprit à travers cette force divine qui vient ainsi au secours de notre impuissance, le voile qui nous cachait les abîmes de la divinité s'écarte en quelque sorte. C'est le sens même du mot révélation qu'on pourrait traduire plus exactement par dévoilement. Il signifie que ce voile, qui était celui de notre opacité charnelle et nous cachait ainsi la vie divine, est écarté de manière à ce que nous soyons introduits dans le sanctuaire céleste, au-delà de toute créature, au-delà des chœurs angéliques, dans ce sanctuaire qui est celui dans lequel la Trinité demeure."

74. Ibid., 49. "La révélation . . . nous fait découvrir que cet abîme mystérieux, qui est celui de la vie divine, a un visage, qu'il n'est pas une réalité impersonnelle, un absolu philosophique, mais qu'il est quelqu'un."

75. Ibid., 49–50. "Dieu est . . . quelqu'un avec qui nous pouvons entrer dans cette relation de personne à personne qui est l'amour, un Dieu à qui nous pouvons nous adresser et un Dieu qui nous écoute, un Dieu qui . . . possède d'une façon éminente ce qui

Prayer, Trinity, and Mission

Entering into the personal life of the Trinity is reflected equally in our divine sonship, our divine brotherhood and our standing as temples of the Spirit.[76] Though God appears at first to the believer as a crushing weight of glory, it becomes clear that one is able to relate to God as a child to his Father. Just as the Father is the source of the Son and the Spirit from which they proceed, He is also the eternal source of our own life. Both the fact of our being children of God and siblings to Christ is expressed in Paul's letter to the Romans, "For those who are led by the Spirit of God are children of God. For you did not receive a spirit of slavery to fall back into fear, but you received a spirit of adoption, through which we cry, "Abba, Father!" The Spirit itself bears witness with our spirit that we are children of God, and if children, then heirs, heirs of God and joint heirs with Christ, if only we suffer with him so that we may also be glorified with him" (Rom 8:14–17; NAB). As adopted children of the Father, it is revealed that God the Father is the "Principle of the life of the Trinity, and it is from Him that the Son and the Holy Spirit proceed. He also appears as the principle in all our relations with Him, since He is the eternal origin of all things."[77] Just as the nature of the Father as source is revealed through one's entrance into Trinitarian life, so also the nature of the Son and the Spirit. "It is through the Son that another aspect of God's human face is revealed to us. This is God's communication of Himself, His eternal fertility, the manner in which the life that is within Him is at the same time totally given and totally received in the Son."[78] The fact of Christ's status as "eternally begotten of the Father"

---

constitue sur le plan humain la vie personnelle, ce qui fait qu'un être est une personne, avec qui on peut entrer en relation. C'est alors que se découvre pour nous en Dieu, dans ses profondeurs, ce qui nous rend possible d'entrer en communication avec lui et d'avoir avec lui tout un ensemble de relations qui constituent l'essence même de la vie spirituelle proprement chrétienne."

76. Sonship expresses our divine adoption better than the term childhood because of the confusion of possibly expressing childlikeness. Also, brotherhood might be better expressed through the term siblinghood. It should be noted that both sonship and brotherhood, as Daniélou uses the terms, are not gender exclusive. The two terms together express the divine adoption of all individuals who obtain this right through a familial relationship with Christ.

77. Daniélou, *La Trinité et le Mystère de l'Existence*, 50. "Il est le Principe de la vie de la Trinité et c'est de lui que precedent le Fils et l'Esprit. Et il apparaît comme principe dans tous nos rapports avec lui dans le mesure où c'est toujours lui qui sera pour tout l'origine."

78. Ibid., 51. "C'est en même temps sous l'aspect du Fils comme étant celui en qui le Père se manifeste pleinement, à qui le Père se communiqué pleinement, qui est la parfait image de Père, qu'un autre aspect de ce visage personnel de Dieu nous est manifesté, c'est-à-dire la communication qu'il fait de lui-même, son éternelle fécondité, la manière

expresses the personal aspect of God as perpetually fecund. This fecundity is an eternally and completely fulfilling gift that is not exhausted in the giving. Indeed, the gift is not lessened in a single degree yet is wholly received by the object. The third aspect is expressed through the Spirit which gives expression to the personal aspect of God by demonstrating the "mutual love of the Father and the Son."

All of this constitutes an unveiling of who the Triune God is. The personal nature of who God is in the Trinity leads one into the "heart of Christian Trinitarian ontology."[79] What Daniélou means by this is that once we are allowed to move into the sphere of Trinitarian life, God reveals that his inner life is inherently personal. This is demonstrated in that the Trinity in itself is relational.[80] "By discovering that the reality of the life of the Trinity is eminently personal . . . we realize that the Trinity is a mystery of love, because God's human face is that of the holy Three in their relations to one another."[81] Instead of emphasizing the relationship of the three as source, begotten and bond, Daniélou chooses to emphasize the aspect of God's personal life as communication between the three persons. Under this rubric, the Father eternally communicates himself to the Son in order to make the Son his "perfect image."[82] This communication—which Daniélou refers to as love—from the Father to the Son is the Holy Spirit—which Daniélou calls "the life of the Father and the Son." It is by means of the intra-trinitarian relationship that the faithful are allowed access to the Trinitarian life. Insofar as one is united to the Father and Son, one is also united with the

---

dont la vie qui est en lui est une vie que en même temps est totalement donnée et totalement recue dans le Fils."

79. Ibid., 52. "Ici nous débouchons sur le fond même de ce qui constitue l'ontologie trinitaire chrétienne."

80. Daniélou, "La Trinité dans la l'Existence Humaine," 11–14.

81. Daniélou, *La Trinité et le Mystère de l'Existence*, 51–52. "C'est en découvrant que la réalité de la vie de la Trinité est éminemment personnelle . . . nous comprenons que la Trinité est un mystère d'amour, du fait que ce visage personnel de Dieu est celui trios Personnes dans leur relation réciproque."

82. See 2 Cor. 4:4, "Christ, who is the image of God"; Col. 1:15, "He is the image of the invisible God"; and Heb. 1:3, "he spoke to us through a son . . . who is the refulgence of his glory, the very imprint of his being" (NAB). The passage in Hebrews uses the term χαραχτήρ which is roughly equivalent to εἰκών ("not a crafted object" but a "living image") and which indicates an "exact representation of," Bauer, *A Greek-English Lexicon of the New Testament and other Early Christian Literature*, 282 and 1078.

Prayer, Trinity, and Mission

Spirit, "who has pervaded our hearts and is the means whereby the Father and Son communicate themselves to us."[83]

This Trinitarian reality teaches the basis of all human existence, of all being. Instead of basing existence on materiality, or individual will, or the absence of meaning, Daniélou insists that the structure and relationality of the Trinity reveals that existence is based on a communion of persons. Indeed, Daniélou expresses it precisely the way John Zizioulas will title his important later work, "The basis of being is communion."[84] Furthermore, this revelation is the apex of God's disclosure to humanity. There is inherent within the structure of the Trinity a mutual interaction which sets the paradigm for the personality of human communion.

> We can understand why all human communion devolves from communion within the Trinity. In the final analysis all reality can be summed up in the phrase: "Let them be as one, as we are one." [John 17:20–22] This means two things: "We are one:" these simple words flash out with a blinding light. Not only do they say that there is a "we" and a "one," but that the one *is* a we. The one is a we: nobody, before Christ had said this! The One, that is the Absolute, is a We. The One is a communion among the Three. The One is an eternal exchange of love. The One is not some vague, ill-defined quantity. The One is Love. And the basis of Being is love among the three members of the Trinity.[85]

Furthermore, within this matrix, our own personal fulfillment is only to be realized in a Trinitarian fashion, that is through self-giving to someone

---

83. Daniélou, *La Trinité et le Mystère de l'Existence*, 48. "Dans la mesure où nous serons unis au Père et au Fils, nous le serons dans l'Esprit-Saint qui a été répandu dans nos cœurs et qui est d'abord la communication que le Père et le Fils se font d'eux-mêmes." See also International Theological Commission document *Communion and Stewardship: Human Persons Created in the Image of God* which states, "Since it is Christ himself who is the perfect image of God, man must be conformed to him in order to become the son of the Father through the power of the Holy Spirit," §12.

84. Daniélou, *La Trinité et le Mystère de l'Existence*, 53. "Le fond de l'être est la communion."

85. Ibid., 53–54. "Nous comprenons pourquoi la communion humaine est suspendue à la communion trinitaire. Finalement toute réalité se résume en un mot: «Qu'ils soient un, comme nous sommes un». Cela signifie deux choses. Nous sommes un, et cette simple phrase est une fulguration extraordinaire. Non seulement elle dit qu'il y a le nous et le un, mais que le un est un nous. Ceci, personne avant Jésus-Christ ne l'a dit: le un est un Nous. Le Un, c'est-à-dire l'Absolu, est un Nous. Le Un est un échange éternel d'amour. Le Un n'est pas je ne sais quelle étoffe. Le Un est Amour. Le fond de l'Être est l'amour entre les Personnes."

other than ourselves. In this regard, prayer is of utmost importance for realizing the communion between persons. Insofar as one's being in communion has its source in the communion of the Trinity, one must strive toward communion to that "primordial origin" of all communion. "Thus, as we ascend in contemplation into the depths of God, the eternal mystery of love reveals itself to our dazzled gaze. It shows us that the foundation of all things . . . is the love of the Trinity. Eternally, God is love, and the radiance He creates and the epiphany of the life of the Trinity will also be caught up in the life of love. . . ."[86]

Communication of the Life of the Trinity

When Daniélou turns to the believer's participation in the life of the Trinity, he first notes the utter self-sufficiency of the Trinitarian communion. There is nothing outside of God which leaves God in want. The Trinitarian relationship expresses all that God is and fulfills all that God requires. As a result, God has no need of anything or anyone from outside to partake of his person or benefits. Daniélou writes:

> The life of the Trinity has no need of outside participation. This must be stressed from the start. It is perfectly self-sufficient. There is something very essential in the fact that God is total fullness of being, and therefore exhausts totally within Himself the totality of what is, so that He needs nothing else. Otherwise he would not be God. There would be an imperfection in Him. And one of the things we must seek tranquilly to understand in God is this fullness, this total perfection and self-sufficiency.[87]

---

86. Ibid., 56. "Ainsi, quand nous nous enfonçons dans les profondeurs de Dieu, dans la contemplation, c'est ce mystère éternel d'amour qui e découvre à nous yeux éblouis et qui nous fait découvrir que le fond de toutes choses, ce fond de toutes choses que nous savions déjà être Dieu, ce fond de toutes choses est l'amour trinitaire lui-même. Dieu est éternellement amour, et l'irradiation créée, l'épiphanie de la vie trinitaire sera aussi appelée à être emportée et saisie dans la vie de l'amour."

87. Ibid., 61. "La vie trinitaire n'a aucun besoin d'être participée. C'est toujours la première chose qu'il faut dire. Elle se suffit parfaitement à elle-même. Il y a quelque chose de très essential dans le fait que Dieu soit plénitude totale d'être et donc épuise totalement en lui la totalité de ce qui est, en sorte qu'il n'a besoin de rien d'autre. Autrement il ne serait pas Dieu. Il y aurait en lui une imperfection. Et une des choses que nous devons chercher paisiblement à comprendre de Dieu, c'est justement cette plénitude et cette totale perfection et suffisance."

Prayer, Trinity, and Mission

For Daniélou, prayer and contemplation is specifically related to this fact. This fullness of being is an aid to the contemplative as he seeks to participate in the Trinitarian sphere. The very essence of contemplation is the incremental disclosure to the faithful of the immensity of the "ocean of Being," of the fullness of the "abyss of divine life."

However, though the Trinity has no need of anything outside itself or to communicate itself to anything else, it nevertheless does seek to communicate itself. In doing so the Trinity seeks to share something of itself—its bliss, its love, its joy—with human beings.[88] This was indeed the original intention of creation. God did not create "beings with souls only to throw them back into nothingness after suffering them to live for a little while," but created human beings in order to share himself. "Revelation shows us that the Trinity breathed life into these beings that surround it and gave them radiance, the world of angels and the world of men, essentially in order to associate them with its own bliss, to lead them into its own infinite joy."[89] This most immediately draws attention to the gratuity of creation since humanity was created not out of necessity but out of God's superabundance of love. Love is both humanity's end and origin. It is what it was created by and what it was created for. Therefore, humanity "exist[s] only to the extent that we are loved. For us, our innermost beings, existing is merely being the condition of an act of love within the Trinity, which communicates being to us only in order to associate us in its life."[90]

In communicating itself to us, the Trinity is aware of our severely limited capacity to experience its superabundance. But, unlike our inability to expand our own "slender capacity," the life of the Trinity is able to "fill out the narrow confines of our heart."[91] By degrees the Trinity is able to enlarge our hearts by its fullness. "Little by little, the Word who has touched our hearts draws us to follow him; he transforms us and introduces us more and

---

88. Daniélou, "La Trinité dans l'Existence Humaine," 14–16.

89. Daniélou, *La Trinité et le Mystère de l'Existence*, 65. "La révélation nous montre que c'est essentiellement pour associer des libertés créées à sa béatitude, pour les introduire dans cette joie infinie qui la sienne, que la Trinité a suscité ces libertés créées qui l'entourent de leur rayonnement, le monde des anges et le monde des homes."

90. Ibid., 66. "Nous n'existons donc que dans le mesure où nous sommes aimés. Exister pour nous, dans notre être le plus intime, c'est être actuellement le terme d'un acte d'amour des Personnes divines qui ne nous communiquent l'être que dans la volonté de nous associer à leur vie."

91. Ibid. "À mesure que cette vie se communiqué à nous, elle dilate en nous, dans la mesure où nous la laissons nous envahir, les espaces étroits qui sont ceux de nos cœurs."

more deeply into the Trinitarian life."[92] Daniélou's use of "peu à peu" recalls Gregory of Nyssa's ideas concerning perpetual progress. Gregory writes, "Participation in the divine good is such that, where it occurs, it makes the participant ever greater and more spacious than before, bringing to it an increase in size and strength, in such wise that the participant, nourished in this way, never stops growing and keeps getting larger and larger. Indeed, as the Source of good keeps flowing and welling up without end, so too the participant, as it becomes larger, grows more and more in desire, by the fact that nothing that it receives is lost or left unused, and everything that flows in produces an increase in capacity."[93] In moving the believer from "glory to glory," the Trinity is able to expand the believer's capacity perpetually in order to accommodate the Trinitarian communion within him.

This expansion and penetration of the believer by the Trinitarian God is achieved through the Father as eternal origin and principle of fecund divine love. "It is the Father, infinitely fertile, infinitely loving, the eternal source and principle of divine life, who strives to communicate this life to Creation in all its superabundance of love. God's limitless fertility perpetually creates life, essentially spiritual life, His life."[94] While the Father is the source of perpetual love, the Son is the means by which the Father eternally communicates himself to his creation. "The Father begets the Son eternally. And since He begets us too, through our participation in the life of His Son, He allows us to partake mysteriously of this eternal process of generation."[95]

92. Daniélou, "L'Experience de Dieu," 10. "Peu à peu le Verbe qui a touché nos cœurs nous attire à sa suite . . ., il nous transforme et nous introduit de plus en plus profondément dans la vie trinitaire." ET: "Experience of God," 94–100. See also Daniélou, *Le Mystère du Salut des Nations*, 43; ET: *The Salvation of the Nations*: "Le Verbe peu à peu prépare l'humanité à recevoir en plénitude le message qu'Il est venu apporter [the Word prepared humanity little by little to receive in its fullness the message He came to give]." All subsequent English translations of this text will be Bouchard's translation unless noted otherwise.

93. Gregory of Nyssa, *De Anima et Resurrectione* (PG 46.105B-C). Daniélou's use of Gregory's notion of *epectasis* will be addressed in a later chapter.

94. Daniélou, *La Trinité et le Mystère de l'Existence*, 67. "C'est le Père qui, dans l'infinie fécondité qui est la sienne, comme source éternelle de la vie divine elle-même, puisque c'est en lui qu'elle subsiste comme en son principe, c'est le Père qui dans son amour créateur veut communiquer cette vie à création dans la surabondance de son amour. Cette fécondité infinie de Dieu suscite perpétuellement la vie et essentiellement la vie spirituelle, la vie même qui est la sienne."

95. Ibid., 67. "Mais cette vie c'est par et dans son Fils que le Père veut nous la communiqué. Le Père éternellement engendre le Fils. C'est une mystérieuse participation à cette génération éternelle à la il nous associe dans le temps en nous engendrant nous aussi dans la participation qui est la nôtre à la vie de son Fils."

Prayer, Trinity, and Mission

This communication of the divine to its creation is the goal of contemplation and also provides the paradigm for the contemplative posture. Daniélou summarizes the Trinitarian communication when he writes:

> It is to this that contemplation leads us. It is to this that love too leads us, since we desire what the Holy Trinity desires, belonging wholly and cooperating mysteriously in its design of love. And the Father's communication of life to the Son—in which we are caught up—is achieved through the communication of the life of the Spirit, which is the Spirit of both the Father and the Son, and which unites them. It is this communication of the Spirit that makes us spiritual—in other words, that leads us to partake of God's life, which is activated by the Spirit which is given to us, so that we may enter the life of the Holy Trinity.[96]

This communication of the three persons of the Trinity is a communication of love of each to the other. While the Trinity has no need to go outside of itself and finds total fulfillment in the internal relations between Father, Son and Spirit, the Trinity does proceed outside itself so that it might order all things to itself in an economy of love.[97]

Father, Son, and Spirit

Daniélou concludes his short work on Trinitarian spirituality by looking briefly at the three persons of the Trinity by considering the Father's love, the mission of the Word, and the Spirit as the bond of love between the Father and the Son.

---

96. Ibid., 68–69. "C'est à cela que nous fait adhérer la contemplation. C'est à cela que nous fait adhérer aussi l'amour, dans le mesure où nous voulons ce que veulent les Personnes divines, où nous adhérons tout entiers et où nous coopérons mystérieusement à leur dessein d'amour. Et cette communication de vie qui est celle que le Père fait au Fils et dans laquelle nous sommes comme entraînés se fait par la communication de la vie de l'Esprit qui est l'Esprit du Père et du Fils et qui les unit. C'est cette communication de l'Esprit qui nous fait spirituels, c-est-à-dire qui nous fait participer à cette vie de Dieu qui est opérée en nous par l'immanence et par la présence même de l'Esprit qui nous est donné, de manière à nous fire entrer dans cette vie des Personnes divines."

97. Daniélou writes, "C'est à cela que nous fait adhérer la contemplation. C'est à cela que nous fait adhérer aussi l'amour, dans le mesure où nous voulons ce que veulent les Personnes divines, où nous adhérons tout entiers [It is to this that contemplation leads us. It is to this that love leads us, since we desire what the Holy Trinity desires, belonging wholly and cooperating mysteriously in its design of love]." *La Trinité et le Mystère de l'Existence*, 68.

Jean Danielou's Doxological Humanism

It must continually be kept in mind that the Father is the source and origin of both the Son and the Spirit and the communication of the Trinity to the world reproduces this generative aspect of the Father. This aspect of the Father's relationship to the Son and the Spirit is expressed in the creedal elements of the Niceno-Constantinopolitan Creed when the faithful say, "We believe in one Lord Jesus Christ, the only Son of God, eternally begotten of the Father" and "We believe in the Holy Spirit, the Lord, the giver of life, who proceeds from the Father and the Son."[98] As Daniélou notes, "In the Holy Trinity, all things proceed from the Father; it is He who eternally begets the Son in His perfect image, and it is from His love for the Son that the Holy Spirit proceeds. And the life communicated to the Son and the Holy Spirit flows back to the Father, since the son is wholly oriented toward Him."[99] This passage succinctly expresses Daniélou's thoughts on the Father in that love is expressed by the Father in generation with the intention that all things sustained by that love will be drawn back into the Trinitarian sphere of existence.

All things proceed from the Father. He is the origin, the first principle, the generative means. Both the Son and the Spirit proceed from the Father. Just as the second and third person of the Trinity proceed from the Father, so also the whole of God's soteriological economy proceeds from the Father. This impetus towards salvation expresses the Father's role as "God's eternal love in that He is both source and origin."[100] As creatures of the God who is love and as co-heirs with Christ, the faithful are enveloped in divine fatherhood. "We bathe in fatherly love. All Creation, every being we encounter, all kinds of gifts—intelligence, affection, goodness—all

---

98. See Kelly, *Early Christian Creeds*. The most recent English translation of the *Ordinis Missae Missalis Romani* (*The Order of Mass I*) renders the first of these creedal elements as "and [I believe] in one Lord Jesus Christ, the Only Begotten Son of God, born of the Father before all ages" (Et in unum Dominum Iesum Christum, Filium Dei unigenitum, et ex Patre natum ante omnia saecula). This translation was signed by Albertus Malcolmus Ranjith of the Congregation for Divine Worship and Discipline of the Sacraments June 23, 2008 and was put into use for Advent of 2011.

99. Daniélou, *La Trinité et le Mystère de l'Existence*, 75. "Dans le Sainte Trinité, c'est du Père que toutes choses procèdent, c'est lui qui éternellement engendre le Fils comme sa parfait image et c'est de son amour pour le Fils que procède l'Esprit-Saint. De même cette vie communiqué au Fils et à l'Esprit, c'est vers lui qu'elle reflue puisque le Fils est tout entier tourné vers le Père."

100. Ibid., 76. "Le Père est donc d'abord l'amour éternel de Dieu en tant qu'il est source, origine."

these originally proceed from the Father's infinite love."[101] God's love for his creation is expressed in the Pauline contention that "the love of God has been poured out into our hearts through the holy Spirit that has been given to us. For Christ, while we were still helpless, yet died at the appointed time for the ungodly. Indeed, only with difficulty does one die for a just person, though perhaps for a good person one might even find courage to die. But God proves his love for us in that while we were still sinners Christ died for us." (Rom 5:5–8; NAB). Christ is the "proof of eternal love" of the Father from which the Son proceeds. This eternal love is both generative and transformative. Through our identification with and participation in Christ, believers are caught up in the love of Father as source and sustenance of eternal love.

Also, the Father's love is also expressed in the mission of the Son to his creation. "In this way the love of God was revealed to us: God sent his only Son into the world so that we might have life through him. In this is love: not that we have loved God, but that he loved us and sent his Son as expiation for our sins" (1 John 4:9–10; NAB). It is through this emanation of love through the Son that the Father draws all things back to himself. In sending his Son, the Father establishes himself as the end toward which all things are oriented and to which all things return. Daniélou describes this movement aptly noting, "the whole movement of the life of the Trinity is the movement in which the Son, issued for the Father, is Himself turned wholly toward the Father. In the same way the Word of God, issuing forth into Creation in order to redeem it, takes hold of Creation and draws it into its own sphere, that is, turns it toward the Father."[102] Entailed in the mission of the Son is his and, by virtue of our kinship with the Son, our return to the Father. It is important to note that the Son always points back to the Father. This aspect of the mission of the Son is emphasized in the Johannine gospel. Jesus says to his disciples, "If you know me, then you will also know my Father. From now on you do know him and have seen him" and "Whoever has seen me has seen the Father" (John 14:7, 9; NAB). This is

---

101. Ibid., 77. "Nous sommes baignés dans cet amour paternel. Toute cette création au milieu de laquelle nous vivons, tous ces êtres que nous rencontrons, toutes espèces de dons, de l'ordre de l'intelligence, de l'ordre de l'affection, de l'ordre de la bonté, tout cela procède originellement de l'amour infini du Père."

102. Ibid., 83. "Le mouvement même de la vie trinitaire est celui par lequel le Fils venant de Père est lui-même tout entier tourné vers le Père. Aussi venant dans l creation, afin de sauver cette création qui est sienne, le Verbe de Dieu la saisit pour l'entraîner dans le mouvement qui est le sien, c'est-à-dire pour la touner vers le Père."

also made clear by the fact of the Ascension. In returning to the "right hand of the Father," Christ goes "to prepare a place" for his followers (John 14:2; NAB). This is a clear indication of the intent of Christ to draw his followers back to their source and origin. This is also clearly indicated when Jesus tells his disciples, "Where I am going, you cannot follow me now, though you will follow later" (John 13:36; NAB). In part, this return to the Father is affected in our participation in the spiritual life of the Church in this life. As one joins his contemplation to the praise and adoration of the Church, one becomes "taken up in the movement of the Son and the Spirit, that come from the Father, and endure through Creation within our souls, allowing us to partake of Their eternal action and movement."[103]

In contemplating the mission of the Word, Daniélou emphasizes Christ's high priestly role. This priestly function is summed up in the Eucharistic doxology which ends the Eucharistic prayer in the Mass: "Through him, with him, in him, in the unity of the Holy Spirit, all glory and honor is yours, almighty Father, for ever and ever."[104] It is through the priestly mission of the Son that all of creation is drawn back to the Father. The Eucharistic doxology expresses "the mission of the Word, which is to draw the whole universe up in the movement that carries Him toward the Father. The Son is eternally turned toward the Father. And He enters Creation to take hold of the whole universe, in order to draw it up in the movement that bears Him eternally toward the Father."[105]

The words of the Eucharistic doxology most clearly express the priestly function of Christ in the sacrifice of praise to the Father. "The Eucharist is also the sacrifice of praise by which the Church sings the glory of God in the name of all creation. This sacrifice of praise is possible only through Christ:

---

103. Ibid., 85. "Glorifiant ainsi le Père en sorte que nous soyons comme pris par le movement même du Fils et de l'Esprit qui viennent du Père et qui retournent au Père, et qui, traversant ainsi la création et demeurant dans nos âmes, nous font participer a ce geste, à ce mouvemnent éternel qui est le leur."

104. The new translation of the doxology to Eucharistic Prayer 1 reads, "Through Him, and with Him, and in Him, to you, O God, almighty Father, in the unity of the Holy Spirit, is all honor and glory, for ever and ever" (Per ipsum, et cum ipso, et in ipso, est tibi Deo Patri omnipotenti, in unitate Spiritus Sancti, omnis honor et gloria per omnia saecula saeculorum).

105. Daniélou, *La Trinité et le Mystère de l'Existence*, 89. "Cette finale du Canon de la messe exprime le terme même de la mission du Verbe qui est d'entraîner l'univers entier dans ce mouvement qui l'emporte vers le Père. Le Fils éternellement est ainsi tourné vers le Père; dans la création il vient ressaisir l'univers entier pour l'entraîner dans ce mouvement qui le porte éternellement vers le Père."

Prayer, Trinity, and Mission

he unites the faithful to his person, to his praise, and to his intercession, so that the sacrifice of praise to the Father is offered *through* Christ and *with* him, to be accepted *in* him."[106] At the same time, *per ipsum, cum ipso,* and *in ipso* express more generally the mission of the Son drawing all things back to the Father. In the first place, *per ipsum* expresses the role that Christ played in creation. In the words of the prologue to the Gospel of John, "All things came to be through him, and without him nothing came to be" (John 1:3; NAB). The Letter to the Colossians says, "For in him were created all things in heaven and on earth, the visible and the invisible, whether thrones or dominions or principalities or powers; all things were created through him and for him" (Col 1:16; NAB). These passages from scripture indicate to Daniélou that "the Word is above all else the life-giving Word from which all existence must come. When we contemplate the mystery of the Word, we must always acknowledge its cosmic vastness. It encompasses the whole of Creation in its action."[107] All existence finds its sustenance through the Son. It is only to the extent that one participates in the creative power of the life-giving Word that existence is able to persist.

The next aspect of the mission of the Son is expressed in the words *cum ipso*. This phrase indicates Christ's activity of drawing creation back to the Father through the incarnation. Though all of reality has been created through the Son, it has cut itself off from that source and origin through sin. "Once Creation cuts itself off from the light of life, it becomes dead. This dead life . . . , this dead existence cut off from the source of life, constitutes the abode of sin in all its forms: inertia, heaviness, lack of response to divine things, everything that still represents the burden of sin within us, everything . . . that still separates us from the source of life."[108] Creation being cut off from its source, the Word seeks out everything through the Incarnation in order to redeem it though the "reassumption by the Word of what the Word had already created in the beginning." This brings one

---

106. *Catechism of the Catholic Church*, §1361.

107. Daniélou, *La Trinité et le Mystère de l'Existence*, 90. "Le Verbe est donc d'abord le Verbe créateur, celui dont procède absolument toute existence. Quand nous contemplons ce mystère du Verbe, nous devons toujours lui donner son amplitude cosmique. Il embrasse dans son action la totalité de la création."

108. Ibid., 93. "Dans la mesure où la création se sépare de la lumière de la vie, elle devient morte. C'est cette vie morte . . ., cette existence morte coupée des sources de vie, qui constitue la sphère du péché sous toutes ses formes: cette sorte d'inertie, cette pesanteur, cette insensibilité aux choses divines, tout ce qui en nous est encore le poids du péché, . . . tout ce qui reste encore qui nous sépare de la source de vie."

Jean Danielou's Doxological Humanism

to the restoration of life by the Word through the Ascension. Through the Incarnation and the Ascension, Christ "seize[s] hold of mankind, . . . [and] raises it up 'with Him' and carries it toward the Father 'with Him.'"[109] God's redemptive economy is accomplished by virtue of God's condescension and subsequent ascension. With Christ's return to the right hand of the Father, humanity is raised up "with Christ" through his ascension.

The final aspect of the mission of the Son is expressed through the phrase *in ipso*. In the first place, all things were made by him. Then, all things were remade by him. Finally, all things are fulfilled "in Him." Daniélou expresses this fact when he writes, "all things are already consummated in Him, in the sense that the meaning of all Creation is fully realized in Him. In Him, through the humanity He has assumed, God is perfectly glorified, man is perfectly sanctified, all things have returned to their origin, and the loving design of the Trinity is perfectly accomplished."[110] Nothing can be added to the work of the Son in that all things have found their complete fulfillment in the Trinity. The divine economy achieves its eternal end in the person of the Son.

Daniélou ends his reflections concerning the Trinity with an exposition on the Holy Spirit. For Daniélou, when one speaks of the Holy Spirit, one must always see the Spirit's mission as "an extension of eternal relations."[111] These eternal relations are also expressed well in the Eucharistic doxology, which continues, "through Him, with Him, in Him, *the unity of the Holy Spirit*, all glory and honor are yours almighty Father, for ever and ever." The Holy Spirit is in fact a personal expression of the bond of love between the Father and Son. "This love," Daniélou expounds, "is not merely something that exists in the Father or in the Son. This love itself is personal. . . . [T]he love binding the Father and Son has its being in the reality of a Person. It is an expression of the fertility of love of the Father and Son."[112]

---

109. Ibid., 94. "Cette humanité qu'il a ressaisie, le Verbe l'entraîne à nouveau vers le Père «avec lui», c'est-à-dire que c'est avec lui que se réalise ce dessein."

110. Ibid., 96–97. "En lui déjà tout est consommé dans le mesure où en lui est déjà pleinement réalise le sens de toute création. En lui, à travers l'humanité qu'il s'est unie, Dieu est parfaitement glorifié, l'homme est parfaitement sanctifié, toutes choses sont revenues à leur origine, le dessein de l'amour trinitaire est parfaitement accompli."

111. Ibid., 103. "C'est-à-dire qu'il est l'expression même de cet amour éternel qui unit le Père au Fils."

112. Ibid., 103–4. "Cet amour n'est pas simplement quelque chose qui existerait dans le Père ou dans le Fils. Lui-même est personnel. . . . Cet amour qui unit le Père et le Fils subsiste donc dans la réalité d'une Personne. Il est l'expression de la fécondité de l'amour du Père et du Fils."

Prayer, Trinity, and Mission

The Spirit, being personal, is sent—or communicated—by the Father and the Son to the Church at Pentecost in order to pour out God's gratuity upon his people. In turn the Church, which has been endowed with gifts by the Spirit dispenses graces through the sacraments in which the "life of the Spirit blooms."[113] So the mission of the Holy Spirit "leads to its goal, its fulfillment, its ultimate perfection the design that originated in the Father's love, the design already fulfilled in substance through the Incarnation of the Word. In Christ, humanity is wholly consecrated and turned toward the Father. But this consecration must embrace and imbue all humanity; and this is the labor of the Spirit in the Church."[114]

The Extension of Adoration

Trinitarian existence—both the internal self-subsistence of the Trinity itself and personal Trinitarian participation—constitute the summit of all divine and human existence. Daniélou, over and over again, maintains that the Trinity expresses the fullness of "ultimate reality." The Father's communication of the Son and the personal bond of love that is the Holy Spirit is the "source both of personal spiritual life and of the missionary vocation."[115] The believer finds his own spiritual life informed by the structure of the Trinitarian interrelations. This fact in turn informs his understanding of the life of the apostolate which is "nothing more than belief in the growth of Christ in the whole universe of souls."[116] While Daniélou certainly sees the active aspect of the apostolate, he also sees the apostolate equally in terms of the "extension of adoration" or the "extension of prayer" (d'étendre notre prière à l'universe entier)[117] rather than solely in terms of personal

---

113. Ibid., 106. "Elle [l'Église] la distribue dans ses sacrements qui constituent le milieu vital, le nouveau paradis, à l'intérieur duquel seul la vie de l'Esprit s'épanouit."

114. Ibid. "L'Esprit-Saint vient ainsi mener à son terme et à sib achèvement, conduire à sa perfection dernière, progressivement, le dessein dont l'origine est l'amour du Père, dont nous avons dit qu'il était accompli substantiellement dans l'Incarnation du Verbe. Dans le Christ l'humanité est entièrement consacrée et rapportée au Père. Mais cette consécration doit venir saisir et pénétrer toute l'humanité et c'est l'œuvre de l'Esprit dans l'Église."

115. Ibid., 68. "C'est la source aussi bien de la vie spirituelle personnelle que de la mission, qui n'est pas autre chose que l'adhésion à la croissance du Christ dans l'univers entier des âmes."

116. Ibid.

117. Daniélou, *Le Mystère du Salut des Nations*, 11.

salvation, though that is certainly an element in the dynamic. In fact, ultimately, the purpose of missions is to Christianize the natural religious impulses of the unevangelized. Therefore, Daniélou contends that "Revelation must be carried to these people, so that their prayer may be a genuine prayer and so that it may be addressed to the true God."[118] In the end, the extension of Christianity throughout the world equates to the reform of the contemplative life of the various religions of the world.

In fact, Daniélou maintains that in praying the *Our Father* one seeks the extension of Trinitarian life in praise, adoration and contemplation of the Trinity. For Daniélou, the Lord's Prayer

> is a prayer that speaks of God's love, a prayer that brings us to seek the extension of praise, which first presupposes that we ourselves are souls of praise, because it is to the extent that we love God that we suffer from his not being loved, that we desire for him to be loved, and that the wish that "his name be hallowed" takes on its full meaning. And, what is very important for us, it helps us to reach that mysterious point where adoration, contemplation, and mission coincide. Mission is the extension of adoration, because adoration means that we desire that God be known and loved by everyone and not just certain people.[119]

Trinity is the root of mission which in turn leads to contemplation: "For there is not one single human being who is not destined, one day, to be transformed in Christ and to contemplate the Trinity. The missionary perspective anticipates the fulfillment of this vocation."[120] Indeed, the Church is the participant in God's current work in sacred history. Daniélou notes Leonce de Grandmaison's contention that the continuing work of the Word

---

118. Ibid. "A ces peoples il faut apporter la Révélation, faire que leur prière soit une prière veritable et que ce soit au vrai Dieu qu'elle s'adresse."

119. Daniélou, *Contemplation: Croissance de l'Église*, 43–44. "C'est une prière qui parle de l'amour de Dieu, une prière qui nous fait demander l'extension de la louange, ce qui suppose que nous soyons d'abord des âmes de louange, car c'est dans la mesure où nous avons commencé à aimer Dieu que nous souffrons que Dieu ne soit pas aimé, que nous désirons qu'Il soit aimé et que cette demande, «que ton Nom soit sanctifié», prend tout son sens. Elle nous aide à toucher, et c'est très important pour nous, ce point mystérieux où adoration, comtemplation et mission coïncedent, puisque la mission c'est l'extension de l'adoration, c'est la fait que l'on désire que Dieu soit connu et aimé de tous et non pas seulement de quelques-uns."

120. Ibid., 150–51. "Car il n'y a aucune âme humaine qui ne soit destinée à être, un jour, transformée dans le Christ et à contempler la Trinité. Le regard missionnaire en anticipe la réalisation."

Prayer, Trinity, and Mission

and the Spirit in the world aims at "all men becoming Christians and all Christians becoming saints."[121] In this regard, the mission of the Church and the expansion of the Church entail an interior dimension. In fact, Daniélou regards the missionary nature of the Church as divisible into two aspects. What most people think of as missionary activity, he describes as the active aspect of mission. But, he also maintains the equally important contemplative aspect of mission.[122] This interior aspect of mission plays a large role in Daniélou's missiology and figures prominently when one is considering the relationship between Daniélou's theology of prayer, Trinity and mission.

When one is speaking of *missions* within the realm of Christian theology it is important to be precise about what exactly the term means. It is by no means a univocal term though the different connotations are intimately related and derive their meanings from each other. The primary sense of the term *missions* is related to the sending of the Son and the Spirit by the Father.[123] It is from this sense of the term that the more common understanding of *mission* is derived. This aspect of mission indicates: "those particular undertakings by which the heralds of the Gospel, sent out by the Church and going forth into the whole world, carry out the task of preaching the Gospel and planting the Church among peoples or groups who do not yet believe in Christ. These undertakings are brought to completion by missionary activity and are mostly exercised in certain territories recognized by the Holy See. The proper purpose of this missionary activity is evangelization, and the planting of the Church among those peoples and groups where it has not yet taken root."[124] In Daniélou's parlance, mission indicates "the mandate given by Christ to the Church in its full scope. More particularly it designates the portion of this mandate that concerns the preaching of the Gospel to non-Christians."[125] Yet, it is also clear that the term "encompasses the whole plan of redemption, and not merely the preaching of the Gospel to pagans."[126] It is within this context that Daniélou emphasizes some different aspects of *mission*.

---

121. Quoted in Daniélou, "The Missionary Nature of the Church," 14.
122. Ibid., 16–17.
123. *Ad Gentes: Decree on the Missionary Activity of the Church*, Vatican II, §2–5.
124. *Ad Gentes*, §6.
125. Daniélou, "The Missionary Nature of the Church," 11.
126. Ibid.

While reflecting on the relationship between prayer, Trinity, and mission, Daniélou's emphasis on both the active and interior aspects of mission becomes pertinent. Clearly, Daniélou admits to the active aspect of the apostolate. Mission is constituted by the effort of the Church "to extend itself without cease in gathering new members to itself."[127] However, unlike some, Daniélou also emphasizes the interiority of mission. For example, Daniélou maintained that St. Anthony, though isolated in the desert was in the midst of the battle for souls. "Anthony buried himself in the desert, that he might be in the thick of the fight."[128]

The Prolongation of the Mission of the Word and Spirit

The missionary activity of the Church has its roots in the divine missions of the Son and the Spirit and derives its meaning from them. "Missionary life is an extension of that first mission, that is the sending by the Father of His Son into the World. That first mission remains the point of departure, the sole origin, the source of all other missions."[129] This aspect of mission illuminates the facet of mission as "the prolongation of the mission of the Word and the Spirit."[130] This is precisely what *Ad Gentes* espouses when the council declared, "The pilgrim Church is missionary by her very nature, since it is from the mission of the Son and the mission of the Holy Spirit that she draws her origin, in accordance with the decree of God the Father."[131] Also, one finds this in Scripture in the Johannine gospel when the Son addresses the Father, "As you sent me into the world, so I sent them into the world" (John 17:18; NAB). The Church's mission finds its meaning in the mission of the Son and constitutes the continuance of the *magnalia Dei* through prayer and the sacraments in the divinized Church. "There is, in truth, only one mission, that one [the mission of the Son]; and all others

---

127. Ibid., 14.
128. Daniélou, *Le Mystère du Salut des Nations*, 58. "Il s'est enfoncé au désert pour être au cœur de la lutte."
129. Ibid., 27. "La vie missionnaire est un certain prolongement de cette première mission qui est l'envoi par le Père de son Fils dans le monde. Cette première mission reste le point de départ, l'origine unique, la source de toute autre mission."
130. Daniélou, "The Missionary Nature of the Church," 11.
131. *Ad Gentes*, §2.

are but its participations and derivations. So, if we return to that primary source, we shall find that it is the origin of all missionary activity."[132]

The mission of the Word was first enacted among the pagans (non-Christians) since Christ is a stranger to no one.[133] Thereafter, the mission of the Word was manifested among the Jewish people in order to accustom people to the incarnation.[134] Finally, after the slow process of pedagogical preparation, the Father sent the Word in the flesh to all people. Therefore, the writer of the book of Hebrews explains, "In times past, God spoke in partial and various ways to our ancestors through the prophets; in these last days, he spoke to us through a son" (Heb 1:1–2; NAB). "Whereas in natural religion the existence of God is grasped, and in the Jewish religion the holiness of God is manifested, in the Christian religion we are introduced into intimacy with God, and this is the great richness of Christ's revelation."[135] This revelation of intimacy with God is the essence of the message of the New Testament: God took on flesh in order to incorporate his creation into a more intimate life through our kinship with his Son. Daniélou narrates the content of this reality:

> the New Testament is the revelation of the mystery of the Trinity, that is, the mystery of God's intimate life: we become aware of this vast life of love in God, by which the Father gives Himself to the Son, and by which the love of the Father and the Son is the Holy Ghost. We know this only because Christ revealed it to us. Thus, we contemplate Christ's life of union with His Father, this being the visible manifestation of the invisible life of the Divine Persons and of the circulation of love within God, of which the Trinity is simply the name. Further, what Christ reveals to us and brings to us is a kind of participation in the intimate life of God. Obviously, this is the essential part of Christ's work. Christ, the Son of God, calls to us and makes us capable of participation in his sonship. He has made us adopted sons of God. In so doing, He has introduced

---

132. Daniélou, *Le Mystère du Salut des Nations*, 27. "Il n'y a en réalité qu'une mission, c'est cella-là, et toutes les autres n'en sont qu'une participation et qu'une dérivation. Donc, en remontant à cette source première, nous trouverons quelle est l'origine de tout esprit missionnaire."

133. Ibid., 27–37.

134. See chapter 2, "History and the Divine Pedagogy."

135. Daniélou, *Le Mystère du Salut des Nations*, 41. "Si dans la religion naturelle c'est avant tout une certain existence de Dieu qui est connue, si dans la religion juive, c'est la sainteté de Dieu qui s'est manifestée, dans la religion chrétienne, c'est dans l'intimité de Dieu que nous sommes introduits, et c'est la grande richesse de la Révélation du Christ."

us into the family of God, into intimacy with God. . . . We now become, in a manner, participants in the Divine nature, and in consequence we have the right to treat with Him as sons, on a footing of equality.[136]

The mission of the Son is not the only Trinitarian mission. The Spirit also proceeds from the Father and the Son with a missionary purpose.

The mission of the Spirit begins at the time of Pentecost and constitutes the alpha point of Christian missions. The missionary significance of Pentecost is highlighted by the passage in I Peter which notes, "It was revealed to them that they were serving not themselves but you with regard to the things that have now been announced to you by those who preached the good news to you (through) the holy Spirit sent from heaven, things into which angels longed to look" (1 Pet 1:12; NAB). It is by means of the presence of the Holy Spirit in them that the gospel is proclaimed. The universality of the missionary force of Pentecost is communicated by the fact that the descent of the Spirit initiated speaking in many languages. "And they were all filled with the holy Spirit and began to speak in different tongues, as the Spirit enabled them to proclaim" (Acts 2:4; NAB). Whereas Pentecost is the beginning of the mission of the Holy Spirit manifested in the Church, the omega point of the mission of the Spirit must be considered. It is through the Spirit that the faithful are made to participate in the sphere of Trinitarian life. For Daniélou, "the effusion of the Spirit on the Apostles . . . is to sanctify us by making the divine life operative in us; in this sense, it is the Holy Ghost Whom we receive in Baptism and Who, as a living principle, gradually transforms us by nurturing in us an awareness of the things of God through faith; by developing in us the love of God

---

136. Ibid., 41–42. "L'essence de la Révélation du Nouveau Testament, c'est la révélation du mystère trinitaire, c'est-à-dire précisément de la vie intime de Dieu: nous reconnaissons qu'il y a en Dieu toute cette vie d'amour par laquelle le Père se donne au Fils, et par laquelle l'amour du Père et du Fils est l'Esprit-Saint. Nous ne la savons que parce que le Christ nous l'a révélé. Nous contemplons la vie d'union du Christ avec Son Père, qui est comme la manifestation visible de la vie invisible des personnes divines et de la circulation d'amour à l'intérieur de Dieu dont la Trinité est tout simplement le nom. Plus encore, ce que le Christ nous révèle et nous apporte, c'est une certaine participation à cette vie intime de Dieu. C'est évidemment l'essentiel de l'œuvre du Christ. Le Christ, Fils de Dieu, nous appelle et nous rend capable de participer à sa filiation. Il a fait de nous des fils adoptifs de Dieu. Ce faisant, Il nous introduit dans la famille de Dieu, dans la familiarité divine. . . . Nous devenons en quelques sorte participants à la nature divine, et par suite, nous avons le droit de traiter avec Lui comme des fils sur le plan d'une certain égalité."

Prayer, Trinity, and Mission

and of others through charity; by increasing in us the hope that makes us adhere to divine realities; by giving us His gifts through which we come to have antennae, as it were, that bring us close to God and enable us to respond to divine touches; by making us capable of being taught and led by the Spirit."[137]

The missions of the Son and the Spirit effect in the Church the divinization of the people of God. We become "sharers in the divine nature."[138] It is by means of the divinized Church that God extends the mission of the Son and the Spirit through the interior life of the body of Christ, through the sacraments of the Church and through the mission spirituality of its members who seek to replicate these effects as the Church extends its life in the Trinity to more and more individuals.

Interiority and Mission

Often, Daniélou speaks of mission as the flowering of contemplation where the apostolate finds its source in interiority. This is certainly the position of Maritain when he writes, "Action then springs from the superabundance of contemplation, *ex superabundantia contemplationis*."[139] Daniélou echoes this maxim when he writes, "I would like to show that the apostolic spirit is authentic only in the measure that it is deeply rooted in the spirit of contemplation, that it is but the blossoming, the fruition of the life of praise."[140] Within the Thomistic understanding of the relationship between the active and the contemplative lives, the apostolate is distinct from, even if it finds

---

137. Ibid., 125. "Cette effusion de l'Esprit sur les Apôtres . . . est de nous sanctifier en opérant en nous la vie divine; c'est l'Esprit-Saint en ce sens que nous recevons au baptême et qui peu à peu nous tranforme comme un principe vivant en développant en nous l'intelligence des choses de Dieu par le foi, en développant en nous l'amour de Dieu et des autres par la charité, en accroissant en nous l'espérance qui nous fait adhérer aux réalités divines, en nous donnant ses dons par lesquels nous avons comme des antennes qui font que les choses divines nous deviennent proches et que nous devenons capable de capter en quelque sorte les touches divines, capable d'être enseignés et conduits par l'Esprit."

138. 2 Pet 1:4.

139. Maritain, *Scholasticism and Politics*. Maritain attributes the phrase *ex superabudanita contemplationis* to Aquinas but it appears to be either an incorrect rendering of the Thomism or absent altogether from Aquinas' works.

140. Daniélou, *Le Mystère du Salut des Nations*, 133. "Ce que je voudrais montrer, c'est comment l'esprit apostolique n'est authentique que dans la mesure où il s'enracine profondément dans l'esprit de contemplation, et comment il n'est que l'efflorescence, l'épanouissement de la vie de louange."

its source in, the contemplative life. Contemplation incites the faithful to seek out others and to invest in them the need for contemplation of God by all. "It is contemplation of God that arouses in us the desire to make Him known and loved."[141] However, though Daniélou often confirms the Thomist understanding of the apostolate and interiority, he often folds the apostolate into the life of prayer and contemplation.

This is clear from Daniélou's comments about St. Anthony noted above. Retaining the need for preaching, Daniélou writes about the defense of the Nicene faith in the early centuries of the Church: "indeed, the real battle was fought in the desert far more than in Nicaea, where outwardly Constantine had all the advantage. It was Constantine who seemed to be Christianizing the world, but in reality it was Anthony who was tearing it away from the power of evil. Anthony buried himself in the desert, that he might be in the thick of the fight. Indeed, Our Lord has told us that souls are to be won away from the Devil first by fasting and vigils, and that the great battle is fought in the heart of the desert, in the depth of solitude, on the summit of Carmel, before it is fought through the ministry of preachers."[142] This passage points to the priority of interiority when speaking of the extension of the mission of the Son and Spirit in the Church. Daniélou refuses to admit to the assertion that mission should prioritize the temporal benefit of humanity. Instead, he maintains that temporal good is only of penultimate value. The mission of the Son and the Spirit seeks to save what is eternal in humanity. With this in view, Daniélou exhorts his reader, the Christian must be "a [person] of contemplation, and if he is not that then he is not a Christian; if his deepest roots are not embedded in the world of the Trinity, if he does not try to penetrate its luminous obscurity . . . , then he is no true Christian. Social, exterior action must not be allowed to take first place in our Christianity. We are called to share the intimate life of the Divine Persons, and there will always be a part of us reserved for that."[143]

Daniélou often speaks of the missionary task solely in terms of interiority and contemplation. This is especially shown in Daniélou's description of missionary spirituality. Following the work which is already accomplished

---

141. Ibid. "C'est la contemplation de Dieu qui suscite en nous le désir de Le faire connaître et aimer."

142. Ibid., 43. See also Daniélou, *Contemplation: Croissance de l'Église*, 154. "La mission apparait donc comme un conflit avec les forces du mal: elle est un combat spirituel qui ne se joue pas d'abord dans l'extérieur, mais dans l'intérieur."

143. Daniélou, *Le Mystère de l'avent*, 150; ET: *Advent*, 131. Subsequent reference to this text will be to the English translation by Sheed.

in Christ, "we can, in our turn, invisibly accomplish, prefigure and prepare universal salvation by assuming inwardly, through prayer, the peoples that are still strangers to the Gospel, so that there may even now exist, though hidden, this mystery of perfect praise that will be manifested at the end of time."[144] Through the interior life and through participation in and imitation of Christ's work, we learn to "live the missionary life within ourselves, like a hidden mystery."[145]

Daniélou also expresses this when commenting on the active and contemplative lives within the context of missions. Meditating on St. Bernard's exhortation to tend to one's own duty before all else, Daniélou tells that one must pray for the "most important interests of the Kingdom, even if they are not the ones we ourselves are engaged in. Charity will then become perfect in us, for it is proportioned to the reality of things, not to our personal point of view."[146] Within this frame of mind, while one goes about one's work, however insignificant, through interiority of mind and soul one is able to participate in the apostolate. "Outwardly, we go humbly about our own work, inwardly we are working out the salvation of the whole world."[147] In a mysterious way, the believer is able to go about the extension of the mission of the Word and the Spirit through one's own inward journey.

Not only is the extension of the Son and Spirit's mission achieved through the interiority of the particular believer, but it is also received by those sought out by the Son and the Spirit in an interior fashion. The conversion of souls is brought about "in Jesus Christ by the action of the Spirit" and constitutes another facet of the interiority of mission.[148] Certainly the exterior aspect of mission entails the external acts of the Church seeking out new members in Christ's body. However, this incorporation into the

---

144. Daniélou, *Le Mystère du Salut des* Nations, 8. "Pouvons-nous à notre tour accomplir invisiblement, préfigure et préparere le salut universel en assumant intérieurement par la prière les nations qui sont encore étrangers à l'Evangile, en sorte qu'existe déjà, mais cache, ce mystère de la louange parfait qui sera manifesté à la fin des temps."

145. Ibid., 7. "Un approfondissement ensuite, en nous apprenant à vivre la vie missionnaire d'abord à l'intérieur, comme un mystère cache."

146. Daniélou, *Le Mystère de l'avent*, 174. "Nous devons prier davantage pour les intérêts les plus importants du Royaume de Dieu, même si ce ne sont pas ceux dont nous sommes charges. Alors la charité devient parfait en nous, elle est proportionnée à la réalité des choses, et non à notre point de vue personnel." The particular passage from St. Bernard is *On the Song of Songs*, Sermon 49.

147. Ibid. "Extérieurement nous faisons très humblement notre petit tâche, intérieurement nous opérons le la salut du monde entier."

148. Daniélou, "Missionary Nature of the Church," 14.

body of Christ entails the "extension of divine life" through the "interior dynamism" of the Church.[149]

The Sacraments and Mission

As the Church continues to extend the mission of the Son and the Spirit, it is important to recall two aspects of the Church's task. First, Daniélou notes, that those benefits endowed to believers by the action of the Word and the Spirit are offered to all of humanity, "inviting each [person], in a mysterious way, to place those acts that will make salvation possible for him."[150] Second, Daniélou notes the primary means by which an individual is engrafted into the body of Christ by partaking of the fruits of the mission of the Son and the Spirit. "It is normally by faith in the word of God and by access to the sacraments of the Spirit, that is, by the institutional Church, that a [individual] opens himself to the divinizing action of the Word and of the Spirit."[151] For Daniélou, the consummation of divine missions in the extension of prayer and adoration is achieved through the sacraments of the one, holy, catholic, and apostolic Church. He indicates as much when he maintains, "For my part I would say that, inasmuch as they are realities of this world, divinization, salvation, and transfiguration are given by faith and the sacraments."[152]

The sacramental aspect of the salvation of the nations is also indicated in the offertory of the Mass. When the priest has offered the host, he then

---

149. Ibid.

150. Ibid., 15.

151. Ibid. It is within this context that Daniélou lodges his reservations about such notions as "implicit Christianity" or "anonymous Christianity."

152. Ibid. In another place Daniélou relates the sacraments to transformed Christian life, "Mais si cette transfiguration commence déjà à s'opérer actuellement, si l'humanité à laquelle nous appartenons dans le Christ plonge déjà dans sa gloire par toute la vie sacramentelle qui nous divinize dès maintenant, qui change notre cœur en l'élargissant à la mesure du cœur du Christ, qui transfigure notre corps lui-même en commençant déjà de le dégager des servitudes, en le rendant capable dans la pauvreté, dans la chasteté, dans la charité, d'une pureté, d'une intégrité qui sont au-dessus des forces de l'homme [This transfiguration is already becoming a reality, and the humanity to which we belong in Christ is already entering its glory through the life of the sacraments, which makes us divine even now, transforms our hearts by enlarging their capacity to the measure of Christ's, transfigures our very bodies by beginning to free them of their bondage, by making them capable, in poverty, in chastity, in charity, of a purity, of an integrity that are beyond the strength of men]." Daniélou, *Le Mystère du Salut des Nations*, 83.

Prayer, Trinity, and Mission

uses it to trace the sign of the cross on the corporal. Having done so, the celebrant then declares, "For the salvation of the whole world"—*pro totius mundi salute*.[153] The sign of the cross expresses the universality of salvation obtained through the sacrifice of Christ and in a mysterious manner this formula during the Mass claims the whole world. Daniélou writes:

> By this gesture he [the celebrant] somehow takes possession, in the name of the Cross, of the whole world, represented by the offerings before him, to consecrate it all to God, signing it with the sign of Christ. And what this sign of the Cross, *pro totius mundi salute*, signifies is the cosmic nature of salvation: it indicates the four points of the compass, so as to embrace all nations, those of the north and of the south, of the east and of the west; they are the *totus mundis* for which the sacrifice of the Mass, the sacrifice of the Cross, is being offered.[154]

By this act the relationship between mission and the sacramental life of the Church is demonstrated.

The Aim of Mission

Within Daniélou's understanding of the purpose of mission as the extension of prayer and adoration, the purpose of mission shifts. This shift moves from solely soteriological to a more holistic spirituality which entails sharing in the divine life, being granted intimacy with God and subsequent divinization of the Church. Each of these components reorients mission toward the conversion of the inward person and incorporation into the life of the Trinity instead of emphasizing personal salvation.

The primary goal of missionary activity is the expansion of Trinitarian life through the believer's sharing in the divine life of the triune God. When Daniélou considers the nature of salvation in relation to the "non-Christian religions" he notes that *religion* in itself does not save.[155] Instead it is only

---

153. Daniélou, *Le Mystère de l'avent*, 145.

154. Ibid. "Par ce geste il prend, en quelque sorte, au nom de la croix, possession du monde tout entier, représenté par les «oblate», par les offrandes, pour ainsi le consacrer au Père par le signe du Christ. Et ce qui est signifié par ce signe de croix, *pro totius mundi salute*, c'est ce caractère cosmique du salut: il désigne les quatre directions, le nord, le sud, l'est et l'ouest, embrassant par conséquent toutes les nations, celles du nord et celles du midi, celles de l'orient et celles de l'occident; c'est cela le *totus mundi* pour lequel le sacrifice de la Messe, la sacrifice de la Croix est offert."

155. For Daniélou it is important to define the term religion as he uses it. Religion,

the divine life of the Trinity extended by the mission of the Son which saves. This salvation is communicated in the incorporation of individuals into the sphere of the Trinity and the sharing in the divine life of the body of Christ. For Daniélou, "God's plan to summon mankind to share in his own life dominates the whole process of unfolding history."[156] Indeed, the whole aim of sacred history is to bring humanity into communion with God. Daniélou contends that the aim of missionary spirituality is unfolded in a mystery "according to a divine plan; prepared by the vocation of the Jewish people, substantially realized by the mission of the Word, Who by His admirable Ascension introduced human nature for all eternity into the sphere of life of the Trinity; and this plan is to be accomplished among the various peoples of the world, one after another, during the time between Pentecost and the Second Coming."[157] Missionary expansion is in its essence the expansion of divine life to all of humankind.

Daniélou believes, "is simply man's attempt to develop that part of himself which is turned toward God." It is a completely natural impulse. Daniélou distinguishes *religion* from *revelation* which is not naturally accessible and is only communicated by God. Within this matrix, religion as such has no saving power. It is only the revelation of Jesus Christ that saves. Though Christianity and religion have a reciprocal relationship, they are not the same. Christianity is revelation not religion. "Religion is a basic aspect of the phenomenon of man. The individual is not fulfilled without God and on a social level faith in God is part of the common good. It is a religious trait of all peoples to see the divine present in nature. And the most profoundly human events such as birth, death, and marriage are usually acknowledged as somehow sacred through accompanying religious rites. Especially in his search for good does man see divine reality reflected in his own self. The diversity of pagan religion show us the different ways in which men recognize God through the world. The religious act, then, is basic to this world, not to the next. A man can no more change his religion than he can change his race. For nothing characterizes a people more than their religion. To become a Christian is not to change one's religion, but to move from the realm of religion to that of revelation. Christianity, therefore, is not a religion of the West. Western religion would rather be the ancient forms of Greek and Roman paganism. What we do have is a western way of being Christian and this way is heavily influenced by our ancient forms of paganism. Therefore, we cannot force upon others our way of welcoming Jesus. Christianity, precisely as revealed religion, testifies to an event that constitutes history. This is the Judeo-Christian act. It is not necessary to be a Christian to worship God, but it is to believe that he became man. Revelation testifies to a movement of God towards man—religion, of man towards God. Revelation is the work of God alone. It is infallible, true, and worthy of God alone. While religion is concerned with the present life revelation is eschatological, it looks toward the future, is prophetic. It testifies to God's response to religion." Daniélou, "Church and Non-Christian Religions," 12.

156. Daniélou, "Non-Christian Religions and Salvation," 57.

157. Daniélou, *Le Mystère du Salut des Nations*, 7–8. "Ce mystère s'accomplit suivant

Prayer, Trinity, and Mission

This sharing in the life of the Trinity yields intimacy with God. Again speaking within the context of sacred history, Daniélou points to the intimacy with God that is garnered by virtue of the revelation of Christ. "Whereas in natural religion the existence of God is grasped, and in the Jewish religion the holiness of God is manifested, in the Christian religion we are introduced into intimacy with God."[158] Indeed, Daniélou argues, this is the whole thrust of the revelation of the New Testament. Scripture reveals that God desires us to be incorporated into the mystery of the Trinity and that in being introduced into this divine life we achieve a familiar intimacy with God. In sum,

> we contemplate Christ's life of union with His Father, this being the visible manifestation of the invisible life of the Divine Persons and of the circulation of love within God, of which the Trinity is simply the name. Further, what Christ reveals to us and brings to us is a kind of participation in the intimate life of God. Obviously, this is the essential part of Christ's work. Christ, the Son of God, calls to us and makes us capable of participating in His sonship. He made of us adopted sons of God. In so doing, He has introduced us into the family of God. Thus, ours is not only a relationship of creature to Creator, as defined by the Old Testament, a relationship founded on fear. We now become, in a manner, participants in the Divine nature, and in consequence we have the right to treat with Him as sons.[159]

---

une divine économie; prepare par la vocation du people juif, réalisé substantiellement par la mission du Verbe, qui introduit à jamais la nature humaine dans la sphère de la vie trinitaire par son admirable Ascension, reçu successivement par les divers peoples Durant le temps qui va de la Pentecôte à la Parousie."

158. Ibid., 41. "Si dans la religion naturelle c'est avant tout une certain existence de Dieu qui est connue, si dans la religion juive, c'est la sainteté de Dieu qui s'est manifestée, dans la religion chrétienne, c'est dans l'intimité de Dieu que nous sommes introduits."

159. Ibid., 42. "Nous contemplons la vie d'union du Christ avec Son Père, qui est comme la manifestation visible de la vie invisible des personnes divines et de la circulation d'amour à l'intérieur de Dieu dont la Trinité est tout simplement le nom. Plus encore, ce que le Christ nous révèle et nous apporte, c'est une certaine participation à cette vie intime de Dieu. C'est évidemment l'essentiel de l'œuvre du Christ. Le Christ, Fils de Dieu, nous appelle et nous rend capable de participer à sa filiation. Il a fait de nous des fils adoptifs de Dieu. Ce faisant, Il nous introduit dans la famille de Dieu, dans la familiarité divine. Ainsi, à l'égard de Dieu, nous n'avons plus seulement ce rapport de créature à Créateur qui définit l'Ancien Testament et qui est fondé sur la crainte, mais nous devenons en quelques sorte participants à la nature divine, et par suite, nous avons le droit de traiter avec Lui comme des fils."

In the end, this intimacy with God and the believer's filial relationship to God through Christ leads to divinization (*theosis*). In fact, this divinization is ultimately the entire aim of missionary effort in the extension of Christ's work in the incarnation. So Athanasius writes in *On the Incarnation of the Word*, "For He was made man that we might be made God."[160] Daniélou indicates that divinization is achieved through the Incarnational act of the Son. This is clearly in accord with the general teaching of the Magisterium, "The Word became flesh to make us '*partakers of the divine nature*': 'For this is why the Word became man, and the Son of God became the Son of man: so that man, by entering into communion with the Word and thus receiving divine sonship, might become a son of God.' 'For the Son of God became man so that we might become God.' 'The only-begotten Son of God, wanting to make us sharers in his divinity, assumed our nature, so that he, made man, might make men gods.'"[161] One of the primary results of the Incarnation is that "in him [Jesus Christ] humanity is united to the divinity in a manner so intimate that there can be no closer union, so that in him human nature is divinized."[162]

Conclusion

For Daniélou, contemplation, trinity, and mission are intimately bound up with one another. It is through contemplation that the believer is granted access to Trinitarian life. In being incorporated into the life of the Trinity, the believer also participates in the activity of the Trinity in the world by prolonging the missions of the persons of the Trinity. It is here where Trinity, contemplation, and mission converge. As Daniélou notes, in praying in intimacy with the Trinity and for the extension of Trinitarian life we "reach that mysterious point where adoration, contemplation and mission coincide."[163]

---

160. Athanasius, *De Incarnatione*, 54.3 (PG 25.192B).
161. *Catechism of the Catholic Church*, §460.
162. Daniélou, "Missionary Nature of the Church," 12.
163. Daniélou, *Contemplation: Croissance de l'Église*, 43. "Elle nous aide à toucher, et c'est très important pour nous, ce point mystérieux où adoration, contemplation et missions coïncident."

FOUR

Prayer and the Spiritual Life

MUCH OF THE SPIRITUAL life is derived from the believer's life of prayer and contemplation. For instance, a major aspect of the spiritual life for Daniélou entails the active engagement with the presence of God. Indeed, one must agree with the statement of the *Dictionnaire de Spiritualité* that all prayer presupposes the presence of the one to whom it is addressed.[1] The divine presence in the soul is a byproduct of intimacy with God. It is from this presence that the whole trajectory for the spiritual life is set and which is achieved through participation in the intimate life of the Trinity. Christian spirituality as advocated by Daniélou has many aspects. In this chapter, the focus will be on select aspects of the spiritual life which are contiguous with each other. Daniélou describes the soul's itinerary as a movement from presence to absence to perpetual progress. These aspects generally correspond to a traditional itinerary of illumination, purgation and union which are represented by mystical texts throughout Catholic tradition.

In a 1972 article for *L'Osservatore Romano*, Daniélou set the course for these practices within the context of the absence and presence of God in the modern, technical and scientific society. He wrote, "God's presence, as we advance, is concealed from us at the same time as it is given to us, in order to oblige us always to advance further in the quest for what is always an absolutely real presence but is at the same time, the presence of him who is beyond our grasp."[2] This passage succinctly sums up a particular spiritual

---

1. Dupuy, "Présence de Dieu," 2107. "Toute prière suppose la présence de celui á qui elle s'adresse."

2. Daniélou, "Absence and Presence of God," 9.

itinerary which includes the presence of God, the darkness of God, the effects of the intensity of God and perpetual progress in the spiritual life. Each aspect of the spiritual life that will be discussed is present in this one place. The presence of God is fundamental to any spiritual journey and constitutes the illuminative stage of the believer's progress toward union with God. As one progresses in the spiritual life, one enters into the purgative stage which is a move from the certainties of the initial illumination due to the presence of God and toward a withdrawal of the divine presence due to its unparalleled immensity and due to its being beyond our feeble means. This requires the soul to seek the presence of God anew. This absence of God is experienced as darkness and is the believer's means of spiritual progress which moves him "from Glory to Glory." In perpetually moving onward and upward, the believer ever renews his intimacy with God and transforms his passability into perfectibility.

The Presence of God

In *Prayer: The Mission of the Church*, Daniélou notes a few specific aims of contemplation. He contends that prayer is "a time of contemplation and silence in a setting that helps us to disengage ourselves from life's immediate concerns. It is an opportunity to live more closely to God, to dwell in his presence, and to nourish ourselves with his Word."[3] Among intimacy with God, Daniélou counts simply being in the presence of God as a substantial aim of the contemplative life. Indeed, Daniélou remarks that the spiritual life "consists precisely in approaching God through all things, discovering God's presence in the ordinary aspects of our lives."[4] Furthermore, one should constantly live with the presence of God in his life. "The extraordinary experience of the presence of God can and should be the normal atmosphere of our lives."[5]

---

3. Daniélou, *Contemplation*, 3. "La prière est un temps de vie contemplative et de silence, dans un cadre qui aide à se dégager de l'actualité immédiate de la vie. Elle est l'occasion de vivre davantage près de Dieu, en sa présence, de se nourrir de sa Parole. ET: *Prayer: The Mission of the Church*, xv. All subsequent English translations of this text will be Schindler's unless noted otherwise.

4. Ibid., 11. "La vie spirituelle consiste à aller à travers toutes choses, à découvrir Dieu présent dans les éléments ordinaires de notre vie."

5. Ibid., 12. "Le sentiment extraordinaire de la présence de Dieu pourrait et devrait être le climat ordinaire de notre vie."

Prayer and the Spiritual Life

It is in prayer that one draws near to the Trinity which dwells within the Christian soul. Because of this fact, when a Christian prays he does so not as a stranger from God but as a child of God who has obtained intimacy with him. Baptismal grace has established a new relationship between the individual and God. Whereas before God could only be approached from the relationship of a creature to its creator, after being initiated into the life of the Trinity a filial relationship is established between God and us. Several Johannine passages from scripture indicate a mutual indwelling due to this fact. The first Epistle of John shows the mutual indwelling by God and the Christian when it says, "God remains in him and he in God" (1 Jn 4:15; NAB). Likewise, this reciprocity is also expressed when the Gospel writer says, "Remain in me, as I remain in you" (Jn 15:4, NAB). Also, Jesus' words indicate the same thing when he tells Judas, "Whoever loves me will keep my word, and my Father will love him, and we will come to him and make our dwelling with him" (Jn 14:23; NAB).

Daniélou deals with the idea of the presence of God at length in his small work *Le Signe du Temple*.[6] For Daniélou, the presence of God is dramatically portrayed throughout scripture by means of a typological reading of the figure (*figura*) of the temple. Therefore, in his exposition of the theme of the presence of God, Daniélou shows how the presence of God is manifested in the cosmic temple, the temple of Moses, the temple of Christ, the temple of the Church, and the temple of the soul. In this excursus, Daniélou moves from the presence of God in his creation, to the presence of God in the Jewish people, to the presence of God in the person of Christ. Once the presence of God in Christ is established, he then moves on to the presence of God in the Mystical body and finally to the presence of God in the Christian soul.

At its most basic level, the presence of God is felt in the cosmos in a general way. This presence is bestowed upon creation due to its divine origin. Daniélou writes of this period of general sacramental presence, "At the birth of mankind, the whole creation, issuing from the hands of God, is holy; the earthly Paradise is nature in a state of grace. The House of God

---

6. *Le Signe du Temple; ou, de la Présence de Dieu*; ET: *The Presence of God*. Subsequent references will be to the English translation by Roberts. The book is also found in an extracted form under the same title, "Le Signe du Temple ou de la Présence de Dieu." See also the much larger work by Yves Congar, *Le Mystère du Temple ou l'Économie de la Présence de Dieu à sa Créature de la Genèse à l'Apocalypse*; ET: *The Mystery of the Temple: or, The Manner of God's Presence to His Creatures from Genesis to the Apocalypse* which acknowledges Daniélou's prior work.

Jean Danielou's Doxological Humanism

is the whole Cosmos. Heaven is his tent, His tabernacle; the earth is His 'footstool.' There is a whole cosmic liturgy, that of the source of the flowers and the birds."[7] At this point there is no hint of the hiddenness of God. The patriarchs of the Old Testament interact with God in very familiar terms which express an idyllic association with the divine presence. This is dramatically illustrated by Abraham's relationship with Yahweh. "The Lord appeared to Abraham by the terebinth of Mamre, as he sat in the entrance of his tent, while the day was growing hot. Looking up, he saw three men standing nearby. When he saw them, he ran from the entrance of the tent to greet them; and bowing to the ground, he said: 'Sir, if I may ask you this favor, please do not go on past your servant. Let some water be brought, that you may bathe your feet, and then rest yourselves under the tree'" (Gen 18:1–4; NAB).[8] Daniélou says of God's relationship with Abraham, "His relationship . . . is that of a friend. . . . Abraham has that *parrhesia* with God, that freedom of speech which, in the days of ancient Greece, was the right of a free citizen, and by which St. Paul and the brethren symbolized the liberty of children of God with their Father."[9] At this early stage, the experience

---

7. Daniélou, *Le Signe du Temple*, 9. "A l'origine de l'humanité, la création tout entière, sortant des mains de Dieu, est sainte; le Paradis terrestre, c'est la nature en état de grâce. La Maison de Dieu, c'est la Cosmos tout entier. La Ciel est sa tente, son tabernacle; la terre, l' «escabeau de ses pieds». Il y a tout une liturgie cosmique, celle des sources des fleurs, des oiseaux."

8. Traditional iconography has understood this episode as a representation of the Trinitarian relationship. Perhaps the most well known of all the icons of the hospitality of Abraham is Andrei Rublev's portrayal of the Old Testament passage. See R. Williams, *Dwelling of the Light: Praying with the Icons of Christ*, 45–63.

9. Daniélou, *Le Signe du Temple*, 10. "Ses rapports . . . sont ceux d'un ami. . . . Abraham a avec Dieu cette parrhésie, cette liberté de parole qui était, dans la Grèce antique, le propre du citoyen libre, et par quoi saint Paul et les frères signifient la liberté des enfants de Dieu avec leur Père." Within the ancient Greek political sphere, *parrhesia* (παρρησία) denoted the freedom of speech granted to rhetors to speak in the assembly. In the private sphere, it indicated an uninhibited candor in nonpublic affairs. *Parrhesia* toward God—which is largely foreign to ancient Greek world—is especially seen later in Hellenistic Jewish literature. In the New Testament *parrhesia* is by no means univocal. In many instances, *parrhesia* refers to the fact of Jesus speaking in public. Therefore, the term is used in the Gospel of John, "Jesus answered him, "I have spoken publicly to the world [ἐγὼ παρρησίᾳ λελάληκα τῷ κόσμῳ]. I have always taught in a synagogue or in the temple area where all the Jews gather, and in secret I have said nothing" (Jn. 18:20, NAB). In other portions of the New Testament, *parrhesia* indicates an openness due to God based on one's faith in Christ and the presence of the Spirit in that individual which in turn leaves the individual with a good conscience and therefore candor with God. Therefore, Gregory of Nysaa writes, "So first my mind must become detached from anything subject to flux and change and tranquilly rest in motionless spiritual repose, so

Prayer and the Spiritual Life

of the presence of God in a primitive fashion has not been superseded by further revelation. The presence of God in the cosmos is common to all of mankind and is enjoyed by every religion to some extent.[10] At this point, all people could equally enjoy the presence of God because the entire cosmos was a "Temple where we are at home with God in the cool of the evening, where man comes forward, silent and composed, absorbed in his task as in a perpetual liturgy, attentive to that Presence which fills him with awe and tenderness."[11]

Though the natural presence of God remains intact for all time, it is superseded by the establishment of the tabernacle and ultimately in the Temple at Jerusalem. It is Moses who was given the task of building a sanctuary of God to be the dwelling place for the presence of God among his people. In the book of Exodus, Yahweh tells Moses to set up a place for God's presence, "You shall erect the dwelling according to the pattern shown to you on the mountain" (Ex 26:30; NAB). Daniélou tells his reader of this dwelling:

---

as to be rendered akin to Him who is perfectly unchangeable; and then it may address Him by this most familiar name and say: Father. What spirit a man mist have to say this word—what confidence, what purity of conscience," *De Oratione Dominica* 2. The sense in which Daniélou understands *parrhesia* seems to be in accord with Origen's usage in *De Oratione* 22.1 (PG 11.481C-484A) where the act of calling God "father" indicated a particular filial candor that is lacking in the Old Testament usage of the appellation. "A specific New Testament παρρησία is expressed when God is called Father . . . . Every prayer demands παρρησία, but especially that in which a filial relationship is expressed." Schlier, *Theological Dictionary of the New Testament*, "παρρησία/παρρησιάζομαι." Daniélou defines *parrhesia* as "the privilege of the free citizen, based on his equality with the other citizens, on the sovereign character of the citizen in the democratic city. The Fathers use this phrase to express the state of a child of God in his relationship with his Father. Being the image of God, he possesses a sovereign dignity; and he enjoys in God's sight the right of free speech, which is proper to a son [le privilege du citoyens, sur le caractère souverain du citoyen dans le cite démocratique. Les Pères reprennent ce langage pour exprimer l'état du fils de Dieu dans ses rapports avec son père. Etant image de Dieu, il possède une dignité souveraine. Et il jouit à l'égard de Dieu du franc-parler, qui et le propre du fils]." See his *Dieu et Nous*, 233-234; ET: *God and the Ways of Knowing*, 225-226. Subsequent references will be to the English translation by Roberts. See also Jean Daniélou, *Le IVème Siècle Grégoire de Nysse et Son Milieu*, 74-75.

10. Daniélou, *Le Signe du Temple*, 10. "This is the primitive level, common to all men, whose traces are still to found, twisted, soiled, perverted in every religion [C'est la religion primitive, originelle, commune à toute l'humanité et dont on retrouve les traces, déformées, souillées, perverties, dans toutes les religions]."

11. Ibid., 14. "L'Univers est redevenu le Temple où un Dieu familier se promène vers le soir où l'homme s'avance, grave, silencieux, appliqué à ses travaux comme à une perpétuelle liturgie, attentive à cette Présence qui remplit de respect et de tendresse."

> The establishment of the Tabernacle, whose ultimate form is the Temple, is the fundamental mission entrusted by God to Moses. The Temple is his concern, as Covenant is Abraham's. This mission is described in the Book of Exodus. Its object is the building of the sanctuary that will be the dwelling of Yahweh alone. This sanctuary is to consist of a threefold enclosure: first of all, an outer court, the *temenos*, the *templum*; then a tent, the tabernacle proper; and finally, within the tent, the sanctuary, divided off by a veil, in which are to be found the Ark, the Mercy Seat, the cherubim. It is here that God was to be present.[12]

However, the external form of the tabernacle or the Temple—whatever the case may be—is of relatively little importance. The importance of the Temple lies in the fact that it houses the presence of God. "The essential religious fact is that of the Presence of God in the Temple, which endured from the time of Moses till the death of Christ."[13] The Temple is often referred to in Scripture as being filled with the glory of the Lord. For instance, in Exodus Moses is unable to enter the tabernacle because of the glory of the Lord. "Then the cloud covered the meeting tent, and the glory of the Lord filled the Dwelling. Moses could not enter the meeting tent, because the cloud settled down upon it and the glory of the Lord filled the Dwelling" (Ex 40:34–35; NAB). Likewise, in Ezekiel, the prophet tells of his vision of the presence of Yahweh filling the Temple.

> Then he led me to the gate which faces the east, and there I saw the glory of the God of Israel coming from the east. I heard a sound like the roaring of many waters, and the earth shone with his glory. The vision was like that which I had seen when he came to destroy the city, and like that which I had seen by the river Chebar. I fell prone as the glory of the Lord entered the temple by way of the gate which faces the east, but spirit lifted me up and brought me to the inner court. And I saw that the temple was filled with the glory of the Lord. Then I heard someone speaking to me from the temple, while the man stood beside me. The voice said to me: Son

---

12. Ibid., 15. "L'institution du Tabernacle, dont le Temple est la forme ultérieure, est la mission fondamentale confiée par Dieu à Moïse. Le Temple se rattache à lui, comme l'Alliance à Abraham. Cette mission est rapportée au livre de l'Exode. L'objet en est l'édification d'un sanctuaire qui sera la demeure spéciale de Iahveh. Ce sanctuaire comprendra une triple enceinte: un parvis d'abord, le *téménos*, le templum; puis une tente, le tabernacle proprement dit; enfin à intérieur de la tente, le sanctuaire, séparé par un voile, où se trouvaient l'Arche, le Propitiatoire, les Chérubs: c'est là que Dieu était présent."

13. Ibid. "Le fait religieux essentiel est celui de cette Présence de Dieu dans le Temple qui a duré de Moïse à le mort de Jésus."

of man, this is where my throne shall be, this is where I will set the soles of my feet; here I will dwell among the Israelites forever (Ez 43:1–7; NAB).

This move from the *parrhesia* of cosmic religion to the specificity of the Judaic cult is indicative of two progressions in Daniélou's estimation. Though at first glance the particularization of the presence of God seems to be a regression, it is in fact a necessary step in the progression. "Up to the time of Moses, sacrifices could be offered anywhere. Henceforth, none are pleasing to God but those that are offered in the tabernacle. There are no longer many places but one. . . . The cult is concentrated in a single place. In the divine plan this was in reality a necessary stage, for the great danger was polytheism; the singleness of the sanctuary was . . . the sign of the oneness of God."[14] Daniélou maintains that this is precisely what Josephus had in mind when he wrote against Apion, "There ought also to be but one temple for one God; for likeness is the constant foundation of agreement. This temple ought to be common to all men, because he is the common God of all men."[15] The localization of the presence of God was in order to educe monotheistic worship of God. This falls within the divine pedagogy of sacred history.

The second aspect of this advance entails the introduction of a chasm between humanity and its creator. Whereas in times before the Jewish Temple the divine presence was enjoyed in parrhesian familiarity, with the advent of the Temple, there now existed a guarded divine presence. This introduces a "barrier between the sacred and the profane—that which is *pro fanum*, outside the Temple."[16] This also may seem to be a regression from the prior ease that humanity enjoyed with God. But, Daniélou contends that this barrier introduces the fact of God's complete otherness, "His essential mystery, His incomprehensibility."[17] This understanding of God constitutes an advance in the knowledge of God. Indeed, true understanding of God can only be achieved in the darkness of his inscrutability. As a

---

14. Ibid., 16–17. "Jusque-là on avait pu offrir partout des sacrifices. Désormais ne seront plus agréés de Dieu que ceux qui sont offerts dans le Tabernacle; il n'y a plus qu'un seul sanctuaire. . . . Le culte est localisé en un lieu unique. En réalité, dans le plan divin, c'était là une étape nécessaire; le grand danger était le polythéisme; l'unité de sanctuaire était comme le signe de l'unicité de Dieu."

15. Josephus, *Contra Apion*, II.24.

16. Daniélou, *Le Signe du Temple*, 17. "Maintenant il y a l'opposition du sacré et du profane, ce qui est hors du Temple, «pro-fanum»."

17. Ibid.

Jean Danielou's Doxological Humanism

result, Gregory of Nyssa tells us: "The true vision and the true knowledge of what we seek consists precisely in not seeing, in an awareness that our goal transcends all knowledge and is everywhere cut off from us by the darkness of incomprehensibility."[18]

Following these disclosures of the presence of God in the cosmos and in the mosaic temple, Daniélou moves to an excursus on the presence of God in the person of Jesus. Though an important stage in the economy of the presence of God, the Temple of Moses recedes from prominence in light of the central event of sacred history, the Incarnation. "The Temple of Moses was only a passing stage. A new order appears with Christ, who is the reality of which the Temple was only a symbol. Henceforth the abode of Yahweh, the *shekinah*, is no longer the Temple, but the Manhood of Jesus."[19] This supersession of the presence of God in the Temple is clearly indicated when the gospel of Matthew reports Jesus' reference to himself, "I say to you, something greater than the temple is here" (Mt 12:6; NAB).[20]

The presence of God is often indicated in the life of Christ by means of the presence of angels throughout the events of his life. An angel watches over each Annunciation of the coming of the Christ child. The annunciation to Mary, to Zechariah, to Joseph, to the shepherds are all carried out by Gabriel.[21] Raphael oversees healings and miracles. According to Daniélou, he is the angel present at the pool of Bethesda who "troubles the waters of healing."[22] According to Daniélou, it is the legions of St. Michael the Archangel who are present in the background of the Passion.[23] The presence

---

18. Gregory of Nyssa, *De Vita Moysis* (PG 44.377A).

19. Daniélou, *Le Signe du Temple*, 20. "Mais le Temple mosaïque n'était qu'un stade transitoire. Un ordre nouveau lui succède avec le Christ qui est la réalité dont le Temple n'était que le figure. Désormais le Demeure de Iahveh, la Schekinah, n'est plus le Temple, mais l'Humanité de Jésus."

20. On supersession see Chapter 2, n. 73.

21. Daniélou, *Le Signe du Temple*, 22. Luke 1:10–38, 2:8–15.

22. Daniélou's reference is to an additional verse in John 5 which was known toward the end of the second century in the West and among the fourth century Fathers of the East. "For [from time to time] an angel of the Lord used to come down into the pool; and the water was stirred up, so the first one to get in [after the stirring of the water] was healed of whatever disease afflicted him." The angel was a popular explanation of the turbulence and the healing powers attributed to it. This verse is missing from all early Greek manuscripts and the earliest versions, including the original Vulgate.

23. Daniélou, *Le Signe du Temple*, 22. Michael—one of the three angels celebrated by the Catholic Church in its liturgy—was regarded "as the captain of the heavenly host, the protector of the Christian against the devil, especially at the hour of death, when he

Prayer and the Spiritual Life

of the archangels during the events of the life of Christ bestow the divine imprimatur on Christ and establish him as the presence of God incarnate.[24] In Daniélou's words,

> They establish around the Word a sacred region, the Temple of the intellectual realm. Everywhere they precede and follow the Word. They prepare the way before Him and complete His handiwork. They surround Him not only at the throne of glory, but also in His various missions. They go up with Him into the Presence of the Father, bearing in their hands that incense which is the prayer of the righteous. They pass through the spaces of charity with a swiftness that is denied to our fleshly hearts. They are indeed the heaven of heavens, of which Scripture speaks, for heaven is not visible space, but the invisible depths of the intellectual rays of the Word, the splendor of His imagery reflected in innumerable mirrors.[25]

Whereas the Temple of Jerusalem had superseded the presence of God in the cosmic temple, the presence of God within the humanity of Jesus in turn supersedes the Mosaic Temple as the place where the glory of God resides. "Jesus is not of the order of Moses, He is not a higher kind of Moses. Moses and the Temple are figures, but Jesus is the reality. The divine Presence is no longer to be found in an enclosure of stone, it dwells in Jesus Himself."[26] Jesus has fulfilled the entire line of typology in reference to the temple and the presence of God. The presence of God in Jesus is not simply another instantiation in a progressive stage of figures, he is the reality to which all prior figures point. Christ is the fulfillment which results in a new economy at the acme of the pedagogy of typology. God accustomed his

---

conducts the soul to God." This appears to be the background for the belief that Michael was present at the time of Jesus' crucifixion. See Delaney, "Michael."

24. See chapters 3 and 4 of Jean Daniélou, *Les Anges et leur Mission, d'aprés les Pères de l'Église*; ET: *The Angels and their Mission: According to the Fathers of the Church*.

25. Daniélou, *Le Signe du Temple*, 22–23. "Ils créent autour duVerbe l'espace sacré, le Temple intelligible. Partout ils precedent et suivent le Verbe. Ils préparent ses coies et achèvent son œuvre. Ils l'entourent non seulement dans la session glorieuse, mais dans ses diverses missions. Ils montent vers le Père avec Lui, portant dans leurs mains l'encens qui est la prière des justes. Ils franchissent les espaces de la charité avec l'agilité que n'ont pas nos cœurs enfoncés dans la chair. Ils sont en effet les cieux, don't parle l'Ecriture, car le ciel, ce ne sont pas les espaces visibles. Mais les profondeurs invisibles des rayons intelligibles du Verbe, sa splendeur d'Image unique reflétée dans les innombrables miroirs."

26. Ibid., 25. "Mais précisément Jésus n'est pas dans l'ordre de Moïse, il n'est pas un Moïse supérieur. Moïse, le Temple sont des figures. Et la réalité est là. La Présence divine n'est plus dans l'enceinte de pierres , elle est en Jésus lui-même."

people to the presence of God in various forms until the time was ready for the presence of God to be manifested in its fullest form.

It is not enough, however, to leave it at that. It is not, according to Daniélou, enough to extol the presence of God in the person of Christ in Jesus. One must also consider the presence of God in the *totus Christus*. In his first homily on 1 John, Augustine, addressing issues of unity in the body of Christ, quotes the prologue to the Gospel of John, "'the Word was made flesh, and dwelt in us.' To that flesh the Church is joined, and so there is made the *whole Christ*, head and body."[27] Daniélou remarks that when one considers the presence of God in the person of Christ, it must be remembered that Christ's humanity must be considered in its entirety. "It is the Manhood of Jesus that is the Temple of the New Law, but this Manhood must be taken as a whole, that is to say, it is the Mystical Body in its entirety, this is the complete and final Temple."[28] Because of the humanity of Jesus, the presence of God now dwells within the community of the Church which is the body of Christ. Of course, St. Paul describes the Church as the body of Christ in a number of places. In the letter to the Romans he speaks of it in reference to unity, "For as in one body we have many parts, and all the parts do not have the same function, so we, though many, are one body in Christ and individually parts of one another" (Rom 12:4–5; NAB).[29] The imagery of the unity of the Church with Christ is not limited to corporal imagery. The first epistle of Peter to the Churches in Asia Minor writes in architectural terms when the author states, "Come to him, a living stone, rejected by human beings but chosen and precious in the sight of God, and, like living stones, let yourselves be built into a spiritual house to be a holy priesthood to offer spiritual sacrifices acceptable to God through Jesus Christ" (1 Pet 2:4–5; NAB). Elsewhere, Paul also refers to the Church and its head in a similar fashion: "So then you are no longer strangers and sojourners, but you are fellow citizens with the holy ones and members of the household of God, built upon the foundation of the apostles and prophets, with Christ Jesus himself as the capstone. Through him the whole structure is held together and grows into a temple sacred in the Lord; in him you also

---

27. Augustine, *Tractatus in epistolam Ioannis*, 2.1 (PL 35.1979). The Latin reads: "quia *Verbum caro factum est, et habitavit in nobis*. Illi carni adjungitur Ecclesia, et fit Christus totus, caput et corpus."

28. Daniélou, *Le Signe du Temple*, 28. "C'est l'Humanité de Jésus qui est le Temple de la Loi Nouvelle, mais cette Humanité doit être prise dans sa totalité, c'est-à-dire qu'elle est le Corps Mystique tout entier: c'est là le Temple total et définitif."

29. See also 1 Cor 12:12–27; Eph 3:6, 5:23; Col 1:18.

Prayer and the Spiritual Life

are being built together into a dwelling place of God in the Spirit" (Eph 2:19–22; NAB).[30]

Christ's body which is the Church becomes the receptacle of the presence of God by virtue of its relation to Christ who is the head of the body. Now, by extension, the "dwelling of God is the Christian community whose Head is in heaven, and whose members are still making their earthly pilgrimage; it is the true Temple of which the Temple of stone was the figure."[31] This movement from "shadow to reality," from temple of stone to the temple of the body of Christ, constitutes a move from the letter to the spirit. The need for a particular place for the presence of God to reside has been dispensed with by the succession of the tabernacle or temple by the *ecclesia*. In moving from the temple to the body of Christ, the presence of God is no longer local but ecclesial.

> This is an extraordinary fact, as extraordinary in its own order as the Presence of God in the Temple at Jerusalem. God enters into relationship not with isolated souls, but with the community, and only with souls who are part of the community. Through the baptismal rites, the entry of the catechumen into the church of stone is a figure of his entry into the living Church, into the community which is the place of his meeting with God. Of this meeting, the Eucharist is the permanent sign, being at once the Sacrament of the Mystical Body and the sign of the real Presence, and bringing about the same union with God and the strengthening of the bonds of charity.[32]

As a result of the relationship between the community of the body and the presence of God in the body, sin—which separates the member from the body in a real way—has the effect of distancing the sinner from the

---

30. Compare these verses to the "Parable of the Stones" in the *Shepherd of Hermas*, I.3:2–3 which also contains architectural imagery in reference to the Church.

31. Daniélou, *Le Signe du Temple*, 28. "La demeure de Dieu, c'est la communauté chrétienne dont la Tête est au ciel, dont les membres achèvent leur pèlerinage. Elle est le Temple véritable, dont le Temple de pierre était l'image."

32. Ibid., 29. "C'est là un fait extraordinaire, aussi extraordinaire en son ordre que la Présence de Dieu dans le Temple hiérosolymite. Dieu entre en rapport non avec les âmes isolées, mais avec la communauté et seulement avec les âmes qui font partie de la communauté. Parmi les rites du baptême, l'entrée du catéchumène dans l'église de pierre figure sone entrée dans l'Église vivante, dans la communauté qui est le lieu de sa rencontre avec Dieu. De cette rencontre l'Eucharistie est le signe permanent qui est à la fois le Sacrement du Corps mystique et le signe de la Présence réelle et qui opèra à la fois l'union à Dieu et le reserrement des liens de la charité."

presence of God. For this reason the sacrament of reconciliation is of extreme importance in that it restores the member not only to the community but restores the believer's access to the presence of God in the community and in the Eucharist.

The distinguishing mark of the presence of God in the body of Christ is the mark of charity. St. Paul makes this clear in his words to the community in Ephesus, "Rather, living the truth in love, we should grow in every way into him who is the head, Christ, from whom the whole body, joined and held together by every supporting ligament, with the proper functioning of each part, brings about the body's growth and builds itself up in love" (Eph 4:15–16; NAB).[33] The building up of the true temple is done through the extension of charity within the body itself. Charity is the mark of the presence of God in the spiritual temple of the Church. These marks of the Church are indicated in the Pauline exposition of the greatest of the theological virtues, charity (love), in 1 Corinthians 13.[34] It is in this that the Christian is able to say in concord with the Psalms of the Church, "Lord, I love the house where you dwell, the tenting-place of your glory" (Ps 26:8; NAB).

The presence of God in the Church is not manifested in a general sense among all ecclesial bodies in the same way. Daniélou is clear in maintaining that the presence of God is expressed most fully in continuity with the figures of the Old Testament which find their fulfillment in the rituals of the Mass.[35] This continuity between the rituals of the Old Testament and the Mass is seen when Daniélou writes:

> Thus the New Temple finally replaced the Temples of Jerusalem and the Cosmos. It was time for these to disappear. The first Law was destroyed because of its weakness and ineffectiveness, but it saw the introduction of a greater hope, by means of which we have access to the Presence of God. The figure has no further part to

33. Daniélou—as is typical of Catholic theologians and exegetes—renders the word translated twice in these verses as "love" in the NAB as "charity" rather than love. The French New Testament renders the verses, "mais que, professant la vérité dans la charité, nous croissions à tous égards en celui qui est le chef, Christ. C'est de lui, et grace à tous les liens de son assistance, que tout le corps, bien coordonné et formant in solide assemblage, tire son accroissement selon la force qui convient à chacune de ses parties, et s'édifie lui-même dans la charité." In the Greek New Testament the word in both instances is ἀγάπη. The Vulgate translates the Greek word *agape* as *charitate* which was hence translated from the Latin to English as "charity."

34. Daniélou, *Le Signe du Temple*, 31.

35. See Daniélou, *Bible et Liturgie*.

Prayer and the Spiritual Life

play, when the fact which it proclaims has come to pass. The New Temple brings with it an infinitely better reality. It is no longer through heavenly signs that man looks for traces of God, but the true sun has finally risen upon a new world. It is no longer in a single place that the living God may be worshipped; it is to the ends of the earth that the New Temple reaches out, and it is enough that two or three are gathered in the Name of Jesus, for Him to dwell among them. But the destruction of the old order is positive; it removes the blemishes of the old order, it preserves all the valuable elements. Nothing is lost, all is retained, organized on a higher level of significance; it is a pure elevation, an absolute progress. Just as the Temple at Jerusalem continued the Cosmic Temple while taking over its functions, so the Church continues the Temples of Jerusalem and the Cosmos. It offers new sacrifices according to ancient ritual patterns. Thus the Mass contains all the breadth of time and space, cosmos and history.[36]

This is generally in line with both Daniélou's ideas concerning sacred history and his typological reading of that history. God is present in all of history which finds its contemporary culmination in the sacramental milieu of the Mass—both the liturgy of the Word and the liturgy of the Eucharist.

To the extent that the believer participates in the sacramental life of the Church, he too becomes a place where God dwells. Here Daniélou turns his attention to a passage from the fourteenth century Flemish mystic John Ruysbroeck. Ruysbroeck says, "Christ, the Son of God, has built for God, for Himself, and for us, and eternal Ark and Tabernacle; and it is none

---

36. Daniélou, *Le Signe du Temple*, 35. "Ainsi le Temple nouveau a-t-il définitivement remplacé le Temple hiérosolymite et le Temple cosmique. Ceux-ci n'ont plus qu'à disparaître: «Ainsi a été abrogée la première ordonnance, à cause de son impuissance et de son inutilité, mais elle a été l'introduction à une meilleure espérance par laquelle nous avons accès auprès de Dieu.» La figure n'a plus rien à faire, quand ce qu'elle avait pour objet d'annoncer est arrivé. Le Temple nouveau apporte une réalité infiniment meilleure. Ce n'est plus à travers les signes célestas que l'homme cherche à trouver les traces de Dieu, mais le soleil véritables s'est levé définitivement sur un nouvel univers. Ce n'est plus dans un seul lieu du monde que l'on peut entrer en présence du Dieu vivant et l'adorer: c'est sur la terre entière que le Temple nouveau s'étend, et il suffit que deux soient réunis au nom e Jésus pour qu'il habite dans leur communauté. Mais l'abolition de l'ordre ancien est toute positive. Elle enlève les imperfections de l'ordre ancien, elle en conserve les richesses: rien n'est perdu, tout est repris, assume, ordonné à une signification plus haute, c'est une pure promotion, un progrès absolu. Et de même que le Temple hiérosolymite prolongeait le Temple cosmique tout en s'y substituent, de même l'Église prolonge le Temple hiérosolymite et le Temple cosmique. Elle offre le sacrifice nouveau selon les registres rituels anciens. Ainsi la messe contient-elle toutes les épaisseurs du temps et de l'espace, du cosmos et de l'histoire."

other than He Himself or the Church and every man of goodwill whose Prince and Head He is.... When a man seeks to obey God with an undivided heart, he is freed and discharged from every sin, by the blood of our Lord. He is bound and united to God, and God with him. And he becomes himself the Ark and the Tabernacle where God wishes to dwell, not in a figure but in reality. For the figure is past, and the reality is revealed to those who wish to turn towards it."[37] This passage from *The Spiritual Tabernacle* indicates three different ways in which God is present in the "true temple." God chooses to dwell in the true temple which is at once the Humanity of Jesus, the Church, and also every soul who is a member of the body of Christ. Daniélou explains that "every soul is thus the authentic Temple of God, of which the Mosaic Temple was the figure."[38] Indeed, Christ indicates the presence of the Trinity within the individual soul when he says, "Whoever loves me will keep my word, and my Father will love him, and we will come to him and make our dwelling with him" (John 14:23; NAB). Within the context of divisions over the spread of the Church, Paul exhorts the Corinthian Church, "Do you not know that you are the temple of God, and that the Spirit of God dwells in you?" (1 Cor 3:16; NAB). Within the context of sexual morality, Paul questions the Christians in Corinth, "Do you not know that your body is a temple of the holy Spirit within you, whom you have from God, and that you are not your own?" (1 Cor 6:19; NAB). Within the context of being joined to unbelievers, Paul states, "For we are the temple of the living God; as God said: 'I will live with them and move among them, and I will be their God and they shall be my people'" (1 Cor. 2:16; NAB). Many of the great mystics have written on the presence of God in the soul of the individual, from Gregory of Nyssa to Teresa of Avila, from Ruysbroeck to Tauler. They all point to the fact that as one progresses through the spiritual life, as one delves further into the "interior castle," the presence of the Trinity comes to dwell more and more fully within the soul of that individual making him a temple of the presence of God. As Teresa tells her sisters concerning the "presence chamber" of God, "for as He has a dwelling-place in heaven, so has He in the soul."[39] And, later on she speaks of the place of union with God in the seventh mansion, "secret union takes place in the innermost center of the soul where

---

37. John Ruysbroeck (Ruusbroec), *Spiritual Tabernacle*.

38. Daniélou, *Le Signe du Temple*, 43. "Toute âme est ainsi le véritable Temple de Dieu, dont le Temple mosaïque était la figure."

39. St. Teresa of Avila, *Interior Castle*, 7.1.3.

Prayer and the Spiritual Life

God Himself must dwell."[40] Concordantly, Daniélou advocates that each individual soul constitutes a "consecrated Temple."[41] For Daniélou, the pattern of the interior life is derived from a figural reading of Mosaic Temple. Initially, the believer is concerned with exterior things. This reality corresponds to the outer court of the tabernacle. Ruysbroeck is again instructive here. He avers, "The outer court of the Tabernacle is a life conformed to the morality according to the exterior man, with all that is connected with it. . . . It is surrounded by a curtain with fine twined linen: by this is understood the purity of manners and life."[42] On Ruysbroeck's spiritual itinerary, the next step is taken into a more holy place where the "life of virtue is not only on this level the practice of the virtues, but also the theological virtues which are of a more excellent order than the virtues, since they unite us directly with God."[43] Moving into closer intimacy with the presence of God entails an inward motion of the soul through interiority. Daniélou never tires of reminding his reader of Augustine's words, "Truth dwells in the inner man." The next step on this spiritual itinerary is moving toward the most inward place of the sanctuary, the holy of holies. This final inward step is characterized by detachment from external realities, withdrawal from the illusory world of appearances, renunciation of *amor sui* and an experience of ecstasy achieved through these acts of "beatifying dispossession."[44] The most secret and holy of all places of the presence of God is, for Daniélou, also characterized by darkness. "This is the Holy of holies, the adyton, the most secret place in the sanctuary. It is the depth of the soul of which Tauler speaks, its centre, the deepest abyss of which St. Teresa tells us. This place cannot be known by the soul. It is a darkness which her glance cannot penetrate."[45] So, for Daniélou, the inward journey toward God is ultimately characterized by absence rather than presence and constitutes a spiritual progression in the life of prayer. The consolation of the presence of God is

---

40. Ibid., 7.2.2.

41. Daniélou, *Le Signe du Temple*, 44. "Ainsi chaque âme chrétienne est un Temple consacré."

42. John Ruysbroeck (Ruusbroec), *Spiritual Tabernacle*. Quoted in Daniélou, *Le Signe du Temple*, 43.

43. Ibid.

44. Daniélou, *Le Signe du Temple*, 44–45.

45. Ibid., 45–46. "C'est là le Saint des saints, l'adyton, le lieu le plus secret du sanctuaire. C'est le fond de l'âme dont parle Tauler, son centre, l'abîme très profond dont parle saint Thérèse. Ce lieu est inconnaissable à l'âme. C'est une ténèbre que son regard ne peut pénétrer."

removed from us as one advances in the spiritual life "in order to oblige us always to advance further and further in the quest for what is always and absolutely necessary."[46]

The Darkness of God

In the early stages of the spiritual journey God is characterized by light, but as one progresses in the spiritual life, one experiences God's intensity and therefore a lack of vision due to the brilliance of God's glory. Indeed, Daniélou maintains in his important work *Platonisme et Théologie Mystique* that "the spiritual life moves from light to darkness."[47] Thus, Gregory of Nyssa contends that Scripture teaches that "spiritual knowledge first occurs as an illumination in those who experience it. Indeed, all that is opposed to piety is conceived as darkness; to shun the darkness is to share in the light. But as the soul makes progress, and by a greater and more perfect concentration comes to appreciate what the knowledge of truth is, the more it approaches this vision, and so much the more does it see that the divine nature is invisible and incomprehensible, and it is there that it sees God."[48] Gregory describes the spiritual progress of Moses in a similar way. "Moses' vision of God began with light; afterward God spoke to him in a cloud. But when Moses rose higher and became more perfect, he saw God in the darkness."[49] Because of God's intensity, once one is granted access to the presence of God, the darkness of God is experienced. Indeed, God tells Moses, "But my face you cannot see, for no man sees me and still lives" (Ex 33:20; NAB). This declaration expresses the inscrutability of God due to his glory. Daniélou argues that this passage in Exodus "means that God's existence is so intense that we find it intolerable: our flesh is not able to bear it; it devours us; it terrifies us."[50] Because of this fact, God agrees to set Moses in the hollow of a rock and to cover him with his hand until he has passed. Only then does God allow Moses to look at him. Still, Moses does not see his face but

---

46. Daniélou, "Absence and Presence of God," 9.

47. Jean Daniélou, *Platonisme et Théologie Mystique: Doctrine Spirituelle de Saint Grégoire e Nysse*, 19. "La vie spirituelle va de la lumiére à la ténèbre." Translation mine.

48. Gregory of Nyssa, *De Vita Moysis* (PG 44.377A).

49. Gregory of Nyssa, *Commentarius in Canticum Canticorum* (PG 44.1000C).

50. Daniélou, *Contemplation*, 10. "C'est-à-dire que son existence est si intense qu'elle nous est intolérable, que notre chair n'arrive pas à le supporter; elle est comme dévorée par elle; elle en est terrifiée."

Prayer and the Spiritual Life

only sees his back because of the unbearable intensity of God's existence. This same glory which Moses was only to glance at askew, moved St. John of the Cross to declare that "God is darkness to our understanding."[51]

Here we are moving from the *parrhesia* of the presence of God to the nescience of the darkness of God. Aptly stated, "God is both alien and familiar, forever more alien and forever more familiar, familiar as the dove and alien as the darkness, known to the little child and unknown to the greatest mystic."[52] For Daniélou, Gregory of Nyssa takes the idea of the darkness of God—which was certainly not unique to Gregory—in a new direction and constitutes a decisive development in the idea. Gregory's notion of darkness is first developed in his treatise against Eunomius. He writes of Abraham, "Nevertheless, what does the Word [Scripture] say about him?—that he went forth 'not knowing where he was going,' and even without being allowed to learn the name of the one he loved, yet neither resentful nor ashamed at such ignorance. It was also a sure guide towards his goal, that in thinking about God he was not led to an understanding by anything material, nor did his thought ever get stuck in anything comprehensible and desist from the journey towards things beyond knowing."[53] Though Gregory intimates his penchant for the doctrine of divine darkness in a number of places (including his homilies on the Song of Songs), he most fully develops his ideas of darkness in his *De Vita Moysis*.[54] Singular in importance for Daniélou is the following passage:

---

51. St. John of the Cross, *Ascent of Mount Carmel*, 2.9. Indispensable to a study of the darkness of God is Turner, *The Darkness of God: Negativity in Christian Mysticism*. Daniélou states, "When we say that He [God] is holy we mean that He is utterly different from everything we can know, we mean that He is Totally-Other; and we try to express the intensity of His existence—an intensity so great that man cannot see Him and live. Saint John of the Cross tells us that God is darkness because the dazzling brightness of His light sears our eyes [Mais en disant qu'il est saint, nous voulons dire qu'il est autre chose que tout ce que nous pouvons connaître, qu'il est le Tout-Autre. Nous voulons exprimer l'intensité de son existence, qui est telle que l'homme ne peut le voir sans mourir. Saint Jean de la Croix nous dit que Dieu est ténèbras, car l'éclat de sa lumière est tel qu'il brûle nos yeux]." *Évangile et Monde Moderne*, 142; ET: *The Christian Today*, 9.

52. "Dieu est à la fois étranger et familier, toujours plus étranger et toujours plus familier, familier comme la colombe et étranger comme la ténèbre, connu du petit enfant et inconnu du plus grand mystique." Jean Daniélou, "La Colombe et la Ténèbre dans la Mystique Byzantin Ancienne," *Eranos-Jahrbuch*, 404 ; ET: "The Dove and the Darkness in Ancient Byzantine Mysticism," 284.

53. Gregory of Nyssa, *Contra Eunomium*, 2.87–88 (PG 45.940C).

54. Daniélou, "Mystique de la Ténèbre chez Grégoire de Nysse," col. 1873.

> The more the spirit in its march forward perfects its endeavor to understand what the grasp of reality is and the closer it comes to contemplation, the more it sees the invisibility of the divine nature. Thus Moses, having left the world of appearance, not only what the sensibility grasps but what the intellect believes it contemplates, progresses more and more inward, until the activity of his spirit penetrates the invisible and the incomprehensible, and sees God. For the true knowledge and vision of God consists in not seeing, because He transcends all knowledge, being cut off on all sides by His incomprehensibility as by a darkness.[55]

This darkness is not merely due to the incapacities of the mind to comprehend the divine. Instead, it is due to the mind being incapacitated by the divine glory. Here we return to the themes of God's intensity and immensity which confounds the mind's abilities to perceive God.

The confounding of our intellect by the intensity of God can be expressed through a number of illuminating symbols. When speaking of the disorienting effects of God's glory, Gregory speaks of ecstasy, inebriation, the passion of love, dizziness, sleep, madness and wounding.[56] Each of these images expresses a different nuance of this disorientation based on the Scriptural context to which the image is related.[57] Therefore, it is not surprising that passionate love is used in reference to the Song of Songs or ecstasy in reference to Paul or sober inebriation. For Daniélou, ecstasy "designates . . . the soul's going out of itself by reason of the intensity of the divine presence."[58] A number of texts from Gregory's writings show the link between ecstasy and darkness. In his *De Virginitate*, Gregory contends that the soul is caught up out of itself due to its awe of the divine glory. In this

---

55. Gregory of Nyssa, *De Vita Moysis* (PG 44.376D–377A). Here Daniélou contends that PG is defective and supplies his own critical text and translation. As a result we have used the English translation supplied in Daniélou, "The Dove and the Darkness in Ancient Byzantine Mysticism," 285. The French reads, "Plus l'esprit, dans sa marche en avant, parvient par un application toujours plus parfait à comprendre ce qu'est la saisie des réalités et s'approche de la contemplation, plus il voit l'invisibilité de la nature divine. Ainsi Moïse, ayant laissé le monde des apparences, non seulement ce que saisit la sensibilité, mais aussi ce que l'intellect croit contempler, s'avance toujours plus à l'intérieur, jusqu'à ce qu'il pénètre par l'activité de l'esprit jusqu'à l'invisible et à l'insaisissable et que là il voie Dieu. La vraie connaissance en effet de celui-ci et sa vision consiste à ne pas voir, parce qu'il transcende toute connaissance, étant séparé de toutes parts son incompréhensibilité comme par une ténèbre."

56. Daniélou, "Introduction," in *From Glory to Glory*, 33.

57. Ibid., 34.

58. Ibid.

state, the soul is utterly incapacitated by the effulgence of God. Gregory writes, "The soul that does see [God's beauty] by some divine gift and inspiration, retains his ecstasy unexpressed in the secret of his consciousness. . . . The great David rightly shows us how impossible this is. Lifted out of himself by the Spirit, he glimpsed in that blessed ecstasy God's infinite and incomprehensible beauty. . . . And though yearning to say something which would do justice to his vision, he can only cry out . . . : Every man is a liar."[59] In another place, Gregory writes of the ecstasy of Abraham after he was able to raise himself above thoughts of earthly things: "After this ecstasy which came upon him as a result of these lofty visions, Abraham returned once more to his human frailty: *I am*, he admits, *dust and ashes*, mute, inert, incapable of explaining rationally the Godhead that my mind has seen. . . . In this life we taught that for those who are advancing in the divine paths there is no other way of drawing near to God than by the intermediary of faith; it is only through faith that the questing of the soul can unite itself with the incomprehensible Godhead."[60] Here, Daniélou contends, Gregory is explicitly linking ecstasy with the presence of God.[61]

Another closely related image which illuminates our understanding of the disorientation of experiencing the presence of God is *sobria inebrietas* (sober intoxication). Daniélou describes this effect as an expression which "is a paradox, very much like 'luminous darkness.' It emphasizes the passivity of true ecstasy as compared with the effects of actual intoxication. And it is called 'sober' to suggest that the state is not infra-rational but rather supra-rational. So too, the expression 'luminous darkness' suggested that the obscurity of the mind was not a defect—as, for example, if one would speak of the darkness of ignorance—but, on the contrary, the effect of an excess of light."[62] Commenting on the text of the Song of Songs which encourages the friends of the bridal party to "Eat, friends, drink, and be drunk with love" (Song 5:1; NRSV), Gregory explains concerning different kinds of inebriation that "all intoxication causes the mind, overwhelmed with wine, to go into an ecstasy."[63] He goes on to explain that there is different kind of ecstatic inebriation which involves "a transformation from a worse to a better condition."[64] He clarifies this with the example of

59. Gregory of Nyssa, *De Virginitate*, 10 (PG 46.361B).
60. Gregory of Nyssa, *Contra. Eunomium* (PG 45.941A).
61. Daniélou, "Introduction," in *From Glory to Glory*, 36.
62. Ibid., 36–37.
63. Gregory of Nyssa, *Commentarius in Canticum Canticorum* (PG 44.989C).
64. Ibid. (PG 44.989D).

Jean Danielou's Doxological Humanism

David. David spoke in his consternation, "I kept faith, even when I said, 'I am greatly afflicted!' I said in my alarm, 'No one can be trusted!'" (Ps 116:11; NAB).[65] Gregory explains, "In this way the mighty David became intoxicated and went out of himself: he saw, while in ecstasy, that divine beauty which no mortal can behold, and cried out in those famous words: *Every man is a liar*."[66] Commenting on a passage in 2 Corinthians, Gregory talks of the ecstasy of Paul in reference to inebriation. He connects Pauline ecstasy with a passage in the Psalter which alludes to "Benjamin a youth, in ecstasy of mind" (Ps. 68:28). Gregory maintains the youth is a figural foreshadowing of the apostle Paul.[67] For Gregory, Paul is the new Benjamin (youth in ecstasy) and helps to explain Paul's comments to the Church in Corinth: "Sive enim mente excedimus Deo: sive sobrii sumus, vobis" (2 Cor. 5.13; Vul.).[68] For Daniélou, each of these examples provides evidence of the fact that sober inebriation points to the reality that the divine nature is ultimately utterly incomprehensible not due to the inability of the human mind to understand but to the immensity and disorienting effects of the presence of God.[69]

Another way in which Gregory communicates the reality of the darkness of God is through the image of vertigo. The symbol of vertigo refers to the vastness of the divine nature. "It expresses the soul's complete confusion in the presence of a reality for which there is no common measure."[70] Gregory explains while commenting on the Beatitudes:

---

65. The Vulgate reads *Credidi, propter quod locutus sum; ego autem humiliatus sum nimis. Ego dixi in excessu me: Omnis homo mendax.* Indeed the Latin translation of Gregory's πας ἄνθρωπος ψεύστης exactly mirrors Gregory's rendering of the last portion of the text where *omnis homo mendax* would be translated as "every man is a liar."

66. Gregory of Nyssa, *Commentarius in Canticum Canticorum* (PG 44.989C-D).

67. Gregory of Nyssa, *Tractatusin Psalmorum Inscriptiones*, 14 (PG 44.577B).

68. The most common English translations do not convey the sense of sober inebriation clearly as the Vulgate. The NRSV reads: "For if we are beside ourselves, it is for God; if we are in our right mind, it is for you." The NAB reads: "For if we are out of our minds, it is for God; if we are rational, it is for you." The NAS reads: "For if we are beside ourselves, it is for God; if we are of sound mind, it is for you." The Greek—which is undisputed—reads εἴτε γὰρ ἐξέστημεν, θεῷ εἴτε σωφρονοῦμεν, ὑμῖν. Of course, the Douay-Rheims—translating from the Latin—expresses the connection between ecstasy and sobriety well: "For whether we be transported in mind, it is to God: or whether we be sober, it is for you."

69. Daniélou, "Introduction," in *From Glory to Glory*, 38.

70. Ibid., 41.

Prayer and the Spiritual Life

> Along the sea-coast you may often see mountains facing the sea, sheer and steep from top to bottom, while a projection at the top forms a cliff overhanging the depths. Now if someone suddenly looked down from such a cliff to the depths below he would become dizzy. So too is my soul seized with dizziness now as it is raised on high by this great saying of the Lord, *Blessed are the clean of heart, for they shall see God*. . . . But *no man hath seen God at any time*, says the great John. . . . This then is the steep and sheer rock that Moses taught us was inaccessible, so that our minds can in no way approach it. For every possibility of apprehension is excluded by the words: *No man can see the Lord and live*.[71]

Following Gregory, Daniélou believes the soul which encounters God is unable to grasp a "nature which has no dimension."[72] The human intellect is completely overwhelmed by the immeasurableness of God and entirely baffled by the presence of transcendent Being itself.

Daniélou uses a final image from Gregory's writing to help explain the effect that the presence of God has on the believer—that of romantic love. For Daniélou, the notion of *eros* "denotes the surge of love which sweeps the soul out of itself in proportion to its awareness of God's infinite loveliness."[73] He contends that Gregory's notion of *eros* has little to do with the Platonic notion of love.[74] Instead, within the context of the imagery associated with the darkness, ecstasy, and inebriation, the image of romantic love helps to describe the disorienting effects of the presence of God on the believer. Daniélou explains: "as God's adorable presence becomes more and more intense, the soul is, as it were, forced to go out of itself by a kind of infatuation, and to withdraw from its usual mode of existence, to be swept along by the ways of God. *Eros*, then, is not a longing for possession in a self-centered way, but a truly ecstatic love."[75] For Gregory, the *eros* of Greek philosophy is equivalent—though in a more intense degree—to *agape* in the gospels.[76] Daniélou contends that Gregory transposes *eros* into the

---

71. Gregory of Nyssa, *De beatitudinibus orationes*, sermon 6 (PG 44.1264B-C).

72. Gregory of Nyssa, *In Ecclesiasten Salomonis*, sermon 7 (PG 44.729C).

73. Daniélou, "Introduction," in *From Glory to Glory*, 43.

74. Daniélou maintains that this is precisely the error that is made by Anders Nygren in his well-known *Den Kristna kärlekstankengenom Tiderna: Eros och Agape*; ET: *Agape and Eros*.

75. Daniélou, "Introduction," in *From Glory to Glory*, 43–44.

76. "L'expression de cette attirance est l'amour, qui porte le nom général d'ἀγάπη, dont les formes les plus brûlantes s'appellent ἔρως." Daniélou, *Platonisme et Théologie*

Christian context because it is more evocative of the transports of ecstasy which is brought about by the divine presence.[77] Indeed this is precisely what makes the Song of Songs so useful in the hands of Gregory. Commenting on the Canticle, he instructs the reader,

> In order to have us understand its profoundest doctrine, the Scriptures use as a symbol that which is the most violent of all our pleasurable inclinations, I mean the passion of love. Thus we are meant to understand that the soul that contemplates inaccessible beauty of the divine nature falls in love with it in much the same way as the body is attracted towards things connatural with it. But here the entire disturbance of the soul has been transformed into impassibility, all carnal passion is extinguished in us and the soul burns with love by the sole flame of the Spirit.[78]

And, while *eros* expresses the visceral quality of the attraction to the divine, at the same time—and more importantly—it conveys the "experience of the soul as the infinite beauty of God becomes more and more present to it. The more the soul is aware of this beauty, the more it sees that it is inaccessible. And it then realizes that it attains this beauty more by desire than by actual possession, just as it comprehends it rather by darkness than in the light."[79]

Though the presence of God serves to disorient, overwhelm, and confound the soul which enters into his intense light, the itinerant has means conferred upon him to comprehend the divine darkness. "Spiritual man is endowed with new powers and new senses, which accustom him to this divine darkness, inaccessible to the carnal man, and enable him to penetrate deeply into it."[80] As the believer progresses and develops the grace given at baptism, God bestows virtues on him which enable the soul to perceive the things of God. These are primarily the theological virtues (faith, hope, and charity) and the gifts of the Holy Spirit. These gifts allow him to penetrate deeply into the darkness and constitute a definitive spiritual progress as the believer moves "from glory to glory."

Mystique, 207. Gregory writes, "For love [*agape*] that is strained to intensity is called desire (*eros*)," *Commentarius in Canticum Canticorum* (PG 44.755).

77. Daniélou, "Introduction," in *From Glory to Glory*, 44.

78. Gregory of Nyssa, *Commentarius in Canticum Canticorum* (PG 44.773C-D).

79. Daniélou, "Introduction," in *From Glory to Glory*, 45.

80. Daniélou, *Dieu et Nous*, 224. "Cette ténèbre divine, inaccessible à l'homme charnel, l'homme spiritual est doué de dispostitions nouvelle, de sens nouveaux, qui le connaturalisent à elle et qui lui permettent d'y pénétrer."

Perpetual Progress (Epectasis)

The divine darkness and the believer's experience of that darkness is not an end in itself. Instead, God's presence is removed from us in order to incite us onward toward a fuller experience of the divine presence. As has been noted earlier, Daniélou believes that "God's presence . . . is concealed from us at the same time as it is given to us, *in order to oblige us always to advance further and further in the quest for what is an absolutely real presence*."[81] The idea that the "soul should never be satisfied with any progress that has been achieved, but should always proceed further" occurs over and again in Daniélou's writings (as well as Gregory of Nyssa's).[82] Indeed, Daniélou affirms Gregory's assertion that the soul has "the veil of sadness [lifted] from her when she learns that to press on unceasingly and never to pause for breath is truly to enjoy the Beloved."[83] This "pressing on unceasingly" is indicative of Daniélou's insistence that the spiritual life entails a progression "from glory to glory" which extends infinitely by virtue of the fact that it is the discovery of one's relation to the infinite presence of the triune God, "the presence of him who is beyond our grasp." As one moves from the experience of apophatic ecstasy, which is according to Daniélou ultimately the experience of the presence of God, one realizes that the ecstatic experience occurs in the same fashion each time and "involves a process of infinite growth."[84] The spiritual life consists in—like the pines of Bourideys in Mauriac's *Le Mystère Frontenac*—seeking to "ever reach towards the sky, and strain and stretch."[85] This insistence—at least in part—derives from Daniélou's extensive interaction with Gregory of Nyssa and the great spiritual writer's notion of *epectasis*.[86]

---

81. Emphasis added. Daniélou, "Absence and Presence of God," 9.

82. Daniélou, "Gregory of Nyssa," 104.

83. Daniélou, *Dieu et Nous*, 246–247. Gregory of Nyssa, *Commentarius in Canticum Canticorum*, sermon 12 (PG 44. 1037B).

84. Daniélou, "Introduction," in *From Glory to Glory*, 46.

85. François Mauriac, *Le Mystère Frontenac*, 255; ET: *The Frontenacs*, 184.

86. See Deseille, "Épectase," in *Dictionnaire de Spiritualité, Ascétique et Mystique, Doctrine et Histoire*, Tome IV, col. 785–88. A theory of perpetual progress is not unique to Gregory. Everett Ferguson notes that "hints and components of the idea" are scattered among Gregory's predecessors, e.g., Philo, Irenaeus, Clement of Alexandria and Origen. Ferguson, "God's Infinity and Man's Mutability: Perpetual Progress according to Gregory of Nyssa," 60–61. See also, Blowers, "Maximus Confessor, Gregory of Nyssa and the Concept of 'Perpetual Progress,'" 151–71.

Jean Danielou's Doxological Humanism

Daniélou begins his exegesis of Gregory's notion by outlining a general philosophy of change.[87] He tells his reader that for Gregory "the φύσις, the 'reality' of man is not to *be* spiritual, but continuously to *become* so."[88] The implication here is that perpetual change is fundamental to progress in the spiritual life. But Daniélou contends that in general the ancient Greek mindset—and within Platonism in particular—change was viewed as a debasement. "For Platonism change is regarded with distrust. The intelligible world as opposed to the sensible world is characterized by immutability. Origen's Christian Platonism does not surmount this difficulty. Change is conceived as a degradation from an initial perfection. The object of the transmutation effected by Christ is solely to restore immutability, hence to destroy change."[89] The divine in its perfection is seen as absolutely impassibility. Humanity on the other hand—as part of the sensible world—is mutable by its very nature. "Change," Daniélou tells us, "is a constitutive factor of man's existence."[90] It is "essential to man's nature; it is that which distinguishes him from God."[91] It is here that Daniélou and Gregory both use human mutability in order to derive good from a key difference between the human and the divine. Whereas certain strains of ancient thought viewed human mutability as a defect, Daniélou sees this quality as a means of achieving human salvation and the realization of a perpetual human potential. It is imperative that one move beyond the simple equation of change with evil and immobility with good. Daniélou sees Gregory's understanding of human fluctuation as the resolution to the dilemma posed by such an equation. He argues, "If change is essential to the human condition, and change is essentially degeneration, then it follows that the possibility of degeneration must be essential to man, and that good can never be secure. In this case the activity of God would be a continual restoration of man to his

---

87. Daniélou notes, "Le problème de la mutabilité (τροπή) est au cœur de la pensée théologique de Gregoire de Nysse." Daniélou, *L'Être et le Temps chez Grégoire de* Nysse, 95. See also Daniélou, "Le Problème du Changement chez Grégoire de Nysse," 323–47.

88. Daniélou, "La Colombre et la Ténèbre dans la Mystique Byzantine Ancienne," 400.

89. Daniélou, "La Colombre et la Ténèbre dans la Mystique Byzantine Ancienne," 400. "Pour le platonisme le changement . . . est considéré avec défiance. L'immutabilité caractérise le monde intelligible par opposition au monde sensible. Le platonisme chrétien d'Origène ne surmonte pas cette difficulté. Le changement est conçu comme une dégradation à partir d'une perfection initiale. La transmutation opérée par le Christ a seulement pour objet de restaurer l'immutabilité, donc de détruire le changement."

90. Ibid. "Le changement est constitutive de l'existence de l'homme."

91. Daniélou, "Introduction," in *From Glory to Glory*, 47.

primitive immortality, and man would constantly tend to fall from it. Such a movement would be a continual back-and-forth, a continual falling and rising and beginning over again."[92] But, Daniélou contends, there is a solution to the problem that does not require a perpetual ascent and descent. Following Gregory, Daniélou exhorts his reader that inconstant humans who are degenerative by nature acquire "consistency through the power of God" through the conversion of human mutability to its advantage.[93] In Gregory's understanding, humanity remains changeable but this mutability is converted to the benefit of the soul which experiences the ecstasy and resulting darkness of the presence of God.

Within the matrix of mystical knowledge—which is an alternation between illumination and darkness, absence and presence, knowledge and ignorance—the soul embarks on a perpetual journey toward the unchangeable divinity of God. Of this itinerary Daniélou maintains, "This movement tends towards the Immovable, and under this aspect it is at the opposite pole to the meaningless motion of the material world: it is a process of unification and concentration. But the ultimate unity and stability are never achieved; the soul is conceived as a spiritual universe in eternal expansion towards the infinite darkness."[94] Gregory aptly describes this spiritual journey in his exegesis of Exodus 33. Gregory, faced with an untenable literal interpretation of the events in the passage, turns toward a spiritual interpretation of the encounter between Moses and God:

> All heavenly bodies that receive a downward motion, even if they receive no further impulse after the first contact, are rapidly carried downwards of themselves, provided that any surface on which they are moving is graded and sloping, and that they meet no obstacle to interrupt their motion. So too, the soul moves in the opposite direction, light and swiftly moving upwards once it is released from sensuous and earthly attachments, soaring from the world below up towards the heavens. And if nothing comes from above to intercept its flight, seeing that it is of the nature of Goodness to attract those who raise their eyes toward it, the soul keeps rising ever higher and higher, stretching with its desire for heavenly things *to those that are before*, as the Apostle tells us, and thus it will always continue to soar ever higher. For because

---

92. Ibid.

93. Gregory of Nyssa, *Oratio Catechetica Magne*, XXI (PG 45.57D) (κατὰ θείαν δύναμιν εἰς οὐσίαν μεθισταμένης).

94. Daniélou, "Introduction," in *From Glory to Glory*, 57.

> of what it has already attained, the soul does not wish to abandon its heights that lie beyond it. And thus the soul moves ceaselessly upwards, always reviving its tension for its onward flight by means of the progress it has already realized. Indeed, it is only spiritual activity that nourishes its force by exercise; it does not slacken its tension by action but rather increases it.
>
> This is the reason why we say that the great Moses, moving ever forwards, did not stop in his upward climb. He set no limit to his rise to the stars. But once he had put his foot upon the ladder on which the Lord had leaned, as Jacob tells us, he constantly kept moving to the next step; and he continued to go ever higher because he always found another step that lay beyond the highest one that he had reached.[95]

The initial penchant of the soul encumbered by worldly matters is to be constantly pulled down by lower things. However, the soul which is detached from sensuality "strain[s] forward to what lies ahead" (Phil 3:13; NAB). Attracted by the Good, the soul embarks on a perpetual progression to ever higher heights of incorporation into the life of God. The grace bestowed on the soul at baptism and the developed graces of the spiritual life act as a pledge of further ecstasy. The soul increasingly desires to move onward and upward to a more intense and fuller glory.

Within the above passage Gregory uses the term *epectasis* to communicate the notion of straining forward in the spiritual progress of the soul. Gregory further explains the term in the context of the ecstasy of Paul spoken of in 2 Corinthians. Paul writes, "I must boast; not that it is profitable, but I will go on to visions and revelations of the Lord. I know someone in Christ who, fourteen years ago (whether in the body or out of the body I do not know, God knows), was caught up to the third heaven. And I know that this person (whether in the body or out of the body I do not know, God knows) was caught up into Paradise and heard ineffable things, which no one may utter" (2 Cor 12:1–4; NAB).[96] Elaborating on Paul's ecstasy, Gregory tells his audience that though Paul himself experienced a "mystical initiation in Paradise," he continued to strain for that which he desired most intensely, namely an ever-increasing participation in the triune God.[97]

---

95. Gregory of Nyssa, *De Vita Moysis* (PG 44.400D–401B).

96. On the ecstasy of Paul, see Stolz, *Theologie der Mystik*, 82–96; ET: *Doctrine of Spiritual Perfection*, 72–86. See also Daniélou, *Platonisme et Théologie Mystique*, 299; and *L'Être et le Temps chez Grégoire de Nysse*, 15.

97. Phil 3:13–14 says, "Brothers, I for my part do not consider myself to have taken possession. Just one thing: forgetting what lies behind but straining

> Yet even after listening in secret to the mysteries of heaven, Paul does not let the graces he has obtained become the limit of his desire, but he continues to go on and on, never ceasing his ascent. Thus he teaches us, I think, that in our constant participation in the blessed nature of the Good, the graces that we receive at every point are indeed great, but the path that lies beyond out immediate grasp is infinite. This will constantly happen to those who thus share in the divine Goodness, and they will always enjoy a greater and greater participation in grace throughout all eternity.[98]

The spiritual life achieved through prayer and contemplation consists of the perpetual movement to ever higher heights, "from glory to glory." Of these perpetual stages, Daniélou observes analogically, "the brilliance of each stage is always being obscured by the new 'glory' that is constantly rising. So too the sun of the new creation, the New Testament, obscures the brightness of that first sun, the Old Law. And the laws of the soul's growth are parallel with those of man's collective history. And yet this is by no means to depreciate the value of each particular stage—all are good, all are stages in perfection. But the mistake would be to try to hold on to any one of them, to put a stop to the movement of the soul."[99]

This progression is also illustrated by another apt symbol, the succession of garments. Commenting on the Canticle, Gregory tells of the soul's progress in these terms,

> After removing her old tunic and divesting herself of all further clothing, she became much purer than she was. And yet, in comparison with this newly acquired purity, she does not seem to have removed her headcovering. Even after the complete stripping of herself she still finds something further to remove. So it is with our ascent toward God: each stage that we reach always reveals something heavy weighing on the soul. Thus in comparison with her new found purity, that very stripping of her tunic now becomes a kind of garment which those who find her must once again remove.[100]

(ἐπεκτεινόμος) forward to what lies ahead, I continue my pursuit toward the goal, the prize of God's upward calling, in Christ Jesus."

98. Gregory of Nyssa, *Commentarius in Canticum Canticorum* (PG 44.940D–941A).

99. Daniélou, "Introduction," in *From Glory to Glory*, 59–60.

100. Gregory of Nyssa, *Comnetarius in Canticum Canticorum*, sermon 11 (PG 1029B–C).

No matter how many or what garments the soul removes, there is always another garment—a further stage—in the spiritual development of the soul towards higher degrees of perfection. This does not indicate that the lower stages are somehow of less value than later ones. Each removed garment is a stage in perfection being as perfection is not a thing achieved but rather an eternal process by which the soul grows in intimacy with God. Furthermore, Daniélou notes, "the soul was indeed denuded, but this nakedness becomes a cloak in comparison to a greater purity that is revealed to it. But this it could not know before. It was right in thinking itself denuded, because it did not know a purer nakedness."[101]

It is tempting to think of this progress as a perpetual ascent—and the idea is not without its merit. However, Daniélou points out that this progress, if thought of in terms of ascent, is a perpetual inward ascent, an ascent to the heights of the inner life through contemplation. He writes, "The successive stripping of the superimposed outer garments permits a progressive entrance into the inner man. All these deaths and resurrections carry the soul closer to the God who lives in its center, but who remains inaccessible; the circles of inwardness are infinite in number, and perfection consists in this perpetual inward movement, which is a perpetual discovery of God."[102]

The question arises of whether or not the soul will ever have its desire fulfilled. Does the soul not despair while what it seeks perpetually recedes the further on it progresses? As noted earlier, Gregory contends that the soul has the "veil of sadness" removed once it learns "that to progress and rise without cease is the true enjoyment of the Beloved, since desire fulfilled engenders at every moment a new desire. She sees the heartbreaking, unencompassable Beauty of the Beloved revealed perpetually more perfect throughout the eternity of the aeons, and is consumed by a more burning desire."[103] Daniélou contends that the desire of the heart is filled

---

101. Daniélou, "La Colombre et la Ténèbre dans la Mystique Byzantine Ancienne," 411. "L'âme était bien dépouillée, mais cette nudité devient un vêtement par rapport à une pureté plus grande qui se découvre à elle. Et cela, elle ne pouvait le savoir avant. Elle avait raison de se croire dépouillée. Mais c'est qu'elle ne connaissait pas une plus pure nudité."

102. Ibid. "Le dépouillement successif des tuniques extérieures superposes permet une entrée progressive dans l'homme intérieur. Toutes ces mortes et ces résurrections approchent progressivement l'âme du Dieu qui habite en son centre, mais qui y demeure inaccessible, si bien que les sphères d'intériorité sont en nombres infini et que la perfection consiste dans cette entrée perpétuelle vers l'intérieur qui et une découverte perpétuelle de Dieu."

103. Daniélou, *Dieu et Nous*, 246–47. Gregory of Nyssa, *Commentarius in Canticum*

á chaque instant ("at every moment"). Daniélou uses an apt analogy to show how the soul is continually filled to its capacity even as its capacity is continually being expanded in this process. "As the brick mold fills, it empties; its capacity does not increase. It is the scene of a continuous passage. But spiritual nourishment increases the capacity of him who receives it. All of it is assimilable. Nothing is lost. And accordingly the spiritual being grows perpetually, perpetually filled in the measure of his capacity, so that he becomes capable of new goods. Thus perpetual growth implies no dissatisfaction."[104] The soul is filled at every moment to the capacity of a given stage in the spiritual life. Satiation does not imply that the heart may not be increased to enable greater intimacy with the divine and while the next stage enlarges the soul it does not mean the prior stage did not fill it completely or was of lesser value.

Thus, spiritual growth is coordinated with the perpetual sustenance of creation by God. In the same way that the *Logos* was the agent of creation and continues to uphold creation, the Word continually draws the soul onward in a perpetual inward creation. In his eighth homily on the Canticle, Gregory tells of this perpetual sustenance, "Now the voice of the Word is ever a voice of power. At the creation, light shone forth at His command, and again at His order the firmament arose; and similarly all the rest of creation came into being at His creative Word. So too now, when the Word calls a soul that has advanced to come unto Him, it is immediately empowered at his command and becomes what the Bridegroom wishes. It is transformed into something divine, and it is *transformed from the glory* in which it exists to a higher glory by a perfect kind of alteration."[105] In another place, writing against Eunomius, Gregory further explores the similarities between creation and spiritual progress: "That which is created has not merely begun to be, but must be considered as always beginning to be in the good through growth toward the better. That is why its attainment

---

Canticorum, sermon 12 (PG 44. 1037B–C). See also Daniélou, "La Colombre et la Ténèbre dans la Mystique Byzantine Ancienne," 412.

104. Daniélou, "La Colombre et la Ténèbre dans la Mystique Byzantine Ancienne," 413. "À mesure que le moule à brique se remplit, il se vide à nouveau, sa capacité n'augmente pas. Il est le lieu d'un passage continuel. Au contraire la nourriture spirituelle augmente la capacité de celui qui la reçoit. Tout en elle est assimilable. Rien n'y est perdu. Et ainsi l'être spiritual grandit perpétuellement, toujours comblé à le mesure de sa capacité en sorte qu'il est capable de biens nouveaux. Ainsi la croissance perpétuelle n'implique aucune insatisfaction."

105. Gregory of Nyssa, *Commentarius in Canticum Canticorum*, Sermon 8 (PG 44.945D–948A).

never ceases, but everything created by participation becomes the beginning of a higher ascension. And according to the words of Paul, it never ceases to stretch forth toward what is ahead and to forget what is behind"[106] Like the progressive stages of creation and recreation—the progressive stages of *histoire sacramentaire*—the journey of the soul moves from stage to stage in an eternal progression toward the infinite. Or, as Daniélou puts it, "Every culmination is merely a beginning and every arrival a point of departure. Everything appears forever new, everything begins again."[107]

Daniélou uses a number of helpful images to express precisely how the contemplative progresses eternally toward the divine end. Perpetual progress is like the runner who having taken a step, uses that foot to propel himself to the next step by which he again propels himself to the next. Importantly, the runner never looks back at the steps he has taken before, but ever has in front of him the goal of the race. Or, perpetual progress is seen using wings to propel the contemplative from one good to another in an eternal ascent towards God. All of this presupposes the fact that one never ceases to regard what has been left behind and is ever oriented toward God and the riches that the contemplative has not possessed before that point.[108] Thus for Daniélou—following Gregory—the perpetual progress of the spiritual life always contains the "double element of support taken

---

106. Gregory of Nyssa, *Adversus Eunomium*, VIII (PG797A–B), in Daniélou, *Dove and the Darkness in Ancient Byzantine Mysticism*, 292. Compare the translation of the *Nicene and Post-Nicene Fathers*, vol. V: "While the creation attains excellence by partaking in something better than itself; and further, not only had a beginning of its being, but also is found to be constantly in a state of beginning to be in excellence, by its continual advance in improvement, since it never halts at what it has reached, but all that it has acquired good becomes by participation a beginning of its ascent to something still greater, and it never ceases, in Paul's phrase, "reaching forth to the things that are before," and "forgetting the things that are behind."

107. Daniélou, "La Colombre et la Ténèbre dans la Mystique Byzantine Ancienne," 416. "Chaque aboutissement n'est qu'un commencement et chaque arrivée un point de depart."

108. Daniélou, *Platonisme et Théologie Mystique*, 306. "Nous avons ici la description la plus achevée de l'épectase. Elle suppose, d'une part, une participation à la vie divine. C'est l'appui pris sur le Christ, qui est le roc. Cet appui s'exprime par diverses images: c'est la piste sur laquelle le pied du coureur prend appui pour s'élancer plus loin; c'est l'aile par laquelle l'âme prend appui sur les biens déjà possédés pour s'élancer plus haut. Ainsi le progrès suppose une acquisition antérieure, un affermissement dans le bien. Mais en même temps il suppose qu'on ne regarde pas en arrière, qu'on ne s'arrête pas aux richesse acquises, qu'il n'y ait aucun regard sur soi-même, mais une orientation de toute l'âme tendue . . . vers ce qui est en avant, orientée vers Dieu et vers toutes les richesses qu'elle ne possède pas encore."

on Christ and of a gaze turned towards the divine Essence. The spiritual life is thus a perpetual transformation of the soul into Jesus Christ in the form of an increasing heat, the increasing thirst for God to the point that it participates more and is increasingly stabilized, the soul ever more unified and fixed on God."[109] Daniélou vividly describes the entirety of the doctrine of perpetual progress when he writes, "Every stage in the spiritual life is an ever new beginning. And that which had seemed to be a limitation, each perfection, which is, at every point, precisely proportioned to the soul's capacity, becomes a new point of departure. Each peak we strive for fills our entire horizon, and, when we reach it, another rises up beyond. Such is the eternal process of man's discovery of the divine glory. And each stage is a nothing before the rest that remains—'a drop of the night dew that dampens the locks of the Beloved.' Indeed it is but a drop of dew in the ocean of infinite Darkness. Dove will give place to Dove, and Darkness to Darkness. There will always be the Dove and always the Darkness, forever obscure and yet forever bright."[110]

Conclusion

In outlining an itinerary for the spiritual life, Daniélou posits a journey that begins with the initial experience of the presence of God. This presence is characterized in the early stages of the spiritual life as a gift of light and enlightenment. Yet, God absents himself in order to compel the contemplative to ascend to a higher and more intimate knowledge of God. However, the darkness of God is mitigated by the fact that each period of absence is soon replaced anew by a deeper understanding of and fuller participation in the divine presence. As it were, we move from dove to darkness in a perpetual ascent toward the divine end.

---

109. Ibid., 306–7. "Toutes les images que nous avons rencontrées pour décrire le mouvement qui va de l'une à l'autre, l'échelle, la montée, la course, l'aile, comportent toujours ce double élément d'un appui pris sur le Christ et d'un regard tourné vers l'Essence divine. La vie spirituelle est ainsi une transformation perpétuelle de l'âme en Jésus-Christ sous forme d'une ardeur croissante, la soif de Dieu augmentant à mesure qu'il est davantage participé et d'une stabilité croissante, l'âme s'unifiant et se fixant toujours davantage en Dieu" (translation mine).

110. Daniélou, "Introduction," in *From Glory to Glory*, 71.

FIVE

The Crisis of Interiority and the Truly Human City

DANIÉLOU TOOK EVERY OPPORTUNITY to point out and address the crises of the contemporary world. He spoke meaningfully concerning the crisis of religious life in the modern world.[1] He spoke cogently concerning the rise of atheistic humanism and the crisis of knowledge in the academic world. This he called *la crise d'intelligence*, which lies at the heart of the life of the University, and its effects on the broader culture.[2] But, perhaps most importantly—and certainly most relevant here—Daniélou continually sought to address the crisis of interiority, i.e., a crisis of contemplation. He continually spoke of the necessity of contemplation, adoration, interiority and silence, experiencing the presence of God in prayer, which is an absolute necessity for a true humanism. Indeed, he addressed his small volume on the Trinity entirely to this lapse of contemplation in contemporary society.[3] Furthermore, in his provocative work *L'Oraison Problème Politique* Daniélou contends that society without the intentional protection of religious life will devolve into an inhuman society which disables its members from realizing their full human potential which, he argues, can only be realized in interiority. In doing so, Daniélou considers whether the Church—properly understood—is a small, pure, devoted gathering of

---

1. Daniélou, "Y a-t-il une Crise de la Vie Religieuse?," 1029–31; "In Connection with the Crisis of Religious Life," 53–58.

2. Daniélou, *La Crise Actuelle d'Intelligence*; ET: *The Crisis in Intelligence*. All subsequent English translations of this text will be Dominic's translatioin unless noted otherwise.

3. Daniélou, *La Trinité et le Mystère de l'Existence*, 7–8.

The Crisis of Interiority and the Truly Human City

believers or an expansive membership which manifests various levels of devotion and piety—what Augustine called a mixed Church. Daniélou then considers the conditions of contemplation in technical society and how such a society represses interiority. Finally, Daniélou argues for the creation of the "truly human city" where contemplation is an integral aspect of the civilization which makes a true humanity possible.

The Church of the Poor: Little Flock or Great People?

Daniélou begins his discussion of the political aspect of prayer by contending that the Church should always be capable of describing itself as the "Church of the poor." However, at the outset, the idea of "the Church of the Poor" demands that one distinguish two separate notions of the Church. The first of these is the idea of a pure church. The demand that the Church be constituted by a pure, holy and devoted membership has occupied theologians since the time of the influx of members of varying degrees of devotion in the Constantinian era of Church history. In a wide variety of times and contexts, the Church has struggled with the relative degrees of devotion expressed by its membership. For instance, the Donatist controversy represents a crystallization of sentiment concerning purity in the early Church in reference to persecution, the lapsed and schism in this period. For the Donatist schismatics, those that had renounced the faith in the face of Roman persecution were too easily allowed to return to communion with the Church, especially in the case of Caecillian who had been consecrated by a *traditor*. For Daniélou, the proponents of a pure Church conception argue that "the Church stands before the world as a sign, giving witness in the world to that which surpasses the world. On this view, the Church should bear witness and make sure of satisfying the first requirement for this, which is purity."[4] In addition, he describes its tendency to distance itself from civilization so as to maintain its purity. From this viewpoint, the Church following the reign of Constantine and especially the endorsement of Christianity as the official religion of the empire under Theodosius I betrayed its role as a pure sign of what the Church should be. From Daniélou's standpoint, "to protect the Church's purity, those who hold this view would

---

4. Daniélou, *L'Oraison Problème Politique*, 9. "L'Église est avant tout un signe dressé parmi les nations. Elle doit témoigner au milieu du monde de ce qui dépasse le monde. L'essentiel est qu'elle rende témoignage. On lui demandera surtout d'être pure."

go so far as to risk the abandonment of the crowd of baptized Christians for whom Christianity is hardly anything more than an external routine."[5]

From another point of view, an "essential character of the gospel is to be the religion of the poor."[6] This attitude is expressed by John Paul II in his *ad limina* visit to the bishops of the Philippines in 2003, in which he emphasized the continuing need to develop this aspect of the Church. He exhorted the Philippino bishops to take heed of three pastoral concerns: the need to become a true community of the Lord's disciples, the need to engage in renewed integral evangelization and the need to be the Church of the poor.[7] In accord with the *Acts and Decrees of the of the Second Plenary Council of the Philippines*, John Paul II maintained that striving to be the church of the poor is a primary means of "following the way of our Lord."[8] The Second Plenary Council maintained the primary qualities of the Church of the poor as the embrasure of "the *evangelical spirit of poverty*, which combines *detachment from possessions* with a *profound trust in the Lord* as the sole source of salvation."[9]

However, Daniélou emphasizes a more Augustinian notion of the Church of the poor which does not accentuate the renunciation of material things.[10] Rather than emphasizing renunciation, Daniélou emphasizes the fact that the Church is composed of the "great mass of mankind."[11] He

5. Daniélou, *L'Oraison Problème Politique*, 9. "Et on préférera sauvegarder cette pureté, fût-ce au prix de l'abandon de ces nombreux baptisés pour qui le christianisme n'est guère qu'une pratique extérieure."

6. Ibid., 10. "C'est un caractère essential de l'Évangile d'être la religion des pauvres."

7. *Address of John Paul II to the Bishops of the Philippines on their Ad Limina Visit*, September 25, 2003, §2.

8. Ibid., §3.

9. Ibid.

10. Daniélou, *L'Oraison Problème Politique*, 10.

11. It is important to note that the poor who are considered the great mass of humanity are not the same as the poor who practice evangelical poverty. Daniélou maintains that evangelical poverty is the poverty referred to in the Beatitudes and consists of being "libre à l'égard de tout sauf de la volonté de Dieu[free in regard to everything save the will of God]." He also notes that evangelical poverty is characterized by a "disposition d'un cœur uniquement occupé des interest du royaume de Dieu et libre à l'égard des biens terrestres [disposition of a heart occupied solely with the interests of the kingdom of God and free in regard to earthly goods]." Daniélou, "Bienheurieux les Pauvres," 331 and 332; ET: "Blessed are the Poor," 384 and 385. All subsequent English translations of this text will be Birmingham's unless noted otherwise. See also Chapter 6 in Daniélou, *Évangile et Monde Moderne*, 67–86; ET: *The Christian Today*, 129–50. All subsequent English translations of this text will be Sullivan's unless noted otherwise. Though Sullivan

maintains that Augustine viewed the Church as a mixture of devoted and inconstant Christians. Augustine uses the symbol of fish caught in a net to illustrate the mixed nature of the Church. In *De Doctrina Christiana*, he wrote,

> Now this rule requires the reader to be on his guard when Scripture, although it has now come to address or speak of a different set of persons, seems to be addressing or speaking of the same persons as before, just as if both sets constituted one body in consequence of their being for the time united in a common participation of the sacraments. An example of this is that passage in the Song of Solomon, "I am black, but comely, as the tents of Cedar, as the curtains of Solomon." For it is not said, I "was" black as the tents of Cedar, but am "now" comely as the curtains of Solomon. The Church declares itself to be at present both; and this because the good fish and the bad are for the time mixed up in the one net.[12]

Likewise, Gregory the Great also uses the image of a net when speaking of the nature of the Church and the different fish caught in the net in a Homily on two parables of the Kingdom. He tells,

> The kingdom of heaven is said to be like a net let down into the sea, gathering all kinds of fish. When full it is brought to shore, and the good fish are sorted into baskets, but the bad ones are thrown away. Our holy Church is compared to a net, because it has been entrusted to fisherman, and because all people are drawn up in it from turbulent waters of the present age to the eternal kingdom, lest we drown in the depths of eternal death. This net gathers all kinds of fish because it calls to forgiveness of sins everyone, wise and foolish, free and slave, rich and poor, brave and weak. Hence the psalmist tells God: *Every human being will come to you.*[13]

Gregory explains that it will not be until the end of the present age that the Church will be purified. Furthermore, he contends that unlike the fish which cannot change, people on the other hand, caught in the net in a bad state, can become good. "Now the net of the faith holds good and bad together, like the different kinds of fish; but on shore is revealed to the holy Church what she has been drawing in. The fish, when they have been

---

took liberties with the ordering and inclusion of the chapters, the translation that she provides is accurate.

12. Augustine, *De Doctrina Christiana*, 3.32.45 (PL 34.82–83).
13. Gregory the Great, *Homiliarum in Evangelia* (PL 76:1116A–1116C).

caught, cannot be changed; but we, who are caught while we are wicked, can become good. Let us bear this in mind as we are in the process of being caught, lest we be thrown aside on shore."[14] The mixed nature of the Church is what makes it the "Church of the poor." For Daniélou, "the Church was most truly itself in the days of Christendom when everybody was baptized and it is this state of affairs which is much to be desired. But this situation supposes a Church which is involved in civilization, for if civilization runs counter to it a Christian people cannot exist. This Church, a great crowd of saints and sinners is intermingled, is found preferable as a Church to one which might be purer but would strongly resemble a sect."[15]

For Daniélou, the message of the Gospel is not the property of a spiritual elite reserved only for those who represent the *beau ideal* of Christian living. Instead, he argues, "the Gospel message is addressed to all men, and especially to the poor, and that the Church, the community of those who have received this message, is therefore open to everybody."[16] This is evidenced when Jesus reads from a scroll of Isaiah, "The Spirit of the Lord is upon me, because he has anointed me to bring glad tidings to the poor. He has sent me to proclaim liberty to captives and recovery of sight to the blind, to let the oppressed go free" (Lk 4:18; NAB). However, it must be remembered that the term *poor* is equivocal. Daniélou emphasizes this plurality in meaning when he notes some different possible meanings: "It can mean those who are in poverty; and Christ then will comfort their misery. It can mean the poor in spirit, those who seek first of all the kingdom and its righteousness, and will risk everything else to gain that. But it means also the undistinguished and unprivileged, those who lack money, education, and rank."[17] In the Gospel of Luke, the poor are seen as the special

14. Ibid.

15. Daniélou, *L'Oraison Problème Politique*, 10. "La condition authentique de l'Église est à leurs yeux celle des âges de chrétienté, où tout le monde était baptisé. Et c'est cette condition qui leur paraît souhaitable. Elle suppose que l'Église s'engage dans la civilisation, car un people chrétien n'est pas possible dans une civilization qui lui est contraire. Et ils préfèrent cet immense people, mêlé de saints et de pécheurs à une église plus pure, mais qui ressemblerait à une chapelle."

16. Ibid. "Que le message évangelique s'addresse à tous les hommes et spécialement aux pauvres, que l'Église, qui est la communauté de ceux qui ont reçu le message évangelique, soit donc ouverte à tous."

17. Ibid., 10–11. "Le mot pauvre peut avoir plusieurs sens. Il peut désigne ceux qui sont dans la misère. Et le Christ alors soulage ces misères. Il peut designer les pauvres en esprit, ceux qui cherchent d'abord le royaume et sa justice et risquent tout pur cela. Mais il désigne aussi ceux qui effectivement ne sont pas des privilégiés, ni d'argent, ni d'esprit, ni d'honneur."

recipients of the gospel message. "And he said to them in reply, 'Go and tell John what you have seen and heard: the blind regain their sight, the lame walk, lepers are cleansed, the deaf hear, the dead are raised, the poor have the good news proclaimed to them'" (Lk 7:22; NAB). The associations in this passage seem to indicate that the poor are those who—like lepers and the disabled—are denied the benefits of society. The poor in this regarded are simply the unprivileged of society.

Daniélou notes that though there are some exceptions (e.g., Nicodemus and Joseph of Arimathea), Christ unhesitatingly associated with all levels of society. To the horror of the Pharisees he sat down to eat with extortionists and prostitutes. Luke tells of the Pharisees' disdain concerning the matter, "The Pharisees and their scribes complained to his disciples, saying, 'Why do you eat and drink with tax collectors and sinners?'" (Lk 5:30; NAB). Jesus also welcomed children into his presence. Furthermore, he spent a great portion of his ministry speaking to large crowds. Without a doubt, these immense gatherings were peopled with every strata of society. These facts indicate that participation in the kingdom of God was due to one's faith not to one's civil or religious status within society.[18]

This phenomenon is what makes the Church the "Church of the poor." In the early Church, it was a point of ridicule for pagan writers in the first centuries. Celsus openly mocked the Christian community because it was peopled by "anyone ignorant, anyone stupid, anyone uneducated, anyone childish."[19] It was also a matter of embarrassment for some Christians in the early Church. Already in the third century, Cyprian of Carthage was complaining of a relative loss of commitment in the growing Christian community.[20] Likewise, Origen bemoans the fact that the more people who enter the Church the greater the laxity of the Church's membership. According to Daniélou, Origen complains in his homilies on Leviticus, "In truth, if we judge matters according to reality and not according to numbers, according to people's dispositions and not according to the crowds who gather, we shall see that we are not believers."[21] In his sermons on Genesis he complains, "But I fear that the Church is still bearing sons in

18. Ibid., 11.

19. Celsus, *On the True Doctrine*, 72–73.

20. Daniélou notes that this complaint is in no way particular to the Constantinian or post-Constantinian era. Complaint about a loss of fervor which accompanies an increase in members pre-dates the large influx of members after the Constantinian period. See *L'Oraison Problème Politique*, 11–12.

21. Daniélou gives the reference to Origen as *Hom. Lev.* IV.3.

sadness and sorrow. Or does it not cause her sadness and sorrow when you do not gather to hear the word of God? And scarcely on feast days do you proceed to the Church, and you do this not so much from a desire for the word as from a fondness for the festival and to obtain, in a certain manner, common relaxation."[22]

Instead of lamenting the situation of a broadened Church, Daniélou sees the opening of the Church as a positive development which makes the Church the Church of all rather than the domain of a spiritual elite.

> This much only is true—the extension of Christianity to an immense multitude, which is of its very essence, was held back during the first centuries by the fact that the social cadres and cultural forms of the society in which it operated were hostile to it. To cleave to Christianity called then for strength of character which the majority of men are not capable. When the conversion of Constantine removed these obstacles the Gospel was made accessible to the poor, that is to say, to those very people who are not numbered among the élite. The man in the street could now be a Christian. Far from distorting Christianity, this change allowed it to become more truly itself, a people.[23]

Daniélou consistently argues that Christianity is not to be the property of a spiritual or intellectual noblesse. Daniélou's attitude is illustrated by his account of the conflict between Hippolytus and the pontificates of Zephyrinus and Callistus. Hippolytus violently castigated both of these pontiffs because "he dreamed of a Church which was a handful of saints in conflict with the world."[24] Contrariwise, Zephyrinus and Callistus sought to secure the interests of the Church by winning the sympathy of the imperial

---

22. Origen, *Homiliæ in Genesim* XI.1 (PG 12.215C).

23. Daniélou, *L'Oraison Problème Politique*, 12. "Ce qui est vrai seulement, c'est que cette extension du christianisme à un immense people, qui est de son essence, s'est trouvée entravée durant les premiers siècles par le fait qu'il se développait à l'intérieur d'une societé dont les cadres sociaux et les structures culturelles lui étaient hostiles. L'appartenance au christianisme demandait donc une force de caractère dont la majorité des homes ne sont pas capable. La conversion de Constantin, en faisant tomber ces obstacles, a rendu l'Évangile accessible aux pauvres, c'est-à-dire précisément à ceux qui ne font pas partie des élites, à l'homme de la rue. Loin de fausser le christianisme, elle lui a permis de s'accomplir dans sa nature de people."

24. Daniélou and Marrou, *Novelle Histoire de l'Église: Des Origines à Saint Grégoire le Grand*,182; ET: *The First Six Hundred Years: The Christian Centuries, Volume One*, 150. "Il rêve d'une Église qui soit une poignée de saints en conflit avec le monde." All subsequent English translations of this text will be Cronin's unless noted otherwise.

The Crisis of Interiority and the Truly Human City

government, by increasing the numbers of the Church and by adapting the Church to the new circumstances of the Church of their times.[25] For this reason, Daniélou maintains that "Hippolytus was mistaken. He did not see that the growth of God's people implied new situations, that Christianity was not a sect of pure people, but a city expressive of its inhabitants. He mocked Callistus's admirable image of the Church as Noah's ark, containing animals of all kinds, who will be sorted out only at the Last Judgment."[26] Daniélou maintains these were the same concerns that were behind the dispute between Novatian and Cyprian. In the Novatian schism, Daniélou tells us, "The ideal of a Church of prophets, confessors and virgins was opposed by the notion of a great Christian people."[27] Furthermore, Daniélou describes both parties' position, "For Novatian, the Church was a small group of the spiritually-minded, in inevitable conflict with the earthly city: a Church of prophets and martyrs. On the other side was the bishops' view; for them the Church was a people which must gather together all men, and must therefore take account of the different levels implied by the arrival of a great many people within the Church. There was a place for an élite of spiritually-minded members; monasticism would satisfy their needs, but there was also room for the immense crowd of ordinary Christians."[28]

That Christianity should become the domain of only the most capable, the most intelligent or the most devout is contrary to the spirit of

---

25. Ibid.

26. Ibid., 183. "Hippolyte se trompe. Il ne voit pas que le développement du people de Dieu implique des situations nouvelles, que le christianisme n'est pas une secte de purs, mais la cité de tous les hommes. Il se moque de l'image admirable de Calixte montrant dans l'Église l'arche de Noé où il y a des animaux de toutes sortes, que le jugement seul discernera." At the same time, Daniélou cautions not to be too harsh in assessing Hippolytus. For Daniélou, he is an authentic vehicle of the pure tradition of the Church. There is no need to qualify him as a schismatic. Instead, Daniélou attributes the violence with which he attacked Zephyrinus and Callistus to the literary form in which he wrote. It is also interesting to note Daniélou's characterization of Hippolytus' position as *intégrisme* which was rightly rejected by the Church hierarchy.

27. Ibid., 231. "La conception d'une Église de prophètes, de confesseurs et de vierges s'oppose à celle grand people chrétien."

28. Ibid., 234. "Pour Novatien, l'Église s'identifie à un petit groupe de spirituels en conflit nécessaire avec la cite terrestre: c'est une église de prophètes et de martyrs A cela s'oppose la conception des évêques. Pour eux l'Église est in people qui doit rassembler tous les hommes. Elle doit donc tenir compte des niveaux divers que représentera nécessairement cette accession des masses dans l'Église. Il y aura place pour une élite de spirituels. C'est à cela que correspondra le monachisme. Mais il y a place aussi pour l'immense foule des chrétiens ordinaire."

the Gospel. For Daniélou, this is the most distressing aspect of the secularization of the western world.[29] With the continuing dechristianization of the masses—of whole societies—it becomes of the utmost importance to determine what measures must be taken to ensure the existence of particular Christian peoples. "Our task, therefore, is to discover what those conditions are which make a Christian people possible. To do that we have to ask what conditions have in fact made a Christian people possible."[30]

More and more, societies and their institutions make the possibility of a Christian people a more distant prospect. One reason for the ebbing of Christianity and the diminishing possibility of a Christian people concerns the way in which Christianity has been instituted in non-Western nations. Often, when Christianity was brought to nations of the East, western Christianity was simply duplicated in a different cultural milieu. This had a dire effect on the long-term viability of Christianity within these contexts. When Christianity was instantiated in a new cultural milieu in its Western forms, it was unable to endure the various pressures on the faithful.

> A major cause of this is that Christianity had become tied to its Western forms and was not incorporated into the systems of thought and art and manners of those countries. Christianity came to seem alien to national traditions. Its future becomes precarious because conversion acquires the smack of treason and becomes a difficult thing, at best forcing a man on the fringe of the life of his country. We see now that before the faith can be truly rooted in a country it must penetrate its civilization and bring into existence a Christendom. Christianity is accessible to a people as revelation only when it is rooted in that people as a religion.[31]

---

29. See Daniélou, "Le Peuple Chrétien selon Péguy," 175–86.

30. Daniélou, *L'Oraison Problème Politique*, 13. "Le problème est donc de s'interroger sur les conditions qui rendent possible un people chrétien. Et pour cela de s'interroger sur les conditions qui ont rendu possible un people chrétien."

31. Ibid., 13–14. "Il est apparu évident que ce recul venait du fait que le christianisme y était resté lié à ses formes occidentales et ne s'était pas incarné dans les structures de pensée, d'art, de mœurs de ces pays. Du coup, il apparaît comme étranger à la tradition nationale. Son existence reste précaire. La conversion est rendue difficile, parce qu'elle semble être une trahison et qu'elle met en quelque manière en marge de la vie nationale. Il en résulte une constatation: la foi ne peut être vraiment enracinée dans un pays que lorsqu'elle a pénétré la civilization, quand il existe un chrétienté. Le christianisme n'est accessible à la masse d'un people comme revelation que quand il est enraciné dans ce people comme religion."

The Crisis of Interiority and the Truly Human City

In this situation, Christianity was not a religion of the masses—a religion of the poor—and as a result its longevity was in serious doubt from the outset. For Daniélou, this is a confirmation of the "legitimacy of the Constantinian process" by which christendoms are established within given cultural contexts as an indigenous cultural expression of the Gospel and is necessary for the full and permanent situation of Christianity in a given cultural milieu. This is precisely what occurred in the Church of the fourth century, according to Daniélou: "It was because from the fourth century Christianity had penetrated Western civilization and formed a Christendom that the immense Christian people of the medieval [and Baroque] West became possible. Of course, this people had the defects common to all people. For many, Christianity was less a supernatural faith than a religious need. But is it not desirable, we should ask, that the Gospel should be taken even to such poor as these, who do after all receive something of its saving power?"[32]

The inability to create a situation suitable for a Christian people in the Western world had more to do with either religious elitism or the oft-cited phenomenon of desacralization. First of all, Daniélou gives the example of a religious elitism that spurns the participation of the laity due to the decreased efficiency associated with their participation. Daniélou contends that "it would be criminal if the crowd of poor confided to [the Church's] care were abandoned on the pretext that [it] could do more effective missionary work without them."[33] This occurrence spurns the idea that the great mass of the poor need be involved in the activity of the Church and prioritizes the position of a religious elite over the identity of the Church as the Church of the poor.

Second, the process of desacralization has eviscerated the Christianity of the masses.[34] The secularization of Western culture is the process of the undoing of the situation which allows a Christian people to exist in the very place where a Christendom *par excellence* has existed in the past. The

---

32. Ibid., 14. "C'est parce qu'à partir du IVe siècle, le christianisme a pénétré la civilization occidentale, parce qu'il y a eu une chrétienté, qu'a été rendu possible l'immense people chretien qui est celui de l'Occident medieval et baroque. Bien sûr, ce people présente le défauts qui sont ceux de tout people. Pour beaucoup, le christianisme a été moins une foi surnaturelle qu'un besoin religieux. Mais la question est de savoir s'il n'est pas précisément souhaitable que l'Évangile puisse s'étendre jusqu'à ces pauvres qui reçoivent cependent quelque chose de son salut."

33. Ibid., 12. "Ce serait un calcul criminal, sous pretext d'alléger l'Église afin de la render plus missionaire, d'abandonner la foule des pauvres qui s'est confiée à elle."

34. See Daniélou, "La Desacralisation," 1056.

removal of those obstacles which allow the great mass of people to enter into the Church has been undone. For Daniélou, this phenomenon constitutes the "drama of Western Christianity" where "the masses are being dechristianized." He bemoans the loss of such a Christianity: "Of course there are crises among the intellectuals, but that is nothing new. It is no more dangerous for a Christian country to have in its midst a few atheistic intellectuals than it is for an atheistic country to have in it a few serious Christian intellectuals. It is much more serious when a Christian people is destroyed, for it can be built up again only after a long and patient effort."[35]

For some, the reduction of the Church to those who are most devoted to the Gospel is a positive development. For these, the manner in which the Church remains most faithful to God is to remain a pure sign as a witness to the world in which it is situated. For Daniélou, it is absolutely necessary to open the Church to the masses with all their varying degrees of devotion and constancy. Therefore, he writes, "The Church has an absolute duty to open herself to the poor. This can be done only by creating conditions which make Christianity possible for the poor. Therefore there is laid upon the Church a duty to work at the task of making civilization such that the Christian way of life shall be open to the poor."[36] However, the contemporary world provides a staggering array of obstacles to life in the Church. Daniélou describes the obstacles to religious life provided by modern technological society when he notes, "In technological civilization [people] tend to be absorbed in care for material things. Socialization and rationalization leave little room for a personal life. Society is so disordered that large numbers have to live in poverty which makes personal life impossible. The result of the secularization of society is that God is no longer present in family, professional or civic life. *A world has come into being in which everything serves to turn [people] away from their spiritual calling.*"[37]

35. Daniélou, *L'Oraison Problème Politique*, 13. "Le drame du christianisme occidental actuel, c'est-à-dire de la partie du monde où un people chrétien a existé, est précisément la déchristianisation des masses. Qu'il y ait des crises dans les élites intellectuelles, il en a toujours été ainsi. Il n'est pas plus dangereux pour un pays chrétien de compter quelques intellectuels athées que pour un pays athée de compter quelques intellectuels chrétiens. Mais ce qui est beaucoup plus difficilement reparable, parce que c'est le résultat d'un long et patient labeur."

36. Ibid., 16.

37. Emphasis added. Ibid., 16. "La civilization technique tend à absorber les hommes dans les preoccupations matérielles. La socialization et la rationalization laissent peu de place à la vie personelle. Les désordres de la société entraînent pour des milliers d'hommes des conditions de misère qui ne leur permettent pas une vie personnelle. La

Interiority and the Technical Society

Perhaps more than elitism, secularism or errors in missiological theory, the technological nature of contemporary society occludes the true vocation of humanity (contemplation) more than any other factor. Nonetheless, Daniélou does admit that technological society can be seen as a means to achieve a true humanism.[38] Indeed, Daniélou claims when responsibility is coordinated with technology it is technology "itself which leads us today to a rediscovery of the permanent values of a complete humanism" if only through exposing what is essential in humanity.[39]

Though technology can at times facilitate that which essential to humanity, for the most part technology and the concomitant society produced by its presence serves as an obstacle to the full blooming of the human person. Even if the Church opens herself up to the great mass of humanity, the context within which the Church finds itself further hampers the total realization of a full human potential. In *Scandaleuse Vérité*, Daniélou noted the obstacles that technological society placed in the way of the full blooming of individuals by hampering religion.[40] The first way in which "a machine civilization threatens to turn man away from adoration is that it causes man to live in a universe made up of his own works."[41] Here the

---

laicization de la société fait que Dieu n'est plus present dans la vie familiale, professionnelle ou civique. *Ainsi se constitue un monde dans lequel tout détourne les hommes de leur vocation spirituelle.*"

38. It is difficult to determine precisely what Daniélou has in mind when he uses the phrase *civilization technique*. At times it appears that it refers to industrial society. Here the picture seems to entail life in large burgeoning cities and factories. Humanity finds himself surrounded by things of his own making. Here the focus seems to be that of invention and the supposed progress associated with human inventiveness. This coordinates well with the electronic technologies associated with computer society commensurate with the end of the twentieth and the beginning of the twenty-first centuries. Daniélou's terminology is certainly pertinent in this new technological and cultural context.

39. Daniélou, *L'Oraison Problème Politique*, 66–67. "Et c'est là la signification même du problème de la rencontre de la responsabilité et de la technique, que montrer que c'est la technique elle-même qui nous amène aujourd'hui à redécouvrir les valeurs permanents d'un humanisme complet."

40. Daniélou, *Scandaleuse Vérité*; ET: *The Scandal of Truth*. All subsequent English translations of this text will be Kerrigan's unless noted otherwise. See also "Christianity and the Machine-Age World," 14–17, which reproduces Chapter IX of *The Scandal of Truth*.

41. Daniélou, *Scandaleuse Vérité*, 130. "Un des traits par lesquels la civilization technique risqué de détourner l'homme de l'adoration, c'est qu'elle fait vivre l'homme ans un univers qui est celui de ses propres œuvres."

magnalia Dei are supplanted by the *magnalia hominis*. Modern humanity surrounds itself with the fruits of its own labor which celebrate his own perceived greatness. "Machine-age man lives surrounded by machines, tools, instruments by which he transforms his life, landscapes, even the skylines of the great modern cities with their immense factories. Thus he finds himself surrounded by the things which reflect his own image back to him from every direction."[42] This self-adulation turns humanity from worship, adoration and contemplation of the divine; instead, it is "himself that he contemplates and that he admires."[43] Within this context, the scientist and the inventor and the technician are the heroes of the modern world, "the one who holds in his hands all the secrets of power."[44] This creates an extremely dire situation for the contemplative in modern society.

> Now this is something serious, for if the heavens proclaim the glory of God, machines proclaim the glory of man. Modern man, it may be said, is apt to be bewitched by a kind of incantation of the whole marvelous world that he finds at his finger tips and that is increasing today on an almost fabulous scale. All this gives him, in his own eyes, a more and more considerable importance and magnitude, and relegates, for him, the reality of God's operations to the background; his practical interest in them is decreased in proportion as his attention is centered on the operations of man. From this point of view, it may be said that the world of technology seems to turn man away from God.[45]

---

42. Ibid. "L'homme de la civilization technique vit entourné de machines, d'outils, d'instruments par lesquels il transforme sa vie, de paysages meme qui sont ces paysages des grandes villes moderns avec leurs immenses usines. Il se trouve ainsi entouré de réalités qui lui renvoient partout sa proper image."

43. Daniélou, "Technical Civilization and Atheistic Humanism," 224.

44. Daniélou, *Scandaleuse Vérité*, 131. "Le savant apparaît à beaucoup de jeunes d'aujord'hui comme le grand héros du monde modern, celui qui tient entre ses mains tous les secrets de la puissance."

45. Ibid. "Voilà qui est grave, parce que si les cieux chantent la gloire de Dieu, les machines chantent la gloire de l'homme: l'homme modern, peut-on dire, subit une espèce d'incantation qui est celle de tout ce monde merveilleux qu'il voit ainsi apparaître sous ses doigts, avec une croissance aujourd'hui quasi fableuse. Tout ceci lui donne, à ses propres yeux, une importance et une grandeur de plus en plus considerable et rejette, pour lui, la réalité des œuvres de Dieu dans un arrière-plan; de sorte qu'il a pour elles un désintérêt pratique, du fait meme que son attention est concentrée sur les œuvres de l'homme. De ce point de vue, par consequent, on peut dire que le monde de la technique apparaît comme détournant l'homme de Dieu."

The Crisis of Interiority and the Truly Human City

If contemplation exists in this situation, it does so in contemplation of humanity's greatness and ability.

Not only does technological society imbue humanity with a sense of its own greatness but also with a sense of its powerfulness. Daniélou notes, "What characterizes this world is the progressive mastery which man achieves over the forces of nature, permitting him to put them to his use. When one compares the situation of primitive man, crushed by cosmic forces, with that of man of today, one grasps the feeling he has of recovering today all that he formerly gave to God simply because he was not the master of it, and of extending his conquest . . . indefinitely toward ever receding limits."[46] This power has been increasingly felt over the material world of physics and matter and seeks to extend its grasp into biological etiology and eschatology. Indeed, Daniélou fully believed that technological progress would lead "to man's conquest of his biological fate . . . to the point where the mysterious world of life, which used to be the very thing that escaped man's grasp, will be progressively mastered, this mastery permitting . . . the gradual possibility of an indefinite prolongation of life. Man, who formerly experienced a feeling of captivity and had recourse to a *deus ex machina* to come and save him, thinks now that he himself is capable of freeing himself from this captivity and bringing about his own salvation."[47] It is interesting to note that biological reproductive technology—though instrumental in the prolongation of life—has instead enabled the "culture of death" to put a limit on the length of life by truncating it both at the very beginnings of life and at its end. In either the prolongation of life or the truncation of life, the power exerted by biological technology has emboldened humanity to see itself as the primary power over its own origins and ends. Daniélou summarizes the attitude of the modern technological individual: "He has

---

46. Ibid., 131–32. "Ce lui caractérise, en effet, ce monde, c'est la maîtrise progressive que l'homme acquiert sur les forces de la nature est qui lui permet de les mettre à son service. Quand on compare la situation de l'homme primitif écrasé par les forces cosmiques à celle de l'homme d'aujord'hui, on comprend que celui-ci ait le sentiment que progressivement il récupère tout ce qu'autrefois il avait donné à Dieu, simplement parce qu'il n'en était pas maître et que cette conquête peut . . . s'étendre jusqu'à des limites qu reculeront toujours."

47. Ibid., 132. "C'est une nouvelle direction dans laquelle les progress peuvent aller très vite; par lesquels . . . l'homme pourrait devenir maître de son destin biologique lui-même, au point que ce monde mystérieux de la vie, qui était essentiellement ce qui échappait à ses prises, soit maîtrisé progressivement; vette maîtrise permettant, comme . . . d'envisager une graduelle possibilité de prolongation de la vie. Ainsi, l'homme qui autrefois éprouvait un sentiment de captivité et recourait à un *deus ex machina* pour venir le délivrer pense maintenant que c'est lui-même qui est capable de se libérer de cette captivité et d'opérer son proper salut."

the feeling that recourse to something outside his world is in fact a kind of laziness; that the need is to devote all man's energies to the struggle for his own liberation; that it is man who will be the demiurge of man and will create the happy and liberated mankind of tomorrow."[48]

Another way in which the technological manner of living serves as an obstacle to religious life is that it "accustoms the mind to approaches very different from those by which the religious world may be attained."[49] For instance, technological society prizes values such as efficiency rather than truth. Daniélou maintains that in the technological world there are only "hypotheses which can be superseded by other hypotheses which are verified by their concrete effectiveness" whether or not the hypotheses are true in and of themselves.[50] In a lengthy description of life in a consumerist society (for which one might easily transpose Daniélou's technological society), Nicholas Boyle narrates the story of consumerist efficiency,

> In a socialist society a society's labor is cheap; in a consumer society people's labor is expensive. This, however, does not mean that in it people themselves are of worth. As people become more expensive—because they are more educated and their skills represent a greater investment, or because payment in status and security becomes less important than payment in purchasing power, or because work is more valuable when there are more satisfactions that it can buy—so it becomes necessary to ration the use made of them and account closely for it. Like expensive computing time, people must be used to the full when switched on and be either instantly transferable to another function when one job is completed or else simply switched off.[51]

Boyle dramatically points to the need for members of technological society to be "switched on" or immediately transferred to another task; efficiency is an ultimate value. In this scenario, individuals are thought of as commodities with value only insofar as they efficiently serve the ends of the market economy.

48. Ibid. "Il a le sentiment que le recours à une forme extérieure est précisément une espèce de pareses; qui'il faut consacrer toutes les forces de l'homme qui sera la demiurge de l'homme, et qui'il créera l'humanité heureuse et libérée de demain."

49. Ibid., 133. "Il habitué l'esprit à des demarches qui sont très différentes de celles par lesquelles le monde religieux peut être abordé."

50. Ibid. "Il n'y a jamais que des hypotheses qui peuvent être remplacées par d'autres hypotheses et qui se vérifient à leur efficacité concrete."

51. Boyle, *Who Are We Now?: Christian Humanism and the Global Market from Hegel to Heaney*, 28. See also his "Understanding Thatcherism," 307–24.

The Crisis of Interiority and the Truly Human City

Religious life, on the other hand, is inherently inefficient. Efficiency entails a speeding up of the tempo of life. Contemplation entails a slowing down of the pace of life. Prayer demands the time and quiet that allows the individual the ability to seek the presence of God. As was noted earlier, Daniélou maintains that prayer is rendered nearly impossible to all except those that are privy to a rule which insures the necessary pace for contemplation. "The first thing that strikes one is that our technological civilization brings about a change in the rhythm of human existence. There is a speeding up of tempo which makes it more difficult to find the minimum of freedom on which a minimum life of prayer depends. These are elementary problems, but none the less basic. Prayer is thus rendered almost impossible for most men, unless they display a heroism and a strength of character of which . . . the majority of men are not capable."[52]

Mauriac dramatically poses the problem and notes the results of the pace of modern life in *Le Mystère Frontenac*. Mauriac's young mystic hero observes the world around him:

> It was the hour when the work-rooms all fill up again, when the Metro sucks in and vomits forth a crowd of ants with human faces. For a long while, Yves, with fascinated gaze, followed this ingurgitation, this spewing out, of human creatures. A day was coming—he felt sure of it, and, from the depths of his despair and weariness, he called upon it—when all men and women would be forced to obey this tidal rhythm, all, without one single exception. . . . Yves thought: "I must live to see that day when the lock-gates will open and close at stated intervals before the human flood. When that time comes, no inherited fortune will make it possible for any Frontenac to stand aloof on pretext of thinking, of indulging in despair, or writing a Journal, of praying, of achieving a personal salvation. . . . Yes, the human being, as such, will have been destroyed, and with his destruction will have disappeared that torment and that dear delight which we call love. No longer will those lunatics exist who can see infinity within the finite.[53]

---

52. Daniélou, *L'Oraison Problème Politique*, 31. "La civilization au milieu de laquelle nous nous trouvons rend la prière difficile. Il est certain tout d'abord que la civilization technique entraîne une modification du rhythme de l'existence humaine, une acceleration du temps qui rendent plus difficile à trouver le minimum d'espace dont a besoin un minimum de vie d'oraison. Ces problems sone élémentaires et pourtant fondamentaux. La prière est ainsi rendue quasi impossible à la plupart des homes, en dehors d'un heroism, d'une force de volonté sont nous devons reconnaître que la majorité des homes n'est pas capable."

53. Mauriac, *Le Mystère Frontenac*, 240–41; ET *The Frontenacs*, 174–75.

Jean Danielou's Doxological Humanism

Mauriac conflates natural imagery and mechanistic imagery to convey the intense pace of modern society. At once, he sees bustling humanity as buzzing flies and dragonflies and swarming ants which quickly move from task to task to task and as the scatological export of the rhythmic mechanical world. This entire existence eviscerates the spiritual human who contemplates the infinite within the framework of the finite world.

The inherent inefficiency of religion is a major critique of Christianity by technological society. Daniélou notes, "this criterion tends to become the measure of all things, spiritual realities are denounced as lacking in pragmatic effectiveness in respect to the concrete transformation of human life. This is one of the objections most current: Christianity is of no use to us for the task that lies before us, namely, the transformation of man's material condition."[54] This is but one among many obstacles the modern world poses to religious life. Indeed, Daniélou notes other impediments in the areas of epistemology, morality, ethics and other points of hindrance.[55] The inefficiency of the required rhythm for a life of contemplation is a stark contrast to the pace that is required by technological civilizations.

Mauriac's vision also points out another aspect that Daniélou pointed to as a primary obstacle to the contemplative vocation of all humans. Because of the nature of modern society, the person of the contemporary world is unable to partake of the necessary amount of solitude to enter into a contemplative state. Daniélou notes, "The problem with which we have to deal here is not simply that of prayer. In a more general manner, we are concerned with the possibility of personal existence. This is not a problem for only the religious man alone. It is of interest to all men, for all are threatened with becoming mere units in a collective existence."[56]

Perhaps the obstacle which is most subversive of Christian spirituality is the general desacralization of society by technology. Prior to the advent of secularization of previously sacral civilization, "collective existence was impregnated with religious values" and by means of this fact "there was

---

54. Daniélou, *Scandaleuse Vérité*, 133. "Or, ce critère tend à devenir la mesure de toutes choses; et *les réalités spirituelles sont dénoncées comme manquant d'efficacité quant à la transformation concrete de l'existence humaine.* Ceci est une des objections que nous rencontrons le plus couramment: le christianisme ne nous sert à rien pour ce que nous avons à faire et qui est de transformer la condition matérielle de l'homme."

55. Ibid., 133–43.

56. Daniélou, *L'Oraison Problème Politique*, 32–33. "Il ne s'agit pas seulement ici du problème de l'oraison, mais, d'une manière plus generale, de la possibilité de l'existence personnelle. Ce problème n'intéresse donc pas seulement l'homme religieux. Il intéresse tout home, menace de n'être qu'un element d'une existence collective."

formed a world in which the very framework of living provide a constantly renewed contact with sacred things."[57] Technological society eviscerated this reality and left many societies without recourse to the divine. If one accepts the radical division between the sacred and the profane, access to the life of prayer will be made nearly impossible for the greater part of mankind. Thus Daniélou maintains, "A world which had built up its culture without reference to God, a humanism from which adoration was completely absent, would make the maintenance of a positive religious point of view impossible for the great majority of [people]."[58]

The problem that these obstacles pose is that if most people are unable to practice a basic function of the Christian life, i.e. contemplation, then the spiritual life of the Church is reserved for the spiritual élite rather than accessible to the great masses of those everyday Christians in the Church. Daniélou continually maintains that "l'Église est l'Église de tous."[59] When the life of the Church is reserved for a small spiritual elite, the full-blossoming of Christian life becomes inaccessible to the large majority of Christians. Technological society is inherently at odds with the facet of Christian life that enables believers to move toward their true vocation and end: contemplation of and participation in the fullness of the life of the Trinity.

Yet, the contemplative posture is essential to the nature of humanity and as a result must be accounted for. It is clear that the positive benefits of technological society are without parallel. At the same time it has introduced an imbalance within the human domain. With the benefits of technological society, there is also "a certain disturbance of the cultural balance, and consequently of the balance of man himself."[60] In order to realize humanity in its fullest stature there must be a place accorded for contemplative practice.

---

57. Ibid., 33–34. Lorsque l'existence collective était imprégnée de valuers religieuses, un univers était créé, où le contact avec le sacré était perpétuellement transmis à travers les structures memes de la vie.

58. Ibid., 35. "Un monde où la culture se constituerait totalement en dehors de Dieu, un humanism dont l'adoration serait totalement absente, rendrait pratiquement impossible à la majorité des hommes le maintien d'une certain attitude religieuse."

59. Ibid., 29.

60. Daniélou, *La Crise Actuelle d'Intelligence*, 13. "Il est evident aussi qu'il risqué d'y avoir, de ce fait, un certain déséquilibre de culture, et par suite un certain déséquilibre de l'homme lui-même."

Prayer and the Common Good: Toward a Truly Human City

When examining the relationship between the spiritual life and public affairs, it is important to keep in mind Daniélou's declaration that "For us, for who a relationship to God represents an essential human dimension, for us, where there is no civilization where the function of adoration is not represented, this problem is a vital one."[61] This profession lies at the crux of Daniélou's thought concerning prayer and its relationship to political societies. First, it points to the fact that one's relationship to God and the means by which his presence is experienced is not something that one can either take or leave. The encounter with God through prayer and adoration is essential to the very nature of human being. In contrast to the idea that the totality of the human person is expressed through his engagement with temporal affairs, Daniélou argues that the human person is only ascertained in his fullness when societies allow him to reach his fullness in prayer and contemplation. As such, it is by virtue of its bearing on the core of the human person that prayer and adoration are prerequisite for the individual's "full blooming."[62] Secondly, it points to the fact that since prayer is an essential dimension of the human person and since civil societies purport to create an "order in which personal fulfillment is possible, where man might be able completely to fulfill his destiny," then it is necessary for these societies to maintain an order which allows for spiritual fulfillment as well as material fulfillment.[63]

For Daniélou, one who—either by choice or by deprivation—does not participate in the contemplative life is missing an essential aspect of human activity. He insists that "a man who does not pray is not a man. He lacks something essential. He is in part mutilated."[64] If as Daniélou maintains prayer and adoration are constitutive elements of human existence and if

61. Daniélou, "L'Oraison comme Problème Politique," 62. "Pour nous, pour qui la relation à Dieu représente une dimension essentielle de l'homme, pour nous, pour qui il n'y a pas de civilization sans que la function de l'adoration y soit représentée, ce problème est un problème vital."

62. Daniélou, "Schema 13 . . . The Theology of Temporal Action: Guidelines for Constructing the World of Tomorrow," 345. "Schema 13" was the provisional title for *Gaudium et Spes*.

63. Daniélou, *L'Oraison Problème Politique*, 25–26. "La politique doit le souci du bien commun, c'est-à-dire le souci de créer un ordre où l'epanouissement de la personne soit possible, où l'homme puisse réaliser pleinement sa destinée."

64. Daniélou, *Évangile et Monde Moderne*, 57. "Un home qui ne prie pas n'est pas un home. Il lui manqué quelque chose d'essentiel. Il est motile d'une part de lui-même."

it is the task of political society to allow for the full human development of the objects of its governance, then a place must be secured where such a full human blooming may occur. It is in this regard that prayer becomes an object for societal consideration, or, as Daniélou provocatively refers to it, prayer becomes a "problème politique."

Within the context of civic protection of religious practices, it is important to note precisely what Daniélou means by the terms *oraison* and *politique*. Importantly, Daniélou uses within this context either *oraison* or *prière* rather than the term *contemplation* which he reserves for more advanced forms of prayer and which is a perfection of the more basic and universal *oraison*. In this very general sense of the word, prayer is very simply "spiritual experience oriented towards God."[65] Because of the intentionally general quality of his definition of prayer within this context, it is necessary to limit out some of the more nebulous notions that might fit the description of *oraison* provided by Daniélou. First, by prayer he does not mean a general spiritual experience which is constituted by an awakening of a person to himself.[66] Secondly, by *oraison* (within this specific context) Daniélou occludes any particularly Christian notions of prayer and instead focuses on prayer as the interior aspect of all religions and as a fundamental aspect of all humanism.[67] For Daniélou, any prayer that seeks an encounter with the presence of the Trinitarian God of Christianity is most often—though not exclusively—referred to as contemplation rather than prayer. However, when Daniélou seeks to foster an environment where prayer is possible, at the same time he ensures a place for Christian contemplation as well.

For Daniélou, *politique* simply refers to the "sphere of the temporal common good."[68] But, unlike many conceptions of the common good, he believes that the common good entails securing the benefits of the human person in its entirety rather than simply the material good of the individual. In viewing the human individual as a unity which is constituted not merely by its material existence but also by its spiritual existence. "To deny this," he declaims, "would be to fall victim to that most detestable form of idealism which separates spiritual existence from its material and sociological

---

65. Daniélou, *L'Oraison Problème Politique*, 23. "J'entends ici par oraison l'expérience spirituelle orientée vers Dieu."

66. Ibid. "D'une part, l'expérience spirituelle qui serait seulement une certain prise de conscience par l'homme de lui-même."

67. Ibid., 23–24.

68. Ibid., 25. "J'entends ici car politique la sphère du bien commun temporal."

substratum."[69] Instead, he argues that "man is a unity; that is to say, that there is a fundamental connection between the problems of the body and those of the soul."[70] Politics, as such, must secure an order where total human flourishing is possible by providing for the opportunity to achieve both material and spiritual fulfillment. Within this context, the political realm is not an end in itself, but provides conditions where proper ends may be achieved. In this respect, Daniélou notes Jeanne Hirsch's contention that "politics is not in itself creative, but it does provide the conditions in which something can be done." The political sphere is neutral and only becomes a positive or negative value by virtue of the values that flourish given the conditions of political systems. This is the case with prayer and politics. Politics is negative, if it "does not create the conditions in which man can completely fulfill himself, it becomes an impediment to that fulfillment."[71]

Some have argued that the realms of politics and prayer are foreign to each other. This is not a separation of Church and the state but an argument that the one can contribute nothing to the other. Daniélou gives voice to this position when he notes, "One wonders whether this is not a false impression. Indeed politics and prayer are two realities that one is not accustomed to seeing brought near to each other."[72] Many have argued that prayer is a strictly personal matter. They object, "Prayer is a personal relationship with God. Does it not, therefore, belong strictly to personal life?"[73] Daniélou rejoins that while it is true that prayer is indeed personal, a fully developed personal life is impossible to cultivate while society is hostile to an environment which is conducive to spiritual maturation. The society's attitude toward spiritual development bears on the possibility for such a blossoming of personal spiritual life. To this point, Daniélou argues

69. Daniélou, *L'Oraison Problème Politique*, 27. "Le méconnaître serait pécher par cet idealism que nous détestons par-dessus tout, car il sépare l'existence spirituelle de son substrat materiel et sociologique."

70. Ibid. "Or nous croyons profondément que l'homme est un, c'est-à-dire qu'il y a une relation fundamentale entre les problems du corps et ceux de l'âme [However, we profoundly believe that the human person is a unity, that is to say, there is a fundamental relation between the problems of the body and the problems of the spirit."

71. Ibid., 26. "En effet, si la politique ne crée pas un espace où l'homme puisse se réaliser pleinement, elle deviant, en tant qu'elle est responsibilité du collectif, un empêchement à la realization de l'homme."

72. Daniélou, "L'Oraison comme Problème Politique," 63. "On s'est demandé s'il n'y avait pas une faute d'impression. En effet, la politique et l'oraison sont deux réalités que l'on n'a pas l'habitude de voir rapprochées l'une de l'autre."

73. Daniélou, *L'Oraison Problème Politique*, 27. "Est-ce que l'oraison, relation personnelle à Dieu, ne relève pas strictement de l'existence personnelle?"

that there is a necessary interrelation between the realms of public policy and between the interior life of the individuals which are members of a society. He argues that there is a "dialogue between prayer and politics, that both one and the other [are] necessary and in a sense complimentary."[74]

Typically, civil societies seek the common good of its members by the elimination of the exploitation of individuals from without and from within, by the security of peace between it and other societies, by the encouragement of an interchange of knowledge between its members, by the elimination of every sort of racism, as well as innumerable other goods which it seeks to provide. However, Daniélou argues, "politics limited to these objectives would still not assure a complete temporal common good."[75] Daniélou was fond of quoting Giorgio La Pira who contended that a true city is one "in which men have their homes and God has his."[76] For Daniélou, this means that a true city must protect both the material and spiritual well-being of its members else it does not meet the criteria of a truly human city. To this point, Daniélou writes, "A city which does not possess churches as well as factories is not fit for men. It is inhuman."[77] The true city is the one which provides for the complete fulfillment of persons through the realization of those aspects which are essential to a true humanity. It is insofar that the spiritual life in general and prayer in particular express an essential dimension of the individual's ability that prayer becomes *un problème politique*. As Daniélou maintains, "Prayer is a political problem; for a city which would make prayer impossible would fail to fulfill its role as a city."[78]

---

74. Daniélou, "L'Oraison comme Problème Politique," 63. "Il y avait un dialogue de la prière et de la politique, que l'un et l'autre étaient nécessaires et en un sens complémentaires."

75. Daniélou, *L'Oraison Problème Politique*, 26. "Mais si la politique limitait à cela ses objectifs, elle n'assurerait pas un bien commun temporel total."

76. Giorgio La Pira was an Italian jurist and politician who was a professor of Roman law at the University of Florence beginning in 1933. He was the representative of the Christian Democratic Party in the Constituent Assembly. In 1951 he became the mayor of Florence. In his governmental service he sought to improve the conditions of the poor and dialogued with the Communists of the time. He was a committed Catholic who practiced an ascetic lifestyle and worked to realize Catholic ideals through his political activity. *Dictionary of Christian Biography*, 744.

77. Daniélou, *L'Oraison Problème Politique*, 26. "Une cite où il n'y a pas d'églises à côté des usines est une cite inhumaine."

78. Ibid., 27. "C'est en quoi nous pensons qu'en tant qu'elle exprime cet épanouissement personnel d'une dimension particulière de l'homme, l'oraison est un problème politique, dans la mesure où une cite qui la rendrait impossible trahirait son role de cité."

SIX

Daniélou's Doxological Humanism

IN THE PROCESS OF articulating Daniélou's vision of the act of contemplation, an overarching theme has emerged throughout each of the topics covered which relate to his understanding of prayer. This theme can be described as Daniélou's doxological humanism. The human person *qua* human is only able to find true happiness (*eudaimonia*) when he realizes that he has a vocation—an essential human quality—which is realized in worship, adoration, and contemplation. In an effort to elucidate what is meant by this, it seems worthwhile to look into some key texts—both classical and modern—which will help to underscore the nature of the relationship between contemplation and Daniélou's understanding of the essential qualities of the human person.

Contemplation, Habituation, and the City

Daniélou shows a certain familiarity with Platonism—especially given his studies concerning such prominent Christian Platonists as Origen and Gregory of Nyssa.[1] He also seems to be much more attracted to Christian theologians of a Platonic heritage (e.g., Gregory, Augustine, and Origen) rather than their Aristotelian counterparts. With this in mind, a short look at the relationship between contemplation and the well-being of the city will be helpful in developing Daniélou's doxological humanism. In this

---

1. See Daniélou, *Origène* and *Platonisme et Théologie Mystique: Doctrine Spirituelle de Grégory de Nysse*.

Daniélou's Doxological Humanism

regard, the "allegory of the cave" in *The Republic* seems to most directly bear on the topic at hand.[2]

There may be no more well-known philosophical text than Plato's allegory of the cave. Yet, a fresh reading of the text within the context of Daniélou's theology of prayer and contemplation yields some useful thematic connections, particularly in the area of the contemplative's duty toward the city in light of his experience of the truth. In considering the individual who is released from his bonds to climb out of the subterranean cavern, one is given a vivid picture of the responsibility of the contemplative toward the society which he has left behind.

Plato notes the difficulty that the unfettered individual encounters. "When one was freed from his fetters and compelled to stand up suddenly and turn his head around and walk and to lift up his eyes to the light, and in doing all this felt pain and, because of the dazzle and the glitter of the light, was unable to discern the objects who shadows he formerly saw, what do you suppose would be his answer if someone told him that what he had seen before was all a cheat and an illusion, but that now, being nearer to reality and turned toward more real things, he saw more truly?"[3] This passage brings out two important aspects of the contemplative life. First, the ascent to contemplation had the initial effect of dazzling the contemplative. This recalls Gregory of Nyssa's words concerning the disorientation of ecstasy due to the presence of God. The analogy of the steep cliff used by Gregory forms a sort of inverse symbol that expresses the same phenomenon that Plato's allegory describes. Instead of coming out of the dark into the light, Gregory's contemplative stands on the precipice gazing at God's infinity: "And thus the soul, slipping at every point from what cannot be grasped, becomes dizzy and perplexed and returns once again to what is connatural to it."[4] Secondly, this initial disorientation due to the experience of true reality requires a period of habituation as the individual ascends in contemplation. If the process of habituation is not allowed to take place, the "light itself, would . . . pain his eyes" and he would "turn away and flee to those things which he is able to discern and regard them as in very deed more clear and exact" than the light he perceived through contemplation.[5] Unless

---

2. All passages will be from Plato, *The Republic*, trans. by Paul Shorey in *The Collected Dialogues of Plato*.

3. Ibid., 515C–D.

4. Gregory of Nyssa, *In Ecclesiasten Salomonis*, sermon 7 (PG 44.729D–732D).

5. Plato, *Republic*, 515E.

the contemplative is "accustomed" to the light (to use Irenaeus' terminology), the soul seeks to return to what is "connatural to it" (to use Gregory of Nyssa's terminology).[6] Socrates contends, "then there would be need of habituation . . . to enable him to see the things higher up. And at first he would most easily discern the shadows and, after that, the likenesses or reflections in water of men and other things, and later, the things themselves, and from these he would go on to contemplate the appearances in the heavens and heaven itself, more easily by night, looking at the light of the stars and the moon, than by day the sun and the sun's light."[7] After this period of habituation, it is possible for the contemplative to "look upon the sun itself and see its true nature, not by reflections in water or phantasms of it in an alien setting, but in and by itself in its own place."[8]

Importantly, Socrates asks of Glaucon what the result would be if the enlightened one were again to descend into the darkness of the cave and take up his place again with his bondsmen: "If such a one should go down again and take his old place would he not get his eyes full of darkness, thus suddenly coming out of the sunlight?"[9] When the contemplative condescends to contend with the bondsmen he becomes an object of ridicule and harm because the ones who remain in the dark are not able to comprehend what has been seen by the one who ascended to the heights of contemplation. Nonetheless, Socrates contends that anyone who is to act rightly in either private or public affairs must have been privy to these revelations.[10] However, those who have attained such heights are often reluctant to descend in order to seek the welfare of the society which he has left behind. Socrates leads Glaucon further along his line of thought: "Do not be surprised that those who have attained to this height are not willing to occupy themselves with the affairs of men, but their souls ever feel the upward urge and the yearning for that sojourn above."[11] In light of this fact, Socrates contends that it is the duty of "the founders" to compel people of vision to "attain knowledge . . . and to win to the vision of the good, to scale that ascent."[12]

---

6. Irenaeus, *Adversus Haeresus*, IV.14.2 (PG 7.1011A–1011C) and Gregory of Nyssa, *Commentarius in Canticum Canticorum*, Hom. VII (PG 44.732A).

7. Ibid., 516A-B.

8. Ibid., 516B.

9. Ibid., 516E.

10. Ibid., 517C.

11. Ibid., 517C-D.

12. Ibid., 519C-D.

Daniélou's Doxological Humanism

But, while persons of vision and knowledge should be encouraged to seek further enlightenment through contemplative ascent, Socrates argues that they should not be allowed to linger and refuse to come down. The one who sees the light of truth through contemplation must render service to his fellow citizens. Socrates reminds Glaucon that "the law is not concerned with the special happiness of any class in the state, but with trying to produce this condition in the city as a whole, harmonizing and adapting the citizens to one another by persuasion and compulsion, and requiring them to impart to one another any benefit which they are severally able to bestow upon the community, and that it itself creates such men in the state, not that it may allow each to take what course pleases him, but with a view to using them for the binding together of the commonwealth."[13]

For Plato, the contemplative citizen returns from the heights of contemplation in order to lead the city to a greater happiness for all. Only once the contemplative returns to the "habitation of the others and accustoms [himself] to the observances of obscure things there" will the city have true happiness available to all through the reciprocal habituation of its people. This happiness is in turn the enlightenment of others who then take their charge to do the same in their own turn.

Pleasure, Humanism, and Contemplation

Though Daniélou was more directly engaged with Platonism than Aristotelianism, a brief look at Aristotle's understanding of the relationship between pleasure, contemplation and how the relationship between the two is a distinctly and characteristically human possibility further sheds light on Daniélou's vision of the contemplative calling of humanity. Aristotle's most condensed consideration of the topic of pleasure is located in Book X of the *Nicomachean Ethics*.[14]

At the outset of his discussion of pleasure, Aristotle surveys the possible attitudes toward it. In short order, he rejects the notions that 1) pleasure is itself the supreme Good and, in turn, 2) that not only is pleasure not the Good but does not contribute to the Good—indeed it is altogether bad. In the first case, Aristotle tells that Eudoxus maintained that since "all creatures, rational and irrational alike, seek to obtain it," pleasure is the

---

13. Ibid., 519E–520A.
14. All passages will be from Aristotle, *Nicomachean Ethics*, LCL 73.

"the Supreme Good."[15] Eudoxus also postulated that pleasure was the Good because its obverse, i.e. pain, is universally avoided. By this logic, its opposite, pleasure, is universally sought by all. Aristotle does not completely reject Eudoxus' analysis; instead, he argues that while pleasure is *a* good, it is not *the* Good.[16] In the second case, Aristotle argues against those who believe that pleasure is a good at all or only good in certain instances.[17] Despite their arguments, Aristotle dismisses these individuals as "surely talking nonsense."[18]

Aristotle then provides his own assessment of pleasure. He begins with the contention that pleasure is not a form of motion or a process of change which would indicate its nature as a means rather than an end. For Aristotle, pleasure is "a whole, and one cannot at any moment put one's hand on a pleasure which will only exhibit its specific quality perfectly if its duration be prolonged."[19] Unlike motion or generation, pleasure is perfect at any moment of duration. Furthermore, every moment of "pleasurable consciousness is a perfect whole."[20]

Another quality of pleasure is important to note and entails the perceiver and the object of pleasure. The value of the pleasure is affected by the condition of the organ which perceives the pleasure. Likewise, the value of the pleasure is affected by the quality of the object which this organ perceives. Aristotle expresses this when he writes, "Inasmuch as each of the senses act in relation to its object, and acts perfectly when it is in good condition and directed to the finest of the objects that belong to it . . . , it follows that the activity of any of the senses is at its best when the sense-organ being

---

15. Ibid., X.ii.1.

16. "The life of pleasure . . . is more desirable in combination with intelligence than without it; but if pleasure combined with something else is better than pleasure alone, it is not the Good, for the Good is not rendered more desirable by the addition of anything to it. And it is clear that nothing else either will be the Good if it becomes more desirable when combined with something good in itself." Ibid., X.ii.3.

17. Ibid., X.ii.4–X.iii.12. See also VII.xi.2–5.

18. In summary, these arguments are 1) to prove that pleasure is not good at all: a) pleasure is a process toward a state, b) temperate individuals avoid pleasures, c) prudent individuals seek freedom from pain rather than pleasure, d) pleasure distracts from "prudent deliberation," e) there is not an art of pleasure, f) children and animals pursue pleasure; and 2) not all pleasures are good: a) some pleasures are disgraceful, b) some pleasures are harmful. These arguments are followed by an excursus on why pleasure is not the Good even if pleasures are seen as goods in a more general sense.

19. Ibid., X.iv.1.

20. Ibid., X.iv.4.

in the best condition is directed to the best of its objects; and this activity will be the most perfect and the pleasantest."[21] Here Aristotle introduces a hierarchy of pleasure. For instance, Aristotle prefers non-material perception over perception through contact. Therefore, for Aristotle, vision, olfaction and audition are superior to flavor and touch. The importance here is that while each occurrence of pleasure may be entire to itself and be a good (or partake of the Good), they are of relative value dependent on the health of the perceptive faculty and the object which is perceived.

Aristotle then goes on to note that like activities, pleasures differ in their moral value and may be adopted, rejected or have a neutral moral value, "for each activity has a pleasure of its own. Thus the pleasure of a good activity is morally good, that of a bad one morally bad" and that of a neutral one morally neutral.[22] With this in mind, it follows that some pleasures are better than others. Aristotle demonstrates this tendency to hierarchize pleasures in his treatment of the senses. "Sight excels touch in purity, and hearing and smell excel taste; and similarly the pleasures of the intellect excel in purity the pleasures of sensation, while the pleasures of either class differ among themselves in purity."[23] He establishes that the intellectual senses are superior to both immaterial and material senses.

This hierarchy of pleasure extends from animal pleasures to particularly human pleasures and, from within the human species of pleasure, from the immoral person to the good person. There is a great variety of esteem given to different pleasures among people ("the same things delight some men and annoy others," X.v.9), but, Aristotle contends, it is only to the good man that the thing which pleases is rightly understood to be truly pleasant. "If this rule is sound, as it is generally held to be, and if the standard of everything is goodness, or the good man, *qua* good, then the things that seem to him to be pleasures are pleasures, and the things he enjoys are pleasant."[24]

At this point, given that animal pleasures and disgraceful pleasures are not "pleasures at all, except to the depraved," the question arises of which pleasures are "distinctively human" in nature. He notes, "pleasures correspond to the activities which they belong; it is therefore that pleasure, or those pleasures, by which the activity, or the activities, of the perfect and

21. Ibid., X.iv.5.
22. Ibid., X.v.6.
23. Ibid., X.v.7.
24. Ibid., X.v.10.

supremely happy man are perfected, that must be pronounced human in the fullest sense."[25] When one looks to the truly happy person to find what yields the most perfect pleasure and conduces to the most perfect happiness, one finds that the greatest human pleasure is to be found in what is self-sufficient, i.e., it is an end in itself rather than a means to another good and it is not perfected by other goods. For Aristotle, this pleasure is contemplation. "But if happiness consists in activity in accordance with virtue, it is reasonable that it should be the activity in accordance with the highest virtue; and this will be the virtue of the best part in us. Whether then this be the intellect, or whatever else it be that is thought to rule and lead us by nature, and to have cognizance of what is noble and divine, either as being itself also actually divine, or as being relatively the divinest part of us, it is the activity of this part of us in accordance with the virtue proper to it that will constitute perfect happiness; and it has already been stated that this activity is the activity of contemplation."[26] Furthermore, the exercise of the intellect in the activity of contemplation is that which raises humanity into the realm of the divine. Contemplation distinguishes humanity from animal life which is unable to partake of the happiness of contemplation and raises humanity godward establishing contemplation as constitutive of the highest humanity.

Catholic Humanism in the Twentieth Century

Following on the heels of Aristotle's vision of the true happiness of humanity, it is interesting to note a statement that Maritain attributes to him. Aristotle contends, "To propose to man only the human ... is to betray man and to wish him misfortune, because by the principle part of him, which is the spirit, man is called to better than a purely human life."[27] One's response to Aristotle's contention entirely depends on how exactly one conceives the human. And, it is here that the equivocality of the term *humanism* is brought to light. For Aristotle, while it is important for humanity to seek to separate itself from a purely animal life, it is more important still for humanity to press on past what is merely human life. However, Maritain warns, one should not define humanism "by the exclusion of all reference to

---

25. Ibid., X.v.11.
26. Ibid., X.vii.1.
27. Quoted in Maritain. *Humanisme Intégral*, 10; ET: *Integral Humanism*, 2.

the superhuman and by the denial of transcendence."[28] With this in mind, Maritain proposes the following definition of *humanism*: that which "tends essentially to render man more truly human, and to manifest his original greatness by having him participate in all that which can enrich him in nature and in history."[29] Thus, to develop a more true humanism, the demand is put upon humanity to "develop virtualities contained within him, his creative forces and the life of reason, and work to make the forces of the physical world instruments of his freedom."[30] The humanism proposed by Maritain is at odds with those species of humanism which places humanity itself at the center. Instead, Maritain argues for a theocentric humanism which posits a humanity that is informed by its creation in the image of God, its relation to the Incarnation and its ultimate realization designated by the beatific vision.

Besides Maritain, the Catholic world in the twentieth century produced a great many Christian humanists who sought to debunk the prevailing vision of modern humanism. In his *Le Drame de l'Humanisme Athée*, Henri de Lubac argued that the anti-Christian humanism of Marx, Nietzsche and Comte all eventually subvert the human rather than maximize its realization.[31] Indeed, the common element in the Marxist, the Nietzchean and the Comptean humanisms is their eventual "annihilation of the human person."[32] Thus, Susan K. Wood tells us, "de Lubac in his Christocentrism offers an anthropology that is fundamentally communitarian rather than individualistic while at the same time enhancing the dignity of the human individual. By converting anthropology to Christology, de Lubac responds to atheist humanism with a Christian humanism wherein a person realizes his greatness, not by getting rid of God, but by participating in the divine life."[33]

John Paul II was perhaps the greatest witness to a vibrant Christian humanism in the face of humanisms built upon the premise that humanity can and should thrive without reference to the divine. He trenchantly believed that these forms of humanism, rather than raising humanity to a

28. Ibid.
29. Ibid.
30. Ibid.
31. De Lubac, *Le Drame de l'Humanisme Athée*; ET: *The Drama of Atheist Humanism*.
32. Wood, *Spiritual Exegesis and the Church in the Theology of Henri de Lubac*, 138.
33. Ibid. See also de Lubac's "La recherché d'un homme nouveau," 2–92 and *Catholicisme: les Apsects Sociaux du Dogme*.

new stature, "consist[ed] in the first place a kind of degradation, indeed in a pulverization, of the fundamental uniqueness of each human person."[34] In response, John Paul II maintained that "to this disintegration planned at times by atheistic ideologies we must oppose, rather than sterile polemics, a kind of 'recapitulation' of the inviolable mystery of the person."[35] This humanism—what has often been referred to as John Paul II's *personalism*—provides a radical "response to a century in which false humanisms had created mountains of corpses and an ocean of blood."[36]

Benedict XVI has continued the witness of John Paul II in continually calling for a "new humanism" as an alternative to the regnant humanisms of the twentieth century. In 2008, Benedict addressed the Pontifical Council for Justice and Peace and asked, "How can we respond to these challenges? How can we recognize the 'signs of the times'? Certainly, joint action on a political, economic and juridical level is needed but, even before that, it is necessary to reflect together on a moral and spiritual level. What is ever more vital is to promote a 'new humanism.'"[37] Indeed, in Benedict's first encyclical as the Holy Father, he described this true humanism as consisting in "the fact that man, through a life of fidelity to the one God, comes to experience himself as loved by God, and discovers joy in truth and in righteousness—a joy in God which becomes his essential happiness."[38] For Benedict, this Christian humanism is grounded in the truth that *Deus caritas est*, a humanism very different from the anthropocentric humanisms of the previous century.

Each of these thinkers provided an alternative vision for humanism in the twentieth century and beyond. And, in many ways they converge with the Christian anthropology promoted by Daniélou. Daniélou seeks what is essential to the human person. What he locates is the basic human need for prayer, adoration and worship and thus I refer to as his anthropology as a "Doxological Humanism."

---

34. A letter from Karol Wojtyla to Henri de Lubac from February 1968. Quoted in Henri de Lubac, *Mémoire sur l'occasion des mes écrits*; ET: *At the Service of the Church: Henri de Lubac on the Circumstances that Occasioned His Writings*, 171.

35. Ibid., 172.

36. Weigel, "John Paul II and the Crisis of Humanism," 32.

37. "Letter of His Holiness Benedict XVI to Cardinal Renato Raffaele Martino on the Occasion of the International Seminar organized by the Pontifical Council For Justice and Peace on 'Disarmament, Development and Peace: Prospects for Integral Disarmament,'" §1.

38. Benedict XVI, *Deus Caritas Est*, §9.

Daniélou's Doxological Humanism

In a 1972 international Thomistic congress whose proceedings were published under the title *De Homine: Studia Hodiernae Anthropologiae*, Daniélou posed the question: "Y a-t-il Une Nature Humaine?"[39] In his address, he sought to demonstrate the existence of an irreducible human reality.[40] In light of this contention, Daniélou notes three primary oppositions to the irreducible reality of human nature.

The first of these is connected with the development of the modern sciences and the extension of its domain to include all areas of human life. Whereas modern science and its concomitant disciplines began with the physical world, it soon began to extend its reach into the domain of the human person. Once this process was begun, the scientific worldview gave its own estimation of human nature and allowed the human person "to throw off constraints and to model himself according to his own will."[41] From this point of view, there is no objective human reality; humanity is what it makes itself out to be by the exertion of its own power and knowledge. While there are certain validities in this attitude, for the most part it has brought about a crisis in human definition by relieving the *humanum* of its content. Daniélou contends, "On the pretext of reducing reality to what can be known by scientific methods, [a crisis of culture] empties it of its content. In fact, at the level of scientific methods there are only structures and there is no content. In this way the objective reality of the universe is contested, for in fact science does not reach it in its ontological [reality]. *There will be denial too of the reality of man, reduced finally to being a mere aggregate of words.*"[42] Due to the success of the science and its method of discovery for the physical and natural world, other fields have begun to

---

39. Daniélou, "Y a-t-il une Nature Humaine?," 5–12; ET: "Does a Human Nature Exist," 8 and 11. All subsequent English translations of this text will be to the English edition of *L'Osservatore Romano* unless noted otherwise.

40. Ibid., 5. "Mon propos est de montrer l'existence d'une réalité humaine irréducible, quel que soit le nom dont on la désigne."

41. Ibid. "L'artificiel, la technique, la culture permettent désormais à l'homme de n'être plus soumis aux contraintes et de se modeler suivant son vouloir."

42. Emphasis added. Ibid., 6. "En prétendant réduire la réalité à ce qui peut être connu par elles, la méthode scientifique en vient à la vider de son contenu. Elle se situe en effet à un niveau où il n'y a que de structures et où il n'y a pas des contenu. On en viendra ainsi à contester la réalité objective de l'univers, parce qu'en effet la science ne l'atteint pas dans sa réalité ontologique. On contestera la réalité de l'homme, réduit ultimement être un agrégat de mots."

apply scientific technique to their own domains. But, the human element is much more elusive than the physical sciences admit because of its "personal mystery, [its] inaccessible spirituality, [its] high dignity."[43] Contrariwise, Daniélou ardently maintains that there is an objective reality of humanity, an objective human nature with identifiable essentialities. Furthermore, it is clear that the fact "that there is a nature of things is a recognition of the transcendence on which [their nature] is based; it is finally, as the [ancient stoics] had already perceived, to [be conformed] to God's plan."[44]

The second obstacle to establishing an objective human reality is the reduction of the human to a purely social phenomenon. Along with Marxist philosophy, this posture posits that humanity is not *partly* social in nature but *merely* social in nature. While Christian humanism proffers a view of humanity where "it is with participation in social existence that man comes to realize his essence" (at least in part), Marxist humanism sees humanity's complete identity in collective relationships.[45] In this conception of humanity, society defines the human element which yields an absolutely subjective view of humanity since each society provides its own definition of what it means to be human. Ultimately, this sociality ends in a radical individualism once subjectivity is introduced into the equation. What begins as a measure of humanity from society to society ends in each individual being his own standard of what it means to be human. But, Daniélou argues, "it is necessary that there should be an element common to all and therefore [transcendent] to all, that which makes every man a man."[46]

The third opposition to a universal human nature is often manifested in the anthropological sciences which posit that the human is that which is manifested at any given point in human society. "What we call nature is nothing but a state of fact corresponding to a certain moment of civilization."[47] There is inherent within this view a relativism which subverts the contention of Christian humanism that there are inherent qualities of

---

43. Ibid.

44. Ibid., 7. "Il y a une nature des choses, c'est reconnaître la transcendance qui la fonde, que se conformer à la nature, c'est finalement, comme les vieux stoïciens l'avaient vu, se conformer au dessein de Dieu."

45. Ibid., 7–8. "C'est par sa participation à l'existence sociale que l'homme réalise son essence."

46. Ibid., 9. "Il faut qu'il y ait un élément commun à tous et donc transcendant à tous, ce qui fait que tout homme est un homme."

47. Ibid. "Ce que nous appelons nature ne serait qu'un un état de fait correspondant à un certain moment de la civilization."

Daniélou's Doxological Humanism

humanity which make them human or more truly human. In a similar vein, the structuralist conception stresses "not so much evolution," as above, "as the radical heterogeneity of the types of civilization in relation to one another. It is a far more static vision, which recalls Spengler's cycles. But here too the reference to a human nature is utterly uncontested. There is nothing but equilibria that are constituted at a given time and place."[48] Within this framework, each society embodies it own conventions and its own determinations of what it means to be human, which do not have a universal character. Humanity is situated within events which are continually modified and therefore humanity is perpetually in a state of becoming. To the contrary, Daniélou admits—following Gregory of Nyssa—that temporality is a necessary component of the created order. Indeed, he continues, "what characterizes [created] being is that it is a movement from nothingness to being and that temporality always remains a constitutive part of it."[49] Furthermore, he argues—very much in line with Gregory of Nyssa's notion of perpetual progress and his apophaticism—that human nature is a "passing from being to more being" and "a growth of supernatural knowledge in luminous darkness."[50] In the end, Daniélou fervently argues for the irreducible reality of human nature whose qualities remain the same from one era to another and from this society to that society.

Having established that there is an objective human nature, one must turn to the characterization of that nature. At a conference on September 13, 1951, Daniélou addressed himself directly to the topic of Christianity and humanism. In this address, he maintained that Christianity has a definite view of the human person which entails his creation by God, in God's own image, Christ's redemption of humanity and humanity's consequent rebirth. All of this determines the trajectory for a Christian anthropology

---

48. Ibid., 10. "Très différente est la conception structuraliste. Elle soulignera moins l'évolution que l'hétérogénéité radical des types de civilisation les uns par rapport aux autres. Il s'agit d'une vue beaucoup plus statique, qui rappelle les cycles de Spengler. Mais ici encore le référence à une nature humaine est entièrement contestée. Il n'y a que des équilibres qui se constituent à une époque et dans un milieu donné."

49. Ibid., 11. "Qui caractérise l'être créé est qu'il est mouvement du néant à l'être et que ceci en reste toujours constitutive."

50. Ibid. "Il est passage d'être à plus d'être. Mais cette temporalité, ce développement, joue à l'intérieur de chaque ordre, de chaque nature. Autre est l'évolution dans le monde de la matière, autre la transformation par l'homme de ses conditions d'existence, autre la croissance de la connaissance surnaturelle dans la ténèbre lumineuse."

which supplies a particular vision for the human person, his historical situation and his relationship with other humans.[51]

Daniélou was cautious in talking of a "new humanism" because of the ideological deformations that the idea had associated with it. He warns that the idea of the *homme nouveau* is a myth which makes little sense outside of the context of the *novissimus homo* which is Jesus Christ. And yet, Daniélou would have ardently agreed with his younger confreres such as John Paul II and Benedict XVI that a new humanism formed in the image of Christ and due to the individual's status as a co-heir with Christ was consistent with a particularly Christian view of the human person.[52] It is in this light that the Council declared, "The truth is that only in the mystery of the incarnate Word does the mystery of man take on light. For Adam, the first man, was a figure of Him Who was to come, namely Christ the Lord. Christ, the final Adam, by the revelation of the mystery of the Father and His love, fully reveals man to man himself and makes his supreme calling clear."[53] Indeed, Daniélou himself affirms that it is in Jesus Christ that everything essential is already acquired.[54]

In elucidating his vision of a truly Christian humanism, Daniélou draws attention to the humanisms that exist on the purely human plane. Looking primarily at Nietzsche and Malraux, he speaks of a radically mundane humanism which sees "anything like the presence of God, or relationship with a religious life as an adulterant to genuine humanity."[55]

---

51. Daniélou, "Humanisme et Christianisme," 97. "Certes, le christianisme a une conception de l'homme, créé par Dieu, à son image, racheté par le Christ, et ressuscité par lui. Tout ceci définit une anthropologie caractérisée, qui engage une vision de la nature de l'homme, de sa situation historique, de ses rapports avec autrui."

52. Ibid., 104. "Un second aspect de la déformation idéologique que présente le monde des techniques est la fois au progrès. Ici encore il s'agit, bien sûr, d'un vieux thème, mais d'un vieux thème qui nous apparaît comme perpétuellement rajeuni. Il ne s'agit aucunement de nier les acquisitions que les sciences, dans tous les domaines, nous apportent; mais nous sommes en présence d'autre chose. On nous parle de la création d'un home nouveau; on nous parle d'une nouvelle échelle de valeurs; on nous parle d'un nouvel humanisme. Or il, faut dire que tout ceci est un mythe qui, pour un chrétien, n'a pas de sens. Ceci n'a pas de sens parce que, pour un chrétien, il n'y a d'homme nouveau qu'un seul: celui que l'apôtre Paul appelle le *novissimus homo*, l'homme à jamais le plus nouveau, et qui est Jésus-Christ."

53. *Gaudium et Spes*, §22.

54. Daniélou, "Humanisme et Christianisme," 106. "En Jésus-Christ l'essentiel est déjà acquis."

55. Daniélou, *Scandaleuse Vérité*, 48; ET: *The Scandal of Truth*, 38. All subsequent English translations of this text will be Kerrigan's unless noted otherwise. "En sorte que

For Daniélou, the humanism of the 20th century is one where "the essential temptation is not to do evil, but to show that one has no need of God in order to do good—that is, in short, to show that man is perfectly capable by himself of reaching veritable greatness, and that he has nothing to look for from God."[56] But, while this sort of humanism believes that it can order a virtuous life without reference to God, Daniélou, in line with the great Christian humanists of his time, believed that humanity can only find its true happiness and realize its full potential by being ordered toward the divine.[57] In an intense protest against false humanisms of the 20th century, Daniélou declares that "happiness is the heroic vocation of man" which "does not lie in having this or that, but in the discovery of the meaning of existence and in communion with the absolute."[58]

Daniélou further affirms this position when he notes three primary scriptural conceptions of the human person. The first of these conceptions has to do with human mastery of his environment. Daniélou recalls the passages in Genesis where the animals were brought before the first Adam so that he could name them all and exercise his dominion over them all. Then he was placed in the garden in order to cultivate the land and to exercise dominion over it as well. "A first aspect of biblical man is therefore his terrestrial duty, that of acquiring mastery over the world in order to bring it into his service. Contrary to a prejudice which we meet around us, and which must be demolished forthwith, nothing is more conformable with the biblical vocation of man than the inventory of all the riches of the earth

---

toute présence de Dieu, toute relation à une vie religieuse apparaîtrait comme altérant une certain authenticité d'humanité."

56. Ibid. "Or, ceci me paraît être ce qui représente aujourd'hui la tentation essentielle, celle d'un certain humanism social, celle non pas de faire le mal, mais celle de montrer qu'on n'a pas besoin de Dieu pour faire le bien, c'est-à-dire en somme de montrer que l'homme est parfaitement capable par lui-même d'atteindre les veritable grandeurs et qu'il n'a rien à attendre de Dieu."

57. This is very close to Paul VI's contention in *Populorum progressio*: "The ultimate goal is a fullbodied humanism. And does this not mean the fulfillment of the whole man and of every man? A narrow humanism, closed in on itself and not open to the values of the spirit and to God who is their source, could achieve apparent success, for man can set about organizing terrestrial realities without God. But 'closed off from God, they will end up being directed against man. A humanism closed off from other realities becomes inhuman,'" §42. See also Candler, "Logic of Christian Humanism," 84–91.

58. Daniélou, *Scandaleuse Vérité*, 54 and 56. "Le bonheur est la vocation héroïque de l'homme" and "car le bonheur finalement n'est dans la possession d'aucun bien particulier, mais dans la découverte du sens même de l'existence et dans la communion avec l'absolu."

Jean Danielou's Doxological Humanism

and the discovery of all its resources, for the purpose of making them serve personal development."[59]

The second aspect of the biblical vision of humanity is the bond that persons share with each other. The sociality of the human person is most basically expressed in scripture by God's declaration that it was not good for the man to be alone (Gen 2:18). In this connection, Daniélou notes that the "creation of Eve is not put in relation with the problem of the perpetuation of the species, but in relation with the fact that it is not good that man should be alone."[60] This episode shows that it is an essential element of human nature to enter into communion.

The third aspect of a biblical notion of humanity bears most directly on what I wish to refer to as Daniélou's doxological humanism. He notes, "Man was created in the image of God, which is to say that, for one, he masters the world which is inferior to him; that, for another, he is to be in communion with his fellow-creatures, who are his equals; *but, that finally, he must acknowledge the transcendence of what surpasses him.*"[61] This aspect of the biblical vision of humanity is that of adoration which is "constitutive of the very being of man."[62] From this point of view the human person receives his being from God, or, as St. Paul says, it is from God that "we live and move and have our being" (Acts 17:28). Thus Daniélou writes:

> This relationship with God does not represent some kind of accessory truth, fitted on to a humanism which could exist substantially apart from it, but is constitutive of man as such. Hence a man who refuses to consider it, a man without adoration, is mutilated in his person. When we raise our voice today against every sort of

---

59. Ibid., 158–159. "Un premier aspect de l'homme biblique est donc sa tâche terrestre, celle d'acquérir la maître du monde pour le mettre à son service. Contrairement à un préjugé que nous rencontrons autour de nous, et qu'il faut d'abord démolir, rien n'est plus conforme à la vocation biblique de l'homme que l'inventaire qu'il fait de toutes les richesses de l'univers, de manière, après en avoir découvert les ressources, à les mettre au service de l'épanouissement de sa personnne." This passage is a little disconcerting until the final qualifying statement that dominion is only good if it serves the true development of human persons.

60. Ibid., 159. "La création de la femme n'est pas mise en relation avec le problème de la perpétuation de l'espèce, mais avec le fait qu'il n'est pas bon que l'homme soit seul."

61. Emphasis added. Ibid., 160. "L'homme a été créé à l'image de Dieu, c'est-à-dire que, d'une part, il maîtrise le monde qui lui est inférieur; que, de l'autre, il doit être en communion avec ses semblables qui sont ses égaux, mais qu'enfin il doit reconnaître la transcendance de ce qui le dépasse."

62. Ibid. "Cela est constitutif de l'être meme de l'homme."

atheistic humanism, whether this be marxist humanism or liberal humanism, it is not simply God that we are defending, but man himself. A man without God is not fully human."[63]

For Daniélou, any deviation from the doxological essence of humanity is a falling away from that which constitutes the human person as human.[64] Importantly, this attitude of adoration or worship is manifested in the life of individuals in the practice of contemplation. Prayer is an interaction with the presence of God who transcends humanity, but in taking humanity up into himself he transforms humanity into something more truly human.

Contemplation of the holy Trinity is a universal human calling: "For there is not one single human being who is not destined, one day, to be transformed in Christ and to contemplate the Trinity."[65] This contemplation "engages the depths of our being, and how it must help us to rediscover our spiritual vocation in all of its fullness and to rise above anything that might keep us from fulfilling it."[66]

---

63. Ibid., 160–61. "Cette relation avec Dieu ne représente pas je ne sais quelle vérité surajoutée à un humanisme qui pourrait se constituer en dehors d'elle, mais elle est constitutive de l'homme comme tel. Dès lors, un homme qui la méconnaît, un homme sans adoration, est un homme motile. Quand nous protestons aujourd'hui contre tout humanisme athée, que cet humanisme soit un humanisme marxiste ou un humanisme liberal, ce n'est pas simplement Dieu que nous défendons, mais l'homme lui-même. Un homme sans Dieu n'est plus pleinement humain." Elsewhere, Daniélou notes, "Un monde sans Dieu est d'abord un monde sans l'homme, un monde inhumain." "La Vision Chrétienne de l'homme d'apres le Concile," *Cahiers de Neuilly* (Avril 1966): 16.

64. Hanby states the case much more strikingly in his essay "Desire: Augustine beyond Western Subjectivity," 115 and 116. Hanby contends, "The doxological self is thus able to participate in the life of the Trinity by virtue of a doxological character which it cannot escape, but can only pervert" and "nihilism can arise only when doxology fails, and *all that is not doxology is nihilism*."

65. Daniélou, *Contemplation*, 150–51. "Car il n'y a aucune âme humaine qui ne soit destine à être, un jour, transformée dans le Christ et à contempler la Trinité.

66. Ibid., 17. "Nous voyons ainsi comment la prière engage les profondeurs de notre être et comment elle doit nous aider à retrouver, dans toute sa dimension, notre vocation spirituelle et à émerger de tout ce qui nous empêcher de la réaliser."

Bibliography

Monographs

Daniélou, Jean. *Le IVéme Siecle Grégoire de Nysse et son Milieu*. Paris: Institut Catholique de Paris, n. d.

———. *Les Anges et leur Mission d'après les Pères de l'Eglise*. Paris: Éditions du Chevetogne, 1952. English translation: *The Angels and Their Mission according to the Fathers of the Church*. Translated by David Heimann. Westminster, MD: Christian Classics, 1982.

———. *Approches du Christ*. Paris: B. Grassett, 1960. English translation: *Christ and Us*. Translated by Walter Roberts. New York: Sheed & Ward, 1961.

———. *Autorité et Contestation dans l'Église*. Gèneve: Claude Martingay et Centre Catholique d'Etudes, 1969.

———. *L'Avenir de la Religion*. Paris: Fayard, 1968.

———. *Bible et Liturgie: La Théologie Biblique des Sacraments et des Fêtes d'après les Pères de l'Eglise*. Paris: Éditions du Cerf, 1951. English translation: *The Bible and the Liturgy*. Notre Dame, IN: Notre Dame University Press, 1956.

———. *La Catéchèse aux Premiers Siècles*. Paris: Fayard, 1968.

———. *La Colombe et le Tenebre: Textes Extraits des "Homélies sur le Cantique des Cantiques" de Grégoire de Nysse*. Paris: Éditions de l'Orante, 1967.

———. *Au Commencement: Genèse I-XI*. Paris: Éditions du Seuil, 1963. English translation: *In the Beginning . . . Genesis I-III*. Translated by Julien L. Randolf. Baltimore: Helicon, 1965.

———. *Conférence du Cardinal Daniélou: "La Doctrine Patristique du Sacerdoce Hiérarchique."* Paris: Groupe Sacerdotal 'Lumen Gentium,' 1974.

———. *Contemplation: Croissance de l'Eglise*. Paris: Fayard, 1977. English translation: *Prayer the Mission of the Church*. Grand Rapids: Eerdmans, 1996.

———. *Crise de l'Église, Crise de l'Homme*. Paris: Centre d'Études Politiques et Civiques, 1972.

———. *Culture et Mystère*. Paris: Éditions Universitaires, 1948.

———. *La Culture Trahie par les Siens*. Paris: Epi, 1972.

———. *Dialogue avec Israël. Vers un Rapprochment entre les Juifs et les Chrétiens*. Gènéve: La Palantine, 1963. English translation: *Dialogue with Israel*. Translated by Joan Marie Roth. Baltimore: Helicon, 1968.

———. *Dialogues avec les Marxistes, les Existentialistes, les Protestantes, les Juifs, l'Hindoisme*. Paris: Le Postulan, 1948.

Bibliography

———. *Dieu et Nous*. Paris: B. Grassett, 1956. English translations: *God and the Ways of Knowing*. Translated by Walter Roberts. New York: Meridian, 1957. *God and Us*. Translated by Walter Roberts. London: Mowbray, 1957.

———. *L'Église des Apôtres*. Paris: Éditions du Seuil, 1970.

———. *Essai sur le Mystère de l'Histoire*. Paris: Éditions du Seuil, 1953. English translation: *The Lord of History: Reflections on the Inner Meaning of History*. Translated by Nigel Abercrombie. New York: Meridian, 1968.

———. *Et Qui est Mon Prochain?* Paris: Stock, 1974.

———. *L'Être et le Temps chez Grégoire de Nysse*. Leiden: Brill, 1970.

———. *Études d'Exégèse Judéo-Chrétienne (Les Testimonia)*. Paris: Beauschesne, 1966.

———. *Les Évangiles de l'Enfance*. Paris: Éditions du Seuil, 1967. English translation: *The Infancy Narratives*. Translated by Rosemary Sheed. New York: Herder & Herder, 1968.

———. *From Glory to Glory: Texts from Gregory of Nyssa's Mystical Writings*. Translated by Herbert Musurillo. New York: Scribner's, 1961.

———. *Histoire des doctrines chrétiennes avant Nicée Théologie du judéo-christianisme*. Tournai: Desclée, 1958. English translation: *A History of Early Christian Doctrine before the Council of Nicea, Volume One: The Theology of Jewish Christianity*. Translated by John Austin Baker. London: Darton, Longman & Todd, 1964.

———. *Histoire des doctrines chrétiennes avant Nicée: Message évagélique et culture hellénistique au II et III siècle*. Tournai: Desclée, 1961. English translation: *A History of Early Christian Doctrine before the Council of Nicea, Volume Two: Gospel Message and Hellenistic Culture*. Translated by John Austin Baker. London: Darton, Longman & Todd, 1973.

———. *Histoire des doctrines chrétiennes avant Nicée: Les origins du christianisme latin*. Tournai: Desclée, 1978. English translation: *A History of Early Christian Doctrine before the Council of Nicea, Volume Three: The Origins of Latin Christianity*. Translated by David Smith John Austin Baker. London: Darton, Longman & Todd, 1977.

———. *Jean-Baptiste Témoin de l'Agneau*. Paris: Éditions du Seuil, 1964. English translation: *The Work of John the Baptist*. Translated by Joseph A. Horn. Baltimore: Helicon, 1966.

———. *Les Manuscrits de la Mer Morte et les Origines du Christianisme*. Paris: Éditions de L'Orante, 1957. English translation: *The Dead Sea Scrolls and Primitive Christianity*. Translated by Salvator Attanasio. Baltimore: Helicon, 1958.

———. *Le Mystère de l'Avent*. Paris: Éditions du Seuil, 1948. English translation: *Advent*. Translated by Rosemary Sheed. New York: Sheed & Ward, 1951.

———. *Le Mystère du Salut des Nations*. Paris: Éditions du Seuil, 1946. English translation: *The Salvation of the Nations*. Translated by Angeline Bouchard. New York: Sheed & Ward, 1950.

———. *Mythes Païens Mystère Chrétien*. Paris: Fayard, 1966. English translation: *Myth and Mystery*. Translated by P. J. Hepburne-Scott. New York: Hawthorne, 1968.

———. *Nuns: What is Special about them?* London: Catholic Truth Society, 1974.

———. *L'Oraison Problème Politique*. Paris: Fayard, 1965. English translation: *Prayer as Political Problem*. Translated by J. R. Kirwan. New York: Sheed & Ward, 1967.

———. *Origène*. Paris: La Table Ronde, 1948. English translation: *Origen*. Translated by Walter Mitchell. New York: Sheed & Ward, 1955.

———. *Platonisme et Théologie Mystique: Doctrine Spirituelle de Grégory de Nysse*. Paris: Aubier, 1944.

———. *Philon d'Alexandrie.* Paris: Fayard, 1958.

———. *Pourquoi l'Eglise?* Paris: Fayard, 1972. English translation: *Why the Church?* Translated by Maurice F. De Lange. Chicago: Franciscan Herald, 1975.

———. *Le Problème de Dieu et l'Existentialisme.* Montréal: Collège Jean-De-Brébeuf, 1958.

———. *La Résurrection.* Paris: Éditions du Seuil, 1969.

———. *Sacrementum Futuri: Études Sur les Origines de la Typologie Biblique.* Paris: Buschesne, 1950. English translation: *From Shadows to Reality: Studies in the Biblical Typology of the Fathers.* Translated by Dom Wulstan Hibberd. London: Burns & Oates, 1960.

———. *Les Saints «Païens» de l'Ancien Testament.* Paris: Éditions du Seuil, 1956. English translation: *Holy Pagans of the Old Testament.* Translated by Felix Faber. Baltimore: Helicon, 1957.

———. *Sainteté et Action Temporelle.* Belgium: Desclée & Cie, 1955.

———. *Scandaleuse Vérité.* Paris: Fayard, 1961. English translation: *The Scandal of Truth.* Translated by W. J. Kerrigan. Baltimore: Helicon, 1962.

———. *Le Signe du Temple ou de la Présence de Dieu.* Paris: Gallimard, 1942. English translation: *The Presence of God.* Translated by Walter Roberts. Baltimore: Helicon, 1959.

———. *Les Symboles Chrétiens Primitifs.* Paris: Éditions du Seuil, 1961. English translation: *Primitive Christian Symbols.* Translated by Donald Attwater. Baltimore: Helicon, 1961.

———. *La Trinité et le Mystère de l'Existence.* Paris: Desclée de Brouwer, 1968. English translation: *God's Life in Us.* Translated by Jeremy Leggat. Denville, N. J.: 1969.

Daniélou, Jean and Jean Bosc. *L'Église Face au Monde.* Paris: Palantine, 1966.

Daniélou, Jean and M. Jacob Kaplan. *Le Concile et Les Juifs.* Paris: Impr. Moderne de la Presse, 1966.

Daniélou, Jean and Henri Marrou. *Nouvelle Histoire de l'Eglise.* Paris: Éditions du Seuil, 1963. English translation: *The Christian Centuries: The First Six Hundred Years.* Translated by Vincent Cronin. New York: McGraw-Hill, 1964.

Congar, Yves, Jean Daniélou, Edward Shillebeeckx, Piet Schoonenberg, Johannes Metz and Karl Rahner. *The Crucial Questions: On Problems Facing the Church Today.* Paramus, NY: Newman, 1969.

Articles, Essays and Chapters

Daniélou, Jean. "A Propos du Futur Concile." *Les Cahiers du Neuilly* (April 1959) 67–71.

———. "A Propos d'une Introduction à la Vie Spirituelle." *Études* 308 (1961) 270–274, 415.

———. "Abel the First Martyr." *Jubilee* 5 (March 1958) 36–39.

———. "Abraham et Saint Joseph." *L'Anneau d'Or* 9–10 (1946) 86–88.

———. "Abraham dans la Tradition Chrétienne." *Cahiers Sioniens* 5 (1951) 68–87.

———. "Absence and Presence of God." *L'Osservatore Romano* (February 10, 1972) 9.

———. "Actes des Apôtres: La Pentacôte dans l'Histoire du Salut." *Bulletin du Cercle Saint Jean-Baptiste* (December 1961) 7–14.

———. "Actes des Apôtres: L'Evangile Annonce aux Juifs." *Bulletin du Cercle Saint Jean-Baptiste* (January 1962) 7–14.

Bibliography

———. "Actes des Apôtres: Le Concile de Jérusalem." *Bulletin du Cercle Saint Jean-Baptiste* (February 1962) 7–14.

———. "Actes des Apôtres: Conversion, Foi, Baptême." *Bulletin du Cercle Saint Jean-Baptiste* (March 1962) 7–13.

———. "Actes des Apôtres: La Communauté Primitive." *Bulletin du Cercle Saint Jean-Baptiste* (April 1962) 7–14.

———. "Actes des Apôtres: La Mission de Paul." *Bulletin du Cercle Saint Jean-Baptiste* (May 1962) 7–14.

———. "Actualité de Péguy." *La Nouvelle Revue des Deux Mondes* (October 1973) 36–46.

———. "L'Adoration des Mages." *Bulletin Saint Jean-Baptiste* (February 1967) 151–67.

———. "L'Adoration des Mages n'est pas un Mythe." *Ecclesia* 226 (1968) 49–60.

———. "L'Adversus Arium et Sabellium de Grégoire de Nysse et L'Origenisme Cappadocien." *Recherches de sciences religieuse* 54 (1966) 61–66.

———. "After the Synod, II." *L'Osservatore Romano* (April 30, 1970) 8–9.

———. "Akolouthia chez Grégoire de Nysse." *Recherches des Sciences Religieuse* 27 (1953) 219–249.

———. "Alienated Freedoms." *L'Osservatore Romano* (February 1, 1973) 11.

———. "'All Things to All Men': The Church and the Hellenic Tradition." *The Tablet* 198 (September 29, 1951) 207–8.

———. "Allocution du Cardinal Daniélou." In *Fidelité et Ouverture*, 197–202. Paris: Mame, 1972.

———. "L'Ami de l'Époux." *Bulletin du Cercle Saint Jean-Baptiste* (February 1964) 8–16.

———. "Amour de Dieu et Amour des Hommes." *Études* 279 (1953) 334–46.

———. "Amour de Dieu et Apostolat." *Le Christ au Monde* 15 (1970) 299–303.

———. "L'Amour de Dieu, Fondement de la Loi." *Axes* (February 1971) 5–12.

———. "Les Anges et les Desert." *Bulletin du Cercle Saint Jean-Baptiste* (March 1952) 1–2.

———. "L'Angoisse de L'Occident devant le Tiers Monde." *Études* 314 (1962) 3–18.

———. "Les Années Obscures de Jésus." *Études* 307 (1960) 393–95.

———. "L'Annonce à Marie." *Bulletin Saint Jean-Baptiste* (January 1967) 103–12.

———. "L'Apocalypse: Introduction." *Bulletin du Cercle Saint Jean-Baptiste* (November 1958) 31–33.

———. "L'Apocalypse: Un Foule Immense . . . ." *Bulletin du Cercle Saint Jean-Baptiste* (January 1959) 55–60.

———. "L'Apocalypse: Les Témoins de la Vérité." *Bulletin du Cercle Saint Jean-Baptiste* (February 1959) 78–82.

———. "L'Apocalypse: Le Dragon se Tint devant la Femme." *Bulletin du Cercle Saint Jean-Baptiste* (March 1959) 102–5.

———. "L'Apocalypse: L'Epopée de la Parole de Dieu." *Bulletin du Cercle Saint Jean-Baptiste* (April 1959) 126–31.

———. "L'Apocalypse: Le Jérusalem Nouvelle." *Bulletin du Cercle Saint Jean-Baptiste* (May 1959) 150–52.

———. "Apocalyptique Juive et Messianisme Chrétien." In *Espérance Chrétienne et Avenir Humain*, 10–21. Paris: Seuil, 1974.

———. "L'Apocatastase chez Saint Grégoire de Nysse." *Recherches de Science Religieuse* 30 (1940) 328–347.

———. "Apostolic Dynamism." *Christ to the World* 16 (1971) 453–54.

———. "L'Apôtre selon Saint Grégoire de Nysse." *Cahiers de Neuilly* 7 (1943) 23–27.

Bibliography

———. "Les Apparitions du Christ Ressuscité." *Bulletin Saint Jean-Baptiste* (April 1968) 257–68.

———. "L'Appel Missionaire." *Bulletin du Cercle Saint Jean-Baptiste* (November 1946) 1.

———. "Un Artisan de Paix." *Ecclesia* 208 (1966) 18–19.

———. "L'Ascension d'Hénoch." *Irénikon* 28 (1955) 257–67.

———. "Aspects Barthiens du Problème Missionaire." *Dieu Vivant* 6 (1946) 127–33.

———. "Aspects Trinitaires de l'Eglise." *Bulletin du Cercle Saint Jean-Baptiste* (June-July 1959) 173–75.

———. "L'Attente de la Vision." *Bulletin du Cercle Saint Jean-Baptiste* (May-June 1946) 1.

———. "Autour de l'Exégèse Spirituelle." *Dieu Vivant* 8 (1947) 123–26.

———. "Autour de 'la Table Ronde': Politique et Culture." *Études* 257 (1948) 111–13.

———. "Autorité et Liberté dans l'Église d'aujourd'hui." *Les Annales* 247 (1971) 3–14.

———. "Avant-Propos." *Bulletin du Cercle Saint Jean-Baptiste* (November 1945) 1.

———. "L'Avenir du Patriotisme." *Études* 292 (1957) 3–15.

———. "Le Banquet Messianique." *Bulletin du Cercle Saint Jean-Baptiste* (May 1949) 1–2.1

———. "Bases Communes d'Une Civilisation Méditerréene." In *Méditerranée Carrefour des Religions*, 11–22. Paris: Fayard, 1959.

———. "Les Beatitudes." *Bulletin du Cercle Saint Jean-Baptiste* (October-November 1953) 2–4.

———. "La Bible Livre Scellé?" *L'Anneau d'Or* 36 (1950) 392–95.

———. "Bienheureux Ceux Qui Pleurent." *Bulletin du Cercle Saint Jean-Baptiste* (February 1952) 1–2.

———. "Bienheureux les Pauvres." *Études* 288 (1956) 231–338.

———. "Bilan du Synode." *La Documentation Catholique* (16 November 1969) 1036.

———. "Blessed are the Poor." *Cross Currents* 9 (Fall 1959) 379–88.

———. "Le Bon Samaritan." In *Melanges Bibliques: Rédigés en l'Honneur de Andre Robert*, 457–465. Paris: Bloud & Gay, 1956.

———. "Bulletin d'Histoire des Origines Chrétiennes: L'Église aux Premiers Siècles; Spiritualité Patristique;Exégèse Patistique; Hellénisme et Christianisme." *Recherches de Science Religieuse* 35 (1948) 593–617.

———. "Bulletin d'Histoire des Origines Chrétiennes: Judaïsme et Christianisme; Littérature Gnostique; Littérature Grecque Chrétienne; Littérature Latine Chrétienne." *Recherches de Science Religieuse* 36 (1949) 604–31.

———. "Bulletin d'Histoire des Origines Chrétiennes: Judaïsme et Christianisme; Littérature Chrétienne Archaïque; Trois Théologies Bibliques; Les Origines de la Typologie; Théologie et Liturgie." *Recherches de Science Religieuse* 37 (1950) 587–618.

———. "Bulletin d'Histoire des Origines Chrétiennes: Ouvrages Généraux; Anthropologie, Théologie, Christologie; Exégèse et Typologie; Sacrements et Liturgie; Eschatologie." *Recherches de Science Religieuse* 38 (1951) 257–301.

———. "Bulletin d'Histoire des Origines Chrétiennes: Histoire et Hagiographie; Église, Sacrements, Écriture; Anthropologie et Spiritualité." *Recherches de Science Religieuse* 41 (1953) 535–80.

———. "Bulletin d'Histoire des Origines Chrétiennes: Hippolyte et Origène; La Théologie dans la Première Miotié du IVe Siècle; Théologie Sacramentaire; Les Origines de la Spiritualité Monastique." *Recherches de Science Religieuse* 42 (1954) 585–627.

Bibliography

———. "Bulletin d'Histoire des Origines Chrétiennes: Judaïsme et Christianisme aux Deux Premiers Siècles; Les Origines; Autour de Chalcédoine." *Recherches de Science Religieuse* 43 (1955) 556–98.

———. "Bulletin d'Histoire des Origines Chrétiennes: La Théologie au Second Siècle; L'Église au Temps des Grandes Controverses; Spiritualité Patristique." *Recherches de Science Religieuse* 44 (1956) 576–624.

———. "Bulletin d'Histoire des Origines Chrétiennes: La Synagogue Hellénistique; Archéologie et Théologie; Manuels, Mélanges, Collections." *Recherches de Science Religieuse* 45 (1958) 571–627.

———. "Bulletin d'Histoire des Origines Chrétiennes: Autour du Judéo-Christianisme; Le Moyen-Platonisme Chrétien; Christologie et Anthropolgie; Textes Inédits du IVe Siècle; Le Latin Chrétien." *Recherches de Science Religieuse* 47 (1959) 63–124.

———. "Bulletin d'Histoire des Origines Chrétiennes: Judéo-Christianisme et Gnosticisme; Exégèse Patristique; Christianisme et Culture Antique; Sacrements et Institutions." *Recherches de Science Religieuse* 47 (1959) 570–620.

———. "Bulletin d'Histoire des Origines Chrétiennes: Judaïsme et Judéo-Christianisme; Gnosticisme et Christianisme; La Théologie au IIe et au IIIe Siècles; Histoire de la Spiritualité." *Recherches de Science Religieuse* 48 (1960) 588–645.

———. "Bulletin d'Histoire des Origines Chrétiennes: Exégèse Patristique" *Recherches de Science Religieuse* 49 (1961) 146–52.

———. "Bulletin d'Histoire des Origines Chrétiennes: Ouvrages d'Ensemble; Papyrus Bodmer. Théologie Asiate. Évangile de Thomas; Tertullien; Exégèse Grecque, Juive, Chrétienne." *Recherches de Science Religieuse* 49 (1961) 564–620.

———. "Bulletin d'Histoire des Origines Chrétiennes: Judaïsme, Judéo-Christianisme, Gnosticisme; Théologie Prénicéenne; L'Église et l'Empire à la Fin du IVe Siècle." *Recherches de Science Religieuse* 51 (1963) 112–63.

———. "Bulletin d'Histoire des Origines Chrétiennes: Le Judéo-Christianisme et son Héritage; Philosophie Grecque et Théologie Chrétienne; Histoire du Monachisme Lexiques et Éditions." *Recherches de Science Religieuse* 52 (1964) 101–69.

———. "Bulletin d'Histoire des Origines Chrétiennes: Judaïsme et Judéo-Christianisme; Les Testimonia; Platon, Aristote, Plotin; Le Grec Chétien." *Recherches de Science Religieuse* 53 (1965) 121–70.

———. "Bulletin d'Histoire des Origines Chrétiennes: Mélanges, Manuels, Éditions." *Recherches de Science Religieuse* 53 (1965) 285–302.

———. "Bulletin d'Histoire des Origines Chrétiennes: Judéo-Christianisme et Gnosticisme; Platonisme et Christianisme; Histoire de la Christologie; Typologie et Symbolisme." *Recherches de Science Religieuse* 54 (1966) 272–332.

———. "Bulletin d'Histoire des Origines Chrétiennes: Judéo-Christianisme; L'Église à la Fin du IVe Siècle; Théologie Patristique de l'Histoire; Ancienne Littérature Chrétienne." *Recherches de Science Religieuse* 55 (1967) 88–151.

———. "Bulletin d'Histoire des Origines Chrétiennes: Judéo-Christianisme et Gnosticisme; Philosophie Grecque et Révélation Biblique; Sacrements et Liturgie." *Recherches de Science Religieuse* 56 (1968) 110–69.

———. "Bulletin d'Histoire des Origines Chrétiennes: Le Christianisme Asiate au Second Siècle; Tertullien et Novatien; Science et Mystique à l'Âge Patristique." *Recherches de Science Religieuse* 57 (1969) 75–130.

———. "Bulletin d'Histoire des Origines Chrétiennes: Le Judaïsme au Ier Siècle ap. J.-C.; Gnosticisme et Christianisme; Judéo-Christianisme et Théologie du IIe Siècle." *Recherches de Science Religieuse* 58 (1970) 113-54.

———. "Bulletin d'Histoire des Origines Chrétiennes: Le Judaïsme au Ier Siècle ap. J.C.; Textes Gnostique et Manichéens; L'Église aux Premiers Siècles." *Recherches de Science Religieuse* 59 (1971) 37-74.

———. "Bulletin d'Histoire des Origines Chrétiennes: Judéo-Christianisme; Justin, Clément, Tertullien; Théologie Archaïque." *Recherches de Science Religieuse* 61 (1973) 233-76.

———. "Bulletin d'Histoire de la Théologie Sacramentaire." *Recherches de Science Religieuse* 34 (1943) 369-84.

———. "Bulletin de Littérature Patristique." *Recherches de Science Religieuse* 33 (1946) 115-28.

———. "Le Cantique de Moïse et la Vigile Pascale." *Bible et Vie Chrétienne* 1 (1953) 21-30.

———. "The Canticle, A Song of Sacraments." *Orate Fratres* 3 (1951) 97-103.

———. "The Canticle, A Song of Sacraments (II)." *Orate Fratres* 4 (1951) 161-65.

———. "Cardinal Daniélou on Modern Errors on the Trinity." *L'Osservatore Romano* (August 10, 1972) 3.

———. "Cardinal Daniélou: A Self-Portrait." *L'Osservatore Romano* (August, 7 1975) 7-8.

———. "Catéchèses Eucharistique chez les Péres de l'Eglise." In *La Messe et sa Catéchèse*, 33-72. Paris: Cerf, 1947.

———. "Catéchèse Pascale et Retour au Paradis." *La Maison-Dieu* 45 (1956) 99-119.

———. "Catéchèse et Symbole." *Axes* (October-November 1969) 3-6.

———. "La Catéchèse dans la Tradition Patristique." In *Conversion, Catechumenate, and Baptism in the Early Church*, ed. Everett Ferguson, 21-34. New York: Garland Publishing, Inc., 1993.

———. "Catholicisme et Crise des Civilisations." *Bulletin du Cercle Saint Jean-Baptiste* (June-July 1955) 5-10.

———. "Le Célibat Sacerdotal." *L'Osservatore Romano* (13 February 1970) 2.

———. "Celui qui Rassemble." *Bulletin du Cercle Saint Jean-Baptiste* (May 1947) 1.

———. "Le Centenaire de Saint Thérèse de Lisieux." *Axes* (June-July 1973) 61-62.

———. "Centre d'Études: Comment Lire la Bible." *Cahiers de Neuilly* 15 (1947) 27-32.

———. "Ce Qui est Acquis et Ce Qui est Attendu." *Bulletin du Cercle Saint Jean-Baptiste* (December 1951) 1-2.

———. "Ce Que l'Etude des Peres Grecs Apporte a la Theologie Missionaire." *Bulletin du Cercle Saint Jean-Baptiste* (December 1955) 4-7

———. "Le Cercle Saint Jean-Baptiste: Histoire et Orientations." *Axes* (June-July 1969) 4-6.

———. "La Charité de la Vérité." *La Nouvelle Revue des Deux Mondes* 2 (1973) 534-37.

———. "Charité et Vérité." *Bulletin du Cercle Saint Jean-Baptiste* (June-July 1960) 193-96.

———. "Charity or Humanitarianism." *Theology Digest* 3.3 (1955) 151-54.

———. "La Charrue Symbole de la Croix (Irénée, *Adv. haer.*, IV, 34, 4)." *Recherches de Science Religieuse* 42 (1954) 193-203.

———. "Le Chemin dans le Desert." *Bulletin du Cercle Saint Jean-Baptiste* (March 1951) 1-2.

Bibliography

———. "Chrétiens et Marxistes devant le Monde Modern: Débat Télevisé entre le Cardinal Daniélou et Roger Garaundy." *La Documentation Catholique* 67 (1970) 536–47.
———. "Chrismation Prébaptismale et Divinité de l'Esprit chez Grégoire de Nysse." *Recherches de Science Religieuse* 56 (1968) 177–98.
———. "Le Christ Prophète." *La Vie Spirituelle, Supplément* 78 (1948) 154–70.
———. "Christian Faith and the Man of Today." *L'Osservatore Romano* (March 12, 1970) 3, 10.
———. "Christian Faith and Scientific Thought." *L'Osservatore Romano* (May 13, 1971: 7–11.
———. "The Christian View of History." *The Month* 2 (1949) 68–72.
———. "Christianisme et Histoire." *Études* 254 (1947) 166–84.
———. "Le Christianisme Missionaire." *Axes* (October1979-March1980) 138–54.
———. "Christianisme et Patronat." *Les Cahiers de Neuilly* (April 1954) 61–67.
———. "Christianisme et Religions Non Chrétienne." *Études* 321 (1964) 323–36.
———. "Christianisme et Transmigration." *Axes* (June-July 1969) 77–79.
———. "Christianisme et Transmigration." *Bulletin du Cercle Saint Jean-Baptiste* (March 1954) 14–15.
———. "Christianity and History." *The Downside Review* 68 (1950) 182–90.
———. "Christianity and the Machine-Age World." *Jubilee* 10 (February1963) 14–17.
———. "Christiantiy and the Non-Christian Religions." In *Introduction to the Great Religions*, trans. Albert J. La Mothe, Jr., 7–28. Notre Dame, IN: Fides, 1964.
———. "Christos Kyrios: Une Citation des *Lamentations* de Jérémie dans les *Testimonia*." *Recherches de Science Religieuse* 39 (1951) 338–52.
———. "La Chronologie des Œuvres de Grégoire de Nysse." *Text und Untersuchen zur Geschichte der altechristlichen Literatur* 92 (1966) 159–69.
———. "La Chronologie des Sermones de Grégoire de Nysse." *Revue de sciences religieuses* 29 (1955) 346–72.
———. "Church and Communism in the World." *Catholic Worker* 20 (September 1953) n. p.
———. "The Church in Dialogue with the Contemporary World." *Universitas* 27 (1985) 251–55.
———. "The Church and the Modern World." *Studies* 60 (1971) 117–26.
———. "The Church and Non-Christian Religions." In *The Theological Task Facing the Church Today: A Symposium*. Chicago, Ill.: St. Xavier's College, 1966, 12–14.
———. "Chutes d'Anges." *Bulletin Saint Jean-Baptiste* (February 1965) 153–63.
———. "Cinquante Ans de Science Religieuse." *Études* 305 (1960) 3–14.
———. "Circumamicta Varietatisus." *Bulletin du Cercle Saint Jean-Baptiste* (January 1949) 1–2.
———. "Civilisation Technique et Humanisme Athée. Problèmes qu'ils posent à notre apostolate." *Le Christ au Monde* 4 (1959) 216–225.
———. "Collegite Fragmenta." *Bulletin du Cercle Saint Jean-Baptiste* (April 1952) 1–2.
———. "La Colombe et la Ténèbre dans Mystique Byzantine Ancienne." *Eranos-Jahrbuch* 23 (1954) 389–418.
———. "Le Combat et le Repos." *Bulletin du Cerlce Saint Jean-Baptiste* (March 1953) 2–4.
———. "Comble du Mal et Eschatologie chez Grégoire de Nysse." In *Festgabe Joseph Lortz*, 27–45. Baden-Baden: Erschienen Bei Bruno Grimm, 1958.

———. "La Communauté de Jérusalem et son Contexte Politico-Religieux." *Axes* (February 1969) 3–8.

———. "Communauté Méditerranéenne." *Bulletin Saint Jean-Baptiste* (June-July 1966) 377–88.

———. "La Communauté de la Mer Morte." *Études* 277 (1953) 365–72.

———. "La Communauté de Qumrân et l'organisation de l'Eglise Ancienne." *Revue d'Histoire et de Philosphie Religieuses* 35 (1955) 104–16.

———. "La Communication de la Foi." *Bulletin du Cercle Saint Jean-Baptiste* (October-November 1954) 8–11.

———. "Le Complexe d'Antitriumphalisme." *Relations* 332 (November 1968) 325–26.

———. "The Conception of History in the Christian Tradition." *The Journal of Religion* 30 (1950) 171–79.

———. "La Conception de l'Histoire dans la Tradition Chrétienne." *Le Semeur* 48 (1960) 177–88.

———. "Les Conceils Évangeliques et les Aspiriations des Jeunes." *La Vie Spirituelle* 78 (1948) 660–74.

———. "Le Concile a-t-il Trouvé sa Voie?." *Études* 316 (1963) 6–19.

———. "Le Concile Œcuménique." *La Revue de Paris* 69 (1962) 13–28.

———. "Connaissance de Dieu dans les Religions Païennes." *Bulletin du Cercle Saint Jean-Baptiste* (October-November 1955) 5–12.

———. "'Conspiratio' chez Grégoire de Nysse." In *L'Homme devant Dieu: Mélanges Offerts au Père Henri de Lubac*, ed. Marie-Thérèse d'Alverny, 295–308. Paris: Aubier, 1964.

———. "Contestation et Contemplation." *La Documentation Catholique* 65 (1968) 1319.

———. "Contexte du Concile." *The New Morality* 6 (1963) 9–14.

———. "Cours par Correspondence." *Bulletin du Cercle Saint Jean-Baptiste* (December 1944) 1.

———. "Se Convertir n'est Rien Renier." *Bulletin du Cercle Saint Jean-Baptiste* (June-July 1963) 75–83.

———. "La Crise de la Pensée Théologique." In *Les Crises de la Pensée Scientifique dans le Monde Actuel*, 37–56. Paris: Desclée De Brouwer, 1971.

———. "Crise ou Renaissance Religieuse." *La Nouvelle Revue des Deux Mondes* 2 (1973) 112–20.

———. "La Crise de la Morale." *La Nouvelle Revue des Deux Mondes* 1 (1972) 40–49.

———. "Crisis in Christian Theology." *Catholic Mind* 60 (June 1962):19–28.

———. "Crisis in the Church." *L'Osservatore Romano* (November 13, 1969) 8.

———. "Crisis of the Church and Crisis of Civilization." *L'Osservatore Romano* (October 7, 1971) 11.

———. "Crisis of Freedom—Crisis of Intelligence." *L'Osservatore Romano* (June 1, 1972) 11.

———. "Crisis from within Threatens Church." *Our Sunday Visitor* (June 30, 1974) 1, 12

———. "The Crisis in Intelligence." In *Media of Communication*, edited and translated by Mary Dominic, 75–111. Langley, England: St. Paul, 1970.

———. "Critique Rationnelle et Traditions Religieuses." *Axes* (May-June 1972) 3–6.

———. "Les Croissances de Jean-Baptiste." *Bulletin du Cercle Saint Jean-Baptiste* (February 1963) 7–15.

———. "Les Croissances de Jean-Baptiste: Jean Baptiste au Désert." *Bulletin du Cercle Saint Jean-Baptiste* (March 1963) 7–13.

———. "Cross Currents in Modern Protestantism." *Theology Digest* 3.2 (1955) 73–77.

Bibliography

———. "Crucified . . . for Claiming He was God!." *L'Osservatore Romano* (September 16, 1971) 7.

———. "Le Culte Marial et le Paganisme." In *Maria: Études sur la Sainte Vierge*, Vol. 1, 161–181. Paris: Beauchesne, 1949.

———. "Cultural Pluralism and Christianity." In *Symposium on Cultural Pluralism in the Modern World, 3rd August,* 1959, 19–23. Stockhom, Sweden: 1959.

———. "Culture Française et Mystére." *Esprit* 9 (1941) 471–87.

———. "Danel, Juste Païen de la Bible." *Bible et Vie Chrétienne* 12 (1955) 76–82.

———. "Dangers Threatening the Church Today." *L'Osservatore Romano* (May 22, 1969) 7.

———. "Daniel-Rops et son Œuvre." *Ecclesia* 220 (1967) 25–30.

———. "Débra et Jaël." *Bulletin Saint Jean-Baptiste* (January 1966) 115–22.

———. "Les Découvertes de Manuscrits en Égypte et en Palestine." *Études* 265 (1950) 168–183.

———. "Défense du Pratiquant." *Études* 296 (1958) 3–13.

———. "Déluge, Baptême, Jugement." *Dieu Vivant* 8 (1947) 97–112.

———. "Les Démons de l'Air dans la 'Vie d'Antonie'." In *Antonios Magnus Eremita, 356-1956: Studia ad Antiquum Monachismun Spectantia*, 136–147. Roma: Herder, 1956.

———. "La Démythisation dans l'École d'Alexandria." In *Problema della demitizzazione: Atti del Convegno Indetto dal Centro Internazionale di StudiUmanistici e dall'Istituto di Studi Filosofici, Roma, 16–21 Gennaio1961*, 45–49. Roma, Istituto di Studi Filosofici, Universitá, 1961.

———. "Demythologizing the School of Alexandria." In *Rudolf Bultmann in Catholic Thought*, eds. Thomas F. O'Meara and Donald M. Weisser, 51–58. New York: Herder and Herder, 1968.

———. "Deportation & Histoire Sainte." *Bulletin du Cercle Saint Jean-Baptiste* (April 1950) 6–8.

———. "Déracinement et Spiritualité." *Bulletin du Cercle Saint Jean-Baptiste* (May 1960) 168–70.

———. "Le Dernier Advent." *Bulletin du Cercle Saint Jean-Baptiste* (December 1953) 15–17.

———. "La Desacralisation." *La Documentation Catholique* 64 (1967) 1056.

———. "La Descente aux Enfers." *Bulletin du Cercle Saint Jean-Baptiste* (February 1957) 80–84.

———. "Le Desert de la Tentation." *Bulletin du Cercle Saint Jean-Baptiste* (April 1949) 1–2.

———. "Le Dialogue de l'Église et du monde." *Études* 325 (1966) 725–35.

———. "Le Dialogue des Religions." *La Documentation Catholique* 62 (1965) 860.

———. "A Dialogue with Time." *Cross Currents* 2 (Winter 1951) 78–90.

———. "Dieu aujourd'hui." *Bulletin Saint Jean-Baptiste* (October-November 1965) 18–25.

———. "Dieu dans l'Existence de l'Homme." *Dieu Vivant* 20 (1950) 24–32.

———. "Le Dieu d'Ezéchiel." *Bulletin du Cercle Saint Jean-Baptiste* (December 1964) 58–65.

———. "Dieu et le Monde Moderne." *Pédagogie* 18 (1968) 781–83.

———. "Dieu pour Quoi Faire?" *Dieu Vivant* 20 (1950) 127–31.

———. "Le Dimanche comme Huitième Jour." In *Le Dimanche*, 3–89. Paris: Cerf, 1965.

———. "La Direction Spirituelle dans la Tradition Ancienne de l'Église." *Christus* 25 (1960) 6–21.

———. "Discussion sur le Péche." *Dieu Vivant* 4 (1945) 83–133.

———. "Les Divers Sens l'Écriture dans la Tradition Chrétienne Primitive." *Ephemerides Theologicae Lovanienses* 24 (1948) 119–26.

———. "La Doctrine Missionaire de St. Augustin." *Bulletin du Cercle Saint Jean-Baptiste* (December 1959) 34–37.

———. "La Doctrine de la Mort chez les Péres de l'Église." In *Le Mystére de la Mort et sa Célébration*, 134–156. Paris: Editons du Cerf, 1956.

———. "La Doctrine Patristique du Dimanche." In *Le Jour du Seigneur*, 105–30. Paris: R. Laffont, 1948.

———. "Does a Human Nature Exist?" *L'Osservatore Romano* (October 1, 1970) 8, 11.

———. "Does the West have a Missionary Role?" *Theology Digest* 4.2 (1956) 91–92.

———. "Le Dogme de l'Assomption." *Études* 267 (1950) 289–302.

———. "Les Dons du Saint-Esprit." *Cahiers de Neuilly* 10 (April 1945) 13–17.

———. "Les Douze." *Bulletin Saint Jean-Baptiste* (December 1968) 55–70.

———. "Les Douze Apotres et le Zodiaque." *Vigiliae Christianae* 13 (April 1959) 14–21.

———. "The Dove and the Darkness in Ancient Byzantine Mysticism." In *Man and Transformation: Papers from the Eranos Yearbook*, ed. Ernst Benz, 271–96. Pantheon Books, 1964.

———. "Le Dynamisme Apostolique." *Le Christ au Monde* 17 (1971) 477–78.

———. "L'Eau Vive dans le Christianisme Primitif." *Bulletin du Cercle Saint Jean-Baptiste* (May 1957) 153–55.

———. "Écriture et Tradition." *Recherches de Science Religieuse* 51 (1963) 550–57.

———. "Écriture et Tradition dans la Dialogue entre les Chrétiens Séparés." *La Documentation Catholique* 54 (1957) 283–94.

———. "L'Écriture Lieu de rencontre des Chrétiens." In *L'Christ Réconciliaeur des Chrétiens*, eds. Brillet, Jean Clémence and Jean Daniélou, 35–61. Paris: Vitte, 1950.

———. "L'Éducation de l'Homme Nouveau: Une Thése sur la Penséc de Rousseau." *Cité Nouvelle* (1941) 56–66.

———. "Efficacite Surnaturelle et Adaptation Humaine." *Bulletin du Cercle Saint Jean-Baptiste* (February 1946) 5–11.

———. "L'Église et le Communisme dans la Monde." *Bulletin du Cercle Saint Jean-Baptiste* (December 1951) 7–9.

———. "L'Église dans la Monde." *La Documentation Catholique* 68 (1971) 48–49.

———. "L'Église devant le Judaïsme." *La Documentation Catholique* (July 1973) 620–21.

———. "L'Eglise et le Mouvement de l'Histoire." *Bulletin du Cercle Saint Jean-Baptiste* (June-July 1959) 193–99.

———. "Église Primitive et Communauté de Qumran." *Études* 293 (1957) 216–35.

———. "L'Église Spirituelle chez les Judéo-Chrétiens." *Bulletin du Cercle Saint Jean-Baptiste* (April 1957) 129–32.

———. "Émile Brehier." *Études* 273 (1952) 105–6.

———. "The Empty Tomb." *The Month* 39 (1968) 215–22.

———. "L'Encyclique 'In Multiplicibus' sur la Question Palestinienne." *Études* 259 (1948) 260–61.

———. "Engagement et Responsibilité des Chrétiens." In *Notre Foi*, 149–66. Paris: Beauchesne, 1967.

———. "L'Épreuve de l'Amour." *Bulletin du Cercle Saint Jean-Baptiste* (March 1964) 7–17.

Bibliography

———. "Eschatologie et Monde Historique." In *Atti del XXVI Convegno del Centro di Studi filosofici tra professori universitari, Gallarate, 1971*, 19–23. Brescia: Morcelliana, 1972.

———. "Eschatologie Sadocite et Eschatologie Chrétienne." In *Manuscrits de la Mer Morte: Colloque de Strausborg, 25–27 Mai 1955*, 111–25. Paris: Presses Universitaires de France, 1957.

———. "L'Esperance Missionaire." *Bulletin du Cercle Saint Jean-Baptiste* (October-November 1951) 4–7.

———. "L'Espérance et la Libération du Mal." In *Espoir Humain et Espérance Chrétienne*, 58–64. Paris: Editions de Flore, 1951.

———. "L'Éspouse Infidéle." *Bulletin Saint Jean-Baptiste* (January 1965) 111–18.

———. "L'Esprit des Béatitudes dans la Vie d'un Militant Ouvrier." *Masses Ouvrieres* (November 1955) 34–52.

———. "Espoirs Humains et Espérance Chrétienne." *Études* 287 (1955) 145–55.

———. "L'Esprit Missionnaire." In *La Mentalité Missionnaire chez la Religieuse*, 62. Québec: 1960.

———. "L'Esprit Missionaire." *Bulletin du Cercle Saint Jean-Baptiste* (May 1948) 1.

———. "Esprit Missionaire et Foyers Chretiens." *Bulletin du Cercle Saint Jean-Baptiste* (May 1952) 8–9.

———. "Esprit-Saint et Histoire du Salut." *La Vie Spirituelle* 83 (1950) 127–40.

———. "L'etat du Christ dans la Mort d'apres Grégoire de Nysse." *Historisches Jahrbuch* 77 (1958) 63–72.

———. "Etienne Gilson à l'Académie." *Études* 251 (1946) 263–64.

———. "L'Etoile de Jacob et la Mission Chretienne a Damas." *Vigiliae Christianae* 11 (1957) 121–38.

———. "Eunome l'Arien et l'Exégèse Néo-Platonicienne du Cratyle." *Revue des etudes grecques* 69 (1956) 412–32.

———. "Eucharistie et Cantique des Cantiques." *Irénikon* 23 (1950) 257–77.

———. "Evangelical Poverty." *Theology Digest* 11.1 (1963) 57–59.

———. "L'Évêque et l'Amiral." *La Documentation Catholique* 70 (1973) 709–10.

———. "L'Évêque d'Apres Une Lettre de Grégoire de Nysse." *Euntes Docete* 20 (1967) 85–97.

———. "Évêques et Théologiens." *La Revue des Deux Mondes* (February 1970) 257–65.

———. "Exégèse et Dogme." *Dieu Vivant* 14 (1949) 90–94.

———. "L'Existence de Dieu et la Raison." *Bulletin Saint Jean-Baptiste* (May 1966) 307–21.

———. "Existentialism and the Theology of History." *The Month* 1 (1949) 66–70.

———. "Existentialisme et Théologie de l'Histoire." *Dieu Vivant* 15 (1950) 131–35.

———. "L'Experience de Dieu." *Axes* (February-March 1973) 3–10.

———. "Experience of God." *Cistercian Studies* 9 (1974) 94–100.

———. "L'Expression du Sacré dans la Ville de Demain." *Axes* (April-May 1970) 89–101.

———. "Faith and the Modern Mind." *The Clergy Monthly* 19 (1955) 161–70.

———. "Familie et Mission." *Bulletin du Cercle Saint Jean-Baptiste* (June-July 1953) 3–10.

———. "The Fathers and Christian Unity." In *In Honor of Saint Basil the Great*, ed. Maisie Ward, William Meninger and Adalbert de Vogüé, 95–108. Still River, MA: St. Bede's Publications, 1979.

———. "The Fathers and the Scriptures." *Theology* 62 (1954) 83–89.

Bibliography

———. "La Fête des Tabernacles dans l'exégèse Patristique." In *Studia Patristica*, vol. I, eds. Kurt Aland and F. L. Cross, 262–79. Berlin: Akademie-Verlag, 1957.

———. "Figure et Événement chez Méliton de Sardes." In *Neotestamentica et Patristica*, ed. Oscar Cullmann, 282–92. Leiden: Brill, 1962.

———. "Les Figures de la Résurrection." *Bulletin Saint Jean-Baptiste* (December 1967) 55–61.

———. "Le Filet de l'Oiseleur." *Bulletin du Cercle Saint Jean-Baptiste* (April 1953) 5–7.

———. "Le Fils de Perdition (Joh., 17, 12)." In *Mélanges d'Histoire des Religions Offerts à Henri-Charles Puech*, ed. Henri-Charles Puech, 187–189. Paris: Presse Universitaires de France, 1974.

———. "The First and the Last Thing." *The Month* 2 (1949) 329–33.

———. "Une Foi Agissante dans un Monde Exigeant." *Ecclésia* 234 (1968) 36–48.

———. "La Foi aux Dimensions du Monde." In *Foi en Jésus-Christ et Monde d'aujourd'hui*, 206–209. Paris: Éditions de Flore, 1949.

———. "Foi et Mentalité Contemporaine." *Étude* 283 (1954) 289–301.

———. "Les Fondements de la Communauté Méditerréene." *Études* 300 (1959) 145–59.

———. "The Future Church: A Breath of Hope." *Our Sunday Visitor* (November 5, 1972) 1, 11.

———. "Gabriel Marcel: Allocution du Cardinal Daniélou." *La Documentation Catholique* 70 (1973) 928–29.

———. "The Garden of Living Souls." *L'Osservatore Romano* (May 16, 1974) 10–11.

———. "Gédéon." *Bulletin Saint Jean-Baptiste* (February 1966) 163–70.

———. "Un Génie Subversif." *Les Nouvelles Littéraires* (June 18, 1970) 11.

———. "La Gloire d'Israël." *Bulletin du Cercle Saint Jean-Baptiste* (March 1948) 1.

———. "God Intervenes in Our Existence." *L'Osservatore Romano* (August 17, 1972) 3.

———. "Les Grands Priants de l'Ancien Testament." *L'Anneau d'Or* 75 (1967) 174–82.

———. "Les Grands Orants de l'Ancien Testament: David." *Bulletin du Cercle Saint Jean-Baptiste* (March 1958) 108–11.

———. "Les Grands Orants de l'Ancien Testament: Elie." *Bulletin du Cercle Saint Jean-Baptiste* (April 1958) 134–38.

———. "Les Grands Orants de l'Ancien Testament: Jacob." *Bulletin du Cercle Saint Jean-Baptiste* (January 1958) 60–63.

———. "Les Grands Orants de l'Ancien Testament: Jonas." *Bulletin du Cercle Saint Jean-Baptiste* (May 1958) 160–63.

———. "Les Grand Orants de l'Ancien Testament: Moïse." *Bulletin du Cercle Saint Jean-Baptiste* (February 1958) 82–85.

———. "Les Grands Orants de l'Ancien Testament: La Prière Missionnaire de la Bible." *Bulletin du Cercle Saint Jean-Baptiste* (December 1957) 32–34.

———. "Great Preachers—I. Origen." *Theology* 54 (1951) 10–15.

———. "The Greatness and Deficiency of René Guénon." *Eastern Churches Quarterly* 10 (1954) 306–11.

———. "Grégoire de Nysse à Travers les Lettres de Saint Basile et de Saint Grégoire de Nazianze." *Vigiliae Christianae* 19 (1965) 31–41.

———. "Grégoire de Nysse et le Messalianisme." *Recherches de Science Religieuse* 48 (1960) 119–34.

———. "Grégoire de Nysse et le Néo-Platonisme de l'École d'Athéns." *Revue des Études Grecques* 80 (1967) 395–401.

Bibliography

———. "Grégoire de Nysse et l'Origine de la Fête de l'Ascension." In *Kyriakon: Festschrift Johannes Quasten*, edited by Johannes Quasten, Patrick Granfield and Josef A. Jungmann, 663–66. Münster: Aschendorff, 1970.

———. "Grégoire de Nysse et la Philosophie." In *Gregor von Nyssa und Die Philosophie*, edited by Heinrich Dörrie, Margarete Altenburger and Uta Schramm, 3–17. Leiden: Brill, 1976.

———. "Grégoire de Nysse et Plotin." In *Congrés de Tours et Poitiers, 3–9 Septembre 1953. Actes du Congrés*. Paris: Société d'Édition "Le Belle Lettres." 1954: 259–62.

———. "Gregory of Nyssa." *The Month* 25 (1961) 96–105.

———. "Has History a Meaning?." *The Month* 6 (1951) 41–44.

———. "Hellénisme et Christianisme." *Theologia* 33 (1962) 207–10.

———. "Hellénisme, Judaïsme, Christianisme." In *Réponses aux Questions de Simone Weil*, 2–39. Paris: Aubier, 1964.

———. "L'Heresie du XXe Siècle: Le Christianisme Areligieux." *La Documentation Catholique* 65 (1968) 480.

———. "Herméneutique Judéo-Chrétienne." *Archivio di Filosofia* 2 (1963) 255–61.

———. "Hilaire et ses Sources Juives." In *Hilaire et son Temps, Actes du Colloque de Poitiers, 29 Septembre-3 Octobre 1968, á l'Occasion du XVIe Centenaire de la Mort de Saint Hilaire*, 143–47. Paris: Études Augustiennes, 1969.

———. "Histoire et Foi." In *Jésus ou le Christ?*, 35–43. Paris: Desclée de Brouwer, 1970.

———. "Histoire Marxiste et Histoire Sacramentaire." *Dieu Vivant* 13 (1949) 99–110.

———. "Histoire et Prophetie." *La Documentation Catholique* 53 (1956) 1318–27.

———. "L'Histoire du Salut dans la Catéchèse." *La Maison-Dieu* 30 (1952) 19–35.

———. "Histoire du Salut et Formation Liturgique." *La Maison-Dieu* 78 (1964) 22–35.

———. "Histoire et Pensée Religieuse." *Revue de Synthése* 86 (1965) 291–303.

———. "History and Prophecy." *Theology Digest* 6.2 (1958) 109–13.

———. "Holy Scripture: Meeting Place of Christians." *Cross Currents* 3 (Spring 1953) 251–61.

———. "Hommage à Emmanuel Mounier." *La Documentation Catholique* 47 (1950) 693–94.

———. "Homélie du Jubilé de Sœur Marie de l'Assomption." *Axes* (June-July 1973) 20–24.

———. "Hommage à Wladimir D'Ormesson." *La Nouvelle Revue des Deux Mondes* (October 1973) 8–10.

———. "Hope." *Jubilee* 6 (March 1959) 36–39.

———. "L'Horizon Patristique." *Nouvelles de l'Institut Catholique de Paris* 2 (1971) 3–21.

———. "Horizontalism: An Expression of the Crisis of the Sense of God." *Catholic Mind* 67 (April 1969) 20–22.

———. "L'Hospitalite, Grande Realite Humaine." *L'Anneau d'Or* 104 (1962) 104–5.

———. "Humanisme et Christianisme." In *Connaissance de l'Homme au 20e Siècle*, 97–108. Neuchatel: Editions de la Baconniere, 1952.

———. "The Ignatian Vision of the Universe and of Man." *Cross Currents* 4 (Fall 1954) 357–66.

———. "L'Incompréhensibilité de Dieu d'apres Saint Jean Chrysostome." *Recherches de Science Religieuse* 37 (1950) 176–94.

———. "L'Idéal et les Moyens de Perfection dans les Diverses Religions: Trois Visages de la Sainteté Chrétienne." *Bulletin du Cercle Saint Jean-Baptiste* (October-November 1957) 4–7.

———. "The Infallability of the Church." *L'Osservatore Romano* (January 20, 1972) 2.

———. "In Medio Templi Tui." *Bulletin du Cercle Saint Jean-Baptiste* (February 1951) 1–2.

———. "Interpolations Antiorigénistes chez Grégoire de Nysse." In *Überlieferungsgeschichtliche Untersuchungen*, 135–39. Berlin: Akademie-Verlag, 1981.

———. "Intervention au Synode." *La Documentation Catholique* (2 November 1969) 967.

———. "Introduction aux Évangiles de l'Enfance." *Bulletin Saint Jean-Baptiste* (December 1966) 55–62.

———. "L'Introduction a la Poésie Français: L'Anthologie de Thierry Mauliner." *Études* 242 (1940) 545–51.

———. "Introduction to *Sources Chrétiennes*." In Grégoire de Nysse, *La Vie de Moïse*. Paris: Editions du Cerf, 1955.

———. "Iterum Modicum." *Bulletin du Cercle Saint Jean-Baptiste* (June 1949) 2–3.

———. "Jalons pour une Theologie Missionaire: Le Femme Victorieuse du Serpent." *Bulletin du Cercle Saint Jean-Baptiste* (March 1954) 3–6.

———. "Jalons pour une Theologie Missionaire: Marie et la Contemplation Missionaire." *Bulletin du Cercle Saint Jean-Baptiste* (April 1954) 2–5.

———. "Jalons pour une Theologie Missionaire: Marie et la Mission du Verbe." *Bulletin du Cercle Saint Jean-Baptiste* (May 1954) 2–5.

———. "La Jalousie de Dieu." *Dieu Vivant* 16 (1949) 63–73.

———. "Jean-Baptiste et le Temps de l'Advent." *Bulletin du Cercle Saint Jean-Baptiste* (December 1962) 10–16.

———. "Jean, Tèmoin de la Trinité." *Bulletin du Cercle Saint Jean-Baptiste* (December 1963) 7–15.

———. "La Jérusalem Nouvelle." *Bulletin Saint Jean-Baptiste* (May 1965) 301–11.

———. "Je suis dans l'Église.' In *Je Crois en l'Église, que je n'en sois jamais Séparé*, ed. Gabriel Marie Garrone, 47–76. Paris: Mame, 1972.

———. "Jésus Baptisé par Jean." *Bulletin du Cercle Saint Jean-Baptiste* (May 1963) 7–13.

———. "Le 'Jésus-Christ' du P. De Grandmaison." *Les Chahiers de Neuilly* (October 1957) 238–42.

———. "Jésus au Temple." *Bulletin Saint Jean-Baptiste* (May 1967) 295–304.

———. "Jesus et Israël." *Études* 258 (1948) 68–74.

———. "Les Jeunes et Dieu." *La Documentation Catholique* 66 (1969) 343.

———. "Jeunesse 1958." *Les Cahiers de Neuilly* (October 1958) 225–32.

———. "Job ou le Mystere de la Souffrance." *Bulletin du Cercle Saint Jean-Baptiste* (April 1955) 5–7.

———. "Job: The Mystery of Man and of God." In *The Dimensions of Job: A Study and Selected Readings*, edited by Nahum Norbert Glatzer, 100–111. New York: Schocken, 1969.

———. "Joh. 7,38 et Ezéch. 47,1–11." In *Studia Evangelica*, vol. II, pt. I, edited by F. L. Cross, 158–63. Berlin: Akademie-Verlag, 1964.

———. "Les Journées Universitaires de Paris: Sacerdoce et Temoignage." *Études* 231 (1937) 337–42.

———. "Josué." *Bulletin Saint Jean-Baptiste* (December 1965) 59–65.

———. "Les Journées Universitaires de Poitiers." *Études* 227 (1936) 327–35.

———. "Judéo-Christianisme et Gnose." In *Apects du Judéo-Christianisme, Colloque de Strasbourg, 23–25 Avril 1964*, 139–66. Paris: Presses Universitaires de France, 1965.

Bibliography

———. "Justice Biblique et Justice Sociale." *Bulletin du Cercle Saint Jean-Baptiste* (April 1955) 10–13.

———. "The Justice of God." In *Readings in Biblical Morality*, 48–53. Englewood Cliffs, N. J.: Prentice-Hall, 1967.

———. "ΚΑΙΝΗ ΚΤΙΣΙΣ." In *Paulus-Hellas-Oikumene (An Ecumenical Symposium)*, 50–53. Athens: The Student Christian Association of Greece, 1951.

———. "Le ΚΑΙΡΟΣ de la Messe d'apres les Homélies sur l'Incompréhensible de Saint Jean Chrysostom." In *Die Messe in der Glaubensverkündigung*, 71–78. Freiburg: Herder, 1950.

———. "Le Kérygme selon le Christianisme Primtif." In *L'Annonce de l'Évangile aujourd'hui: Rapports du Quatriéme Colloque de "Parole et Mission."* 67–86. Paris: Cerf, 1962.

———. "Les Laïcs Chrétiens et la Sacralisation du Temporel." In *Les Laïcs et la Mission de l'Église*, 115–126. Paris: Éditions du Centurion, 1962.

———. "Les Laïcs Chrétiens dans la Sacralisation du Temporel." *Bulletin du Cercle Saint Jean-Baptiste* (June-July 1962) 55–63.

———. "Lectures Bibliques." *Études* 271 (1951) 206–16.

———. "Lectures et Cantiques." *La Maison-Dieu* 26 (1951) 34–40.

———. "Le Lendemain de la Mort du Maréchal Carmona." *Études* 269 (1951) 402–4.

———. "La Lettre de Mauriac à Cocteau." *Études* 272 (1952):262–63.

———. "La Liberté Chrétienne et l'Église." *Les Cahiers de Neuilly* (July 1952):1–11.

———. "La Liberté Religieuse." *La Revue des Deux Mondes* (October 1971) 25–34.

———. "La Littérature Latine avant Tertullien." *Revue des Études Latines* 48 (1970) 357–75.

———. "Little Flock or Great People?" *The Furrow* 15 (December 1964) 757–61.

———. "Living the Faith." *Theology Digest* 7.1 (1959) 41–46.

———. "Living the Faith." *The Catholic Mind* 57 (December 1959) 515–22.

———. "Un Livre Protestant sur Saint Pierre." *Études* 276 (1953) 206–19.

———. "La Loi et l'Alliance." *Axes* (January 1971) 6–12.

———. "La Loi dans l'Église." *Axes* (May 1971) 3–8.

———. "La Loi, le Peche, la Grace, la Croix." *Axes* (March 1971) 3–11.

———. "Loi ou la Saintete selon la Loi Naturelle." *Bulletin du Cercle Saint Jean-Baptiste* (March 1955) 6–9.

———. "Love of God and Apostolate." *Christ to the World* 15 (1970) 286–89.

———. "Lux in Tenebris." *Bulletin du Cercle Saint Jean-Baptiste* (April 1951) 1–2.

———. "The Magisterium's Authority and Theologians' Liberty." *L'Osservatore Romano* (November 20, 1969) 11.

———. "Man in Search of Himself." *L'Osservtore Romano* (September 28, 1972) 10.

———. "La Manifestation de la Trinité dans l'Incarnation." *Bulletin du Cercle Saint Jean-Baptiste* (February 1956) 4–7.

———. "Les Manuscrits de la Mer Morte et les Origines du Christianisme." *Flambeau* 55 (March 1979) 249–53.

———. "Le Mariage de Grégoire de Nysse et la Chronologie de sa Vie." *Revue des Études Augustiniennes* 2 (1956) 71–78.

———. "Marie dans la Spiritualité Française." *Études* 281 (1954) 145–57.

———. "Marie-Madeleine et l'Église des Nations." *Bulletin du Cercle Saint Jean-Baptiste* (May 1950) 1–2.

———. "Le Marxisme et la Mort." *Bulletin du Cercle Saint Jean-Baptiste* (February 1954) 10–14.
———. "Marxist History and Sacred History." *Review of Politics* 13 (1951) 503–13.
———. "Maternite de Marie et Mission." *Bulletin du Cercle Saint Jean-Baptiste* (January 1954) 2–7.
———. "La Mauvaise Foi d'un Incroyant." *Études* 320 (1964) 513–23.
———. "Le Mauvais Gouvernement du Monde d'aprés le Gnosticisme." In *Le Origini dello Gnosticismo: Colloquio di Messina 13–18 Aprille 1966*, 448–59. Leiden: Brill, 1967.
———. "The Meaning of Job." *Theology Digest* 4.3 (1956) 189.
———. "Medium Silentium." *Bulletin du Cercle Saint Jean-Baptiste* (January 1950) 1–2.
———. "Melchisedech, le Pretre de la Religion Cosmique." *Bulletin du Cercle Saint Jean-Baptiste* (February 1955) 7–10.
———. "Mensonge [l'Illusion] de Satan et Vérité de Jésus." *Bulletin du Cercle Saint Jean-Baptiste* (March 1956) 5–7.
———. "Mépris du Monde et Valeurs Terrestres d'aprés le Concile Vatican II." *Revue d'Ascétique et de Mystique* 41 (1965) 421–28.
———. "Mère Marie de l'Assomption." *Axes* (February-March 1973) 2.
———. "Le Message de la Genèse." *Bulletin du Cercle Saint Jean-Baptiste* (October-November 1960) 8–16.
———. "Le Message de la Genèse: La Création du Monde." *Bulletin du Cercle Saint Jean-Baptiste* (December 1960) 7–12.
———. "Le Message de la Genèse: La Doctrine Biblique de l'Homme." *Bulletin du Cercle Saint Jean-Baptiste* (January 1961) 7–13.
———. "Le Message de la Genèse: Le Mystère du Péche." *Bulletin du Cercle Saint Jean-Baptiste* (February 1961) 7–13.
———. "Le Message de la Genèse: Adam et le Christ." *Bulletin du Cercle Saint Jean-Baptiste* (March 1961) 7–12.
———. "Le Message de la Genèse: Les Peuples de la Terre." *Bulletin du Cercle Saint Jean-Baptiste* (April 1961) 7–14.
———. "Le Message de la Genèse: La Tour de Babel." *Bulletin du Cercle Saint Jean-Baptiste* (May 1961) 7–13.
———. "Le Message Ignatien et Notre Temps." *Études* 290 (1956) 3–17.
———. "Le Message de Lou Tseng Tsiang." *Bulletin du Cercle Saint Jean-Baptiste* (May 1949) 7–8.
———. "Metempsychosis in Gregory of Nyssa." In *The Heritage of the Early Church: Essays in Honor of the Very Reverend Georges Vasilievich Florovsky*, eds. David Neiman and Margaret Schatkin, 227–43. Roma: Pont. Institutum Studorum Orientalium, 1973.
———. "MIA EKKLESIA chez les Pères Grecs des Premiers Siècles." In *1054–1954: L'Église et les Églises: Neuf Siècles Douloureuse Séparation entre l'Orient et l'Occident*, 129–139. Belgique: Éditions de Chevetogne, 1954.
———. "Le Ministère des Femmes dans l'Eglise Ancienne." *La Maison-Dieu* 61 (1960) 70–96.
———. "Le Ministère Sacerdotal chez les Pères Grecs." In *Études sur le Sacrement de l'Ordre*, 147–65. Paris: Éditions du Cerf, 1957.
———. "Le Miracle: Théologie du Miracle." In *Le Livre des Miracles de Notre-Dame de Rocamadour, Rocamadour, 19 au 21 Mai 1972*, 131–55. Rocamadour: n. p., 1973.

Bibliography

———. "La Mission du Chrétien dans un Monde Technique." *Bulletin du Cercle Saint Jean-Baptiste* (June-July 1958) 201–6.
———. "Mission Chrétienne et Mouvement Ouvrier." *Axes* (June-July 1969) 55–60.
———. "Mission Chrétienne et Mouvement Ouvrier." *Bulletin du Cercle Saint Jean-Baptiste* (February 1960) 6–9.
———. "Mission et Colonisation." *Les Cahiers de Neuilly* (January 1956) 1–5.
———. "La Mission Face aux Bouleversements Sociologiques." *Bulletin du Cercle Saint Jean-Baptiste* (October-November 1959) 4–8.
———. "La Mission de Jean." *Bulletin du Cercle Saint Jean-Baptiste* (April 1963) 7–15.
———. "Mission et Martyre." *Bulletin du Cercle Saint Jean-Baptiste* (December 1947) 1.
———. "Missionaire Signe de Contradiction." *Bulletin du Cercle Saint Jean-Baptiste* (January 1951) 4–6.
———. "Missionary Nature of the Church." *Christ to the World* (July-August 1967) 336–45.
———. "The Missionary Nature of the Church." In *The Word in the Third World*, 11–43. Washington: Corpus, 1968.
———. "Le Mois: Le Discours du Saint-Père et La Tactique Communiste." *Études* 257 (1948) 247–49.
———. "Le Mois: Tentation du Communisme." *Études* 249 (1946) 116–17.
———. "Moïse Exemple et Figure chez Grégoire de Nysse." *Cahiers Sioniens* 8 (1954) 267–82.
———. "La Morale des Affaires." *Les Cahiers de Neuilly* (April 1955) 80–83.
———. "La Morale au Service de la Personne." *Études* 317 (1963) 145–53.
———. "La Mort d'Emmanuel Mournier." *Études* 265 (1950) 250–51.
———. "La Mort de Jean-Baptiste." *Bulletin du Cercle Saint Jean-Baptiste* (April 1964) 7–14.
———. "La Mort de Louis Massignon." *Études* 315 (1962) 398–99.
———. "The Moslem Wall." *The Commonweal* 34 (February 17, 1950) 505–6.
———. "Un Mouvement Juif Parmi d'Autres." In J*esus*, ed. Louis Leprinc-Ringuet, 89–109. Paris: Hachette-Réalités, 1971.
———. "Le Mouvement Liturgique aux États-Unis." *La Maison-Dieu* 25 (1951) 90–93.
———. "Le Mouvement Œcuménique." *Relations* 296 (August 1965) 238–39.
———. "Mystere Chretien de la Mort." *Bulletin du Cercle Saint Jean-Baptiste* (October-November 1953) 4–7.
———. "Mystère de l'Église et Mission de Chrétien." *L'Anneau d'Or* 67 (1956) 5–12.
———. "Le Mystère de la Croix chez les Premières Générations Chrétiennes." *Bulletin du Cercle Saint Jean-Baptiste* (March 1957) 105–8.
———. "Le Mystère du Culte dans les Sermones de Saint Grégoire de Nysse." In *Vom christlichen Mysterium: gesammelte Arbeiten zum Gedächtnis von Odo Casel OSB*, 76–93. Düsseldorf: Patmos-Verlag, 1951.
———. "Le Mystère de l'Incarnation dans la Première Littérature Chrétienne." *Bulletin du Cercle Saint Jean-Baptiste* (January 1957) 59–62.
———. "Le Mystére Liturgique Intervention Actuelle de Dieu dans l'Histoire." *La Maison-Dieu* 79 (1964) 28–39.
———. "Le Mystere du Premier-Ne." *Bulletin du Cercle Saint Jean-Baptiste* (February 1955) 1–2.
———. "The Mystery of Life and Death." *Philosophy Today* 1 (June 1957) 118–21.

———. "Mythe et Revelation." *Bulletin du Cercle Saint Jean-Baptiste* (Febraury 1949) 8–10.

———. "Mythologie Paienne et Revelation Chretienne." *Bulletin du Cercle Saint Jean-Baptiste* (July 1949) 12–17.

———. "La Naissance du Christianisme." In *Le Catholisme Hier-Domain*, eds. Jean Daniélou, Jean Honoré and Paul Poupard. Paris: Éditions Buchet/Chastel, 1974.

———. "La Naissance de Jésus." *Bulletin Saint Jean-Baptiste* (March 1967) 199–210.

———. "Les Nationalismes et les Missions." In *La Conscience Chrétienne et les Nationalismes*, 232–42. Paris: P. Horay, 1959.

———. "La Nature Missionnaire de l'Église." *Le Christ au Monde* 12 (1967) 354–63.

———. "Necessity of Preaching, Faith and Baptism, according to the Acts." *Christ to the World* 14 (1969) 237–41.

———. "The Need for Christian Institutions." *The Month* 41 (1969) 32–37.

———. "The New Testament and the Theology of History." In *Studia Evangelica*, edited by Kurt Aland, F. L. Cross, Jean Daniélou, Harald Riesenfeld and W. C. Van Unnik. Berlin: Akademie-Verlag, 1959.

———. "A New Vision of Christian Origins: Judeo-Christianity." *Cross Currents* 18 (Spring 1968) 163–73.

———. "Noe ou l'Attente de la Nouvelle Creation." *Bulletin du Cercle Saint Jean-Baptiste* (January 1955) 7–10.

———. "Les Non-Chrétiens devant le Christ." *Bulletin Saint Jean-Baptiste* (October-November 1966) 7–16.

———. "Non-Christian Religions." *The Critic* 25 (1966) 47.

———. "Non-Christian Religions and Salvation." In *Foundations of Mission Theology*, 54–59. Maryknoll, NY: Orbis, 1972.

———. "Non-Christians and Christ." *The Month* 37 (1967) 137–44.

———. "Non-Christians and their Religion." *The Clergy Monthly* 7 (December 1964) 168–71.

———. "La Non-Violence dans la Pensée de l'Eglise." *Revue de l'Action Populaire* 89 (1955) 641–54.

———. "Note Conjointe." *Dieu Vivant* 22 (1952) 101–6.

———. "Notes sur Trois Textes Eschatologiques de Saint Grégoire de Nysse." *Recherches de Sciences Religieuse* 30 (1940) 348–56.

———. "La Notion de Confins (*Methorios*) chez Grégoire de Nysse." *Recherches de Science Religieuse* 49 (1961) 161–87.

———. "La Notion de Personne chez les Péres Grecs." In *Problémes de la Personne*, ed. Ignace Meyerson, 113–21. Paris: Mouton, 1973.

———. "Notre Cite est dans le Ciel." *Bulletin du Cercle Saint Jean-Baptiste* (February 1950) 1–2.

———. "Nous Sommes Spirituellement des Hellenes." *Bulletin du Cercle Saint Jean-Baptiste* (December 1949) 1–2.

———. "Novatien et le De Mundo d'Apulée." In *Romanitas et Christianitas*, ed. Jan Hendrik Waszink and Willem den Boer, 71–80. London: North Holland, 1973.

———. "La Nuee des Temoins." *Bulletin du Cercle Saint Jean-Baptiste* (October-November 1951) 1–2.

———. "Les Nuits des Nations." *Bulletin du Cercle Saint Jean-Baptiste* (December 1948) 1–2.

———. "La Nuit de Pascal." *Les Cahies de Neuilly* (January 1955) 1–7.

Bibliography

———. "Obéissance a Dieu et Engagement Temporel." *Études* 280 (1954) 289–300.
———. "L'Occident Chrétien a-t-il encore un Role Missionaire?" *Études* 285 (1955) 173–83.
———. "L'Œuvre de Charles du Bos." In *Qu'est-ce que la Litterature?*, 259–65. Paris: Plon, 1945.
———. "Les Oiseaux du Ciel et l'Ombre de l'Arbre." *Bulletin du Cercle Saint Jean-Baptiste* (October-November 1954) 2–4.
———. "Onction et Baptême chez Grégoire de Nysse." In *Le Saint-Esprit dans la Liturgie, Conférences Saint-Serge, XVIe Semaine d'Études Liturgiques, Paris, 1–4 Juillet 1969*, 65–70. Roma: Edizioni Liturgiche, 1977.
———. "The One Church." *L'Osservatore Romano* (September 14, 1972) 3, 11.
———. "Only God's Absoluteness Insures Freedom." *L'Osservatore Romano* (January 1, 1970) 11.
———. "Oraison et Abandon." *Bulletin du Cerlce Saint Jean-Baptiste* (Febraury 1953) 4–6.
———. "L'Oraison comme Problème Politique." *Bulletin du Cercle Saint Jean-Baptiste* (June-July 1964) 62–73.
———. "L'Ordination des Femmes en Suede." *Études* 305 (1960) 398–99.
———. "Oriens ex Alto." *Bulletin du Cercle Saint Jean-Baptiste* (April 1948) 1.
———. "Orientations Actuelles de la Recherche sur Grégoire de Nysse." In *Écriture et Culture Philosophique dasn la Pensée de Grégoire de Nysse*, 3–17. Leiden: Brill, 1971.
———. "Les Orientations Présentes de la Pensée Religieuse." *Études* 249 (1946) 5–21.
———. "Origéne." *Revue de Métaphysique et de Morale* 55 (1950) 111–12.
———. "Origéne comme exegete de la Bible." In *Studia Patristica*, vol. I, eds. Kurt Aland and F. L. Cross, 280–290. Berlin: Akademie-Verlag, 1957.
———. "Origéne et Maxime de Tyr." *Recherces de Scinece Religieuse* 34 (1947) 359–61.
———. "Les Origines de l'Épiphanie et Les *Testimonia*." *Recherches de Science Religieuse* 52 (1964) 538–53.
———. "L'Origine du Mal chez Grégoire de Nysse." In *Diakonia Pisteos: Al Reverendo Padre José Antonio de Aldama*, edited by Antonia Montero, 31–44. Granado: Facultad Teologica de Granada, 1969.
———. "Ou en est le Mouvement Liturgique?" *La Nouvelle revue des Deux Mondes* 3 (1974) 12–18.
———. "Our Real Vocation." *L'Osservatore Romano*(October 16, 1969) 10.
———. "Le Pape et les Evêquees." *La Documentation Catholique* 66 (1969) 796–97.
———. "Pâques et Baptêmes aux Premiers Siècles." *Bulletin du Cercle Saint Jean-Baptiste* (April 1947) 1–2.
———. "Parole de Dieu et Mission de l'Église." in *Le Pretre Ministre de le Parole*, 41–54. Paris: Union des Œuvres Catholiques de France, 1954.
———. "Parole, Foi, Baptême." *Axes* (January 1969) 4–8.
———. "Pascal et la Vérité." In *Pascal: Textes du Tricentenaire*, 17–25. Paris: Fayard, 1963.
———. "Le Pasteur Transperce." *Bulletin du Cercle Saint Jean-Baptiste* (May 1952) 1–2.
———. "Paul dans les Actes des Apotres." *Axes* (May 1969) 4–13.
———. "Paul and the Pagans." *Christ to the World* 17 (1972) 480–87.
———. "Paul et les Religions Paiennes." *Axes* (March 1969) 3–12.
———. "Le Péché Originel." In *Notre Foi*, 113–34. Paris: Beauchesne, 1967.
———. "La Pédagogie Divine d'après Pères Grecs." *Bulletin du Cercle Saint Jean-Baptiste* (January 1956) 5–10.

———. "Péguy devant Dieu." *La Nouvelle Revue des Deux Mondes* 3 (1974) 545–50.
———. "Péguy et les Péres de l'Église." In *Littérature et Société: Recueil d'études en l'Honneur de Benard Guyon*, 173–79. Paris: Desclée De Brouwer, 1973.
———. "La Pensée Chrétienne." *Nouvelle Revue Théologique* 69 (1947) 930–40.
———. "Penseurs et Mystique d'Israël." *Études* 268 (1951) 362–71.
———. "Pentecote, Mystere d'Unite." *Bulletin du Cercle Saint Jean-Baptiste* (June-July 1950) 2–4.
———. "Les Pères de l'Eglise et l'Unité des Chrétiens." *Texte undUntersuchungen zur Geschichte des altchristlichen Literatur* 92 (1966) 23–32.
———. "Une Perspective Chrétienne des Rites." In *Les Rites: Conférence Prononcée par la Cardinal Jean Daniélou le 20 Avril 1970 à Paris*, 41–49. Paris: Alliance Mondiale des Religions, 1993.
———. "Perspectives Eschatologiques: Autour d'un Probléme d'Exégèse." *Études* 264 (1950) 359–68.
———. "The Perversion of Culture." *L'Osservatore Romano* (July 25, 1974) 12.
———. "Le Peuple Chrétien selon Péguy." *Études* 323 (1965) 175–86.
———. "Phenomenology of Religions and Philosophy of Religion." In *The History of Religions: Essays in Methodology*, 67–85. Chicago: University of Chicago Press, 1959.
———. "Philosophie ou Théologie de l'Histoire?" *Dieu Vivant* 19 (1950) 127–36.
———. "The Philosophy of Philo: The Significance of Professor Harry A. Wolfson's New Study" *Theological Studies* 9 (1948) 578–89.
———. "Pierre dans le Judéo-Christianisme Hétérodoxe." In *San Pietro: Atti della XIX Settimana Biblica*, 443–58. Brescia: Paideia, 1967.
———. "La Place du Christianisme dans le Rapport de l'Europe et des Autres Civilisations." *Comprendre* 17–18 (1957) 37–40.
———. "La Place Irremplaçable de la Vie Religieuse dans l'Église et dans la Société." *La Documentation Catholique* (April 21,1974) 384–88.
———. "La Place des Religieux dans la Structure de l'Église." *Études* 320 (1964) 147–55.
———. "The Place of Religious in the Structure of the Church." *Review for Religious* 24 (1965) 518–25.
———. "Les Pleureuses Chassèes du Temple." *Bulletin du Cercle Saint Jean-Baptiste* (March 1955) 1–2.
———. "Plotin et Grégoire de Nysse sur Mal." In *Atti del Covegno Internazionale sul Tema Plotino e il Neoplatonismo in Oriente e in Occidente*, 485–94. Roma: Accademia Nazionale dei Lincei, 1974.
———. "Pluralism within Christian Thought." *Theology Digest* 10.2 (1962) 67–70.
———. "Poétes de Combat." *Études* 244 (1945) 99–111.
———. "The Pope and the Bishops." *Christ to the World* 14 (1969) 417–20.
———. "The Postponement of the Baptism of Infants." *Christ to the World* 16 (1971) 314–18.
———. "Pour les Institutions Chrétiennes." *Relations* 324 (February 1968) 51–52.
———. "Pour une Théologie de l'Hospitalité." *Axes* (June-July 1974) 1–8.
———. "Pour une Thélogie de l'Hospitalité." *Bulletin du Cercle Saint Jean-Baptiste* (June-July 1951) 4–8.
———. "Pour une Théologie de l'Hospitalité." *La Vie Spirituelle* 85 (1951) 339–47.
———. "Pourquoi je n'ai pas Parlé à Florence." *Études* 299 (1958) 256–57.
———. "Praecessit nos Regina Nostra." *Bulletin du Cercle Saint Jean-Baptiste* (October-November 1950) 2.

Bibliography

———. "Présence de Jean-Baptiste." *Bulletin du Cercle Saint Jean-Baptiste* (May 1964) 8–14.
———. "Présence et Transcendance de Dieu." *Les Cahiers de Neuilly* (January 1954) 8–16.
———. "La Présentation au Temple." *Bulletin Saint Jean-Baptiste* (April 1967) 247–57.
———. "Le Prêtre, l'Église et la Civilisation." *Relations* 326 (April 1968) 128–29.
———. "Le Prêtre: Intervention." *Bulletin Saint Jean-Baptiste* (June-July 1967) 382–83.
———. "Des Prêtres Passionnés de Dieu et Passionés des Hommes." *La Documentation Catholique* (November 1, 1970) 978–81.
———. "La Priere du Christ." *Bulletin du Cercle Saint Jean-Baptiste* (May 1953) 5–7.
———. "Priere Liturgique et Priere Mystique." *Bulletin du Cerlce Saint Jean-Baptiste* (January 1953) 4–6.
———. "La Prière de Louange." *Bulletin du Cerlce Saint Jean-Baptiste* (December 1952) 4–5.
———. "La Priere Mystique d'Israel." *Bulletin du Cerlce Saint Jean-Baptiste* (December 1952) 6–8.
———. "Prière et Poésie Fondements de la Civilization." *Études* 279 (1953) 3–17.
———. "Priestly Celibacy." *L'Osservatore Romano* (February 12, 1970) 9.
———. "The Priestly Ministry in the Greek Fathers." In *The Sacrament of Holy Orders: Some Papers and Discussions Concerning Holy Orders at a Session of the Centre de Pastorale Liturgique, 1955*. Collegeville, MN: Liturgical, 1962.
———. "Pro Totius Mundi Salute." *Bulletin du Cercle Saint Jean-Baptiste* (July 1949) 2–4.
———. "Le Problème du Changement chez Grégoire de Nysse." *Archives de Philosophie* 29 (1966) 323–47.
———. "Le Problème de Dieu dans le Monde d'aujourd'hui." *L'Anneau d'Or* 138 (1967) 414–32.
———. "Les Problémes de l'Église." *La Revue des Duex Mondes* (January 1971) 110–27.
———. "Le Problème Théologique des Religions non Chrétiennes." *Archivio di Filosofia* (1956) 209–33.
———. "The Problem of Symbolism." *Thought* 25 (1950) 423–40.
———. "La Profession de Foi de Paul VI." *Études* 329 (1968) 599–607.
———. "La Propriété Privée et sa Fonction: Universalisme ou Solidarisme." *Études* 217 (1933) 165–81.
———. "Le Protestantisme dans des Voies Nouvelles?." *Études* 277 (1953) 145–56.
———. "The Psalms in the Liturgy of the Ascension." *Orate Fratres* 24 (May 1950) 241–51.
———. "Le Psaume 21 dans la Catéchèse Patristique." *La Maison-Dieu* 49 (1957) 17–34.
———. "Le Psaume 22 dans l'Exégèse Patristique." In *Richesses et Déficiences des Anciens Psaultiers Latins*, 189–211. Roma: Abbaye Saint-Jérôme, 1959.
———. "Le Psaume XXII et l'Initiation Chrétienne." *La Maison-Dieu* 23 (1950) 54–69.
———. "Les Psaumes dans la Liturgie de l'Ascension." *La Maison-Dieu* 21 (1950) 40–56.
———. "Psychiatrie et 'Morales sans Péché." In *Monde Moderne et Sens du Péche*, 180–88. Paris: P. Horay, 1957.
———. "Les Quatre Visages de Job." *Études* 286 (1955) 145–56.
———. "Les Quatre-temps de Septembre et la Fête des Tabernacles." *La Maison-Dieu* 46 (1956) 114–36.
———. "Qu'est-ce que la Tradition Apostolique?" *Dieu Vivant* 26 (1953) 73–78.
———. "Qu'est-ce que Typologie." In *L'Ancien Testament et les Chrétiens*, 199–205. Paris: Éditions du Cerf, 1951.

———. "Question à Karl Barth." *Rèforme* 4 (1948) 4.
———. "La Question du Latin." *Études* 245 (1945) 381–82.
———. "Que Ta Volonté Soit Faite." *Bulletin Saint Jean-Baptiste* (February 1967) 197–98.
———. "Rahab, Figure de l'Église." *Irénikon* 22 (1949) 26–45.
———. "Rainer Maria Rilke: La Lutte avec l'Ange." *Études* 233 (1937) 308–23.
———. "Recherche d'un Style." *Études* 316 (1963) 198–204.
———. "Recherche et Traditon chez les Pères du IIe et du IIIe Siècles." *Nouvelle Revue Theologique* 94 (1972) 449–61.
———. "Recherches et Tradition chez les Péres." In *Studia Patristica*, vol. XII, ed. Elizabeth A. Livingstone, 3–13. Berlin: Akademie-Verlag, 1975.
———. "Un Recueil Inédit de Paroles de Jésus?." *Études* 302 (1959) 38–49.
———. "Le Regne de la Mort et la Victoire du Christ." *Bulletin du Cercle Saint Jean-Baptiste* (April 1950) 1–2.
———. "Le Refus de la Foi." In *Notre Foi*, 135–148. Paris: Beauchesne, 1967.
———. "La Reine de Saba." *Bulletin du Cercle Saint Jean-Baptiste* (May 1955) 5–9.
———. "Religion et Civilisation: Réponse à quelques Objections." *Études* 326 (1967) 418–31.
———. "Les Religions Face à l'Athéisme." *Bulletin du Cercle Saint Jean-Baptiste* (June-July 1956) 8–12.
———. "Les Religions et la Paix." *Axes* (January-February 1972) 5–10.
———. "Religious Liberty." *Journal of Ecumenical Studies* 2 (1965) 265–71.
———. "Les Repas de la Bible et leur Signification." *La Maison-Dieu* 18 (1949) 7–33.
———. "Réponse a Oscar Cullman." *Dieu Vivant* 24 (1953) 107–16.
———. "Réponse du Père Daniélou." *Dieu Vivant* 7 (1946) 86–88.
———. "Le Respect de la Vie Humaine." *Axes* (April-May 1973) 5–8.
———. "Le Reste d'Israel." *Bulletin du Cercle Saint Jean-Baptiste* (February 1949) 1–2.
———. "La Résurrection du Christ." *Axes* (July 1970) 3–8.
———. "La Résurrection des Corps." *Bulletin Saint Jean-Baptiste* (March 1965) 201–10.
———. "La Resurrection des Corps chez Grégoire de Nysse." *Vigiliiae Christianae* 7 (July 1953) 154–70.
———. "La Résurrection des Morts." *Bulletin Saint Jean-Baptiste* (June 1968) 351–63.
———. "La Résurrection Mystère de Salut." *Bulletin Saint Jean-Baptiste* (October-November 1968) 7–15.
———. "La Résurrection comme Révélation." *Bulletin Saint Jean-Baptiste* (April 1968) 303–10.
———. "Retraite Ignatienne et Tradition Chrétienne." *Christus* 10 (1956) 152–70.
———. "La Révélation du Mystère." *Cahiers de Neuilly* 2 (January 1942) 60–66.
———. "La Révélation et la Sacre." *Bulletin Saint Jean-Baptiste* (June-July 1965) 387–96.
———. "Les Rites." In *Les Rites: Conférence Prononcée par le Cardinal Daniélou le 20 Avril 1970 à Paris*, 7–25. N. p.: Alliance Mondiale des Religions, 1993.
———. "Rites Païens et Sacraments Chrétiens." *Bulletin du Cercle Saint Jean-Baptiste* (October-November 1956) 5–7.
———. "Le Rôle des Créatures Spirituelles, Anges et Démons, dans l'Économie du Salut." *Bulletin du Cercle Saint Jean-Baptiste* (April 1956) 5–8.
———. "Le Rôle des Laïcs dans l'Église Primitive." *L'Anneau d'Or: Cahiers de Spiritualité Familiale* 26 (1949) 77–82.
———. "Le Royame de la Prière." *Axes* (June-July 1969) 65–67.

Bibliography

———. "Le Royame de la Prière." *Bulletin du Cercle Saint Jean-Baptiste* (October-November 1952) 4–6.
———. "Rudolf Bultmann." *The Month* 16 (1956) 228–33.
———. "Ruth." *Bulletin Saint Jean-Baptiste* (April 1966) 260–66.
———. "Sacrements et Histoire du Salut." In *Parole de Dieu et Liturgie*, 53–69. Paris: Éditions du Cerf, 1958.
———. "The Sacraments and the History of Salvation." In *The Liturgy and the Word of God*, 21–32. Collegeville, MN: Liturgical, 1959.
———. "Sacraments and Parousia." *Orates Fratres* 25 (1951) 400–404.
———. "La Sagesse et la Folie." *Bulletin du Cercle Saint Jean-Baptiste* (June-July 1952) 5–10.
———. "Saint Augustin et le Salut des Païens." *Bulletin du Cercle Saint Jean-Baptiste* (January 1960) 60–63.
———. "Saint Bernard et les Péres Grecs." *Analecta Sacri Ordinis Cisterciensis* 9 (1953) 46–55.
———. "Le Saint-Esprit dans les Actes." *Axes* (April 1969) 4–12.
———. "Saint Grégoire de Nysse." *Bulletin Josephe Lotte* (1938) 171–80.
———. "Saint Grégoire de Nysse dans l'Histoire du Monachisme." In *Théologie de la Vie Monastique: Études sur la Tradition Patristique*, 131–42. Paris: Aubier, 1961.
———. "Saint Hilaire, évêque et docteur." In *Hilaire de Poitiers Évêque et Docteur: Cinq conférences données à Poitiers à l'occasion du XVIe centenaire de sa mort*, 9–18. Paris: Études Augustiniennes, 1968.
———. "Saint Irénée et les Origines de la Théologie de l'Histoire." *Recherches de Science Religieuse* 34 (1947) 227–31.
———. "Saint Jerome et les Pères Grecs." *Bible et Terre Sainte* 148 (1973) 2–3.
———. "Sainteté." *Les Cahiers de Neuilly* (July 1955) 117–21.
———. "Samson." *Bulletin Saint Jean-Baptiste* (March 1966) 211–18.
———. "La Sanctification de Jean-Baptiste." *Bulletin du Cercle Saint Jean-Baptiste* (January 1963) 7–14.
———. "Sanctitas Dei." *Cahiers de Neuilly* 6 (January 1943) 44–52.
———. "Savior aujourd'hui Vivre sa Foi." *Relations* 27 (December 1967) 331.
———. "Le Scandale de la Division entre les Chrétiens." *Bulletin du Cercle Saint Jean-Baptiste* (January1948) 6–8.
———. "Le Scandale de la Vérité." *Études* 304 (1960) 3–17.
———. "Schema 13: The Theology of Temporal Action." *Social Survey* 13 (1964) 345–50.
———. "Scripture, Tradition, and the Dialogue." *Theology Digest* 9.1 (1961) 38–42.
———. "Le Sens de la Loi." *Axes* (December 1970) 5–10.
———. "Le Sens des Mythes." *Ecclesia* 215 (1967) 48–61.
———. "La Sens du Sacré." *La Documentation Catholique* 71 (1974) 47–48.
———. "The Sense of the Sacred." *L'Osservatore Romano* (June 13, 1974) 4.
———. "La Session à la Droite du Pére." In *Studia Evangelica*, eds. Kurt Aland and F. L. Cross, 689–98. Berlin: Akademie-Verlag, 1959.
———. "Un Seul Dieu en Trois Credos." *Realites* 185 (June 1961) 74–79.
———. "Le Signe de la Croix." *La Table Ronde* 120 (1957) 32–38.
———. "Le Signe du Temple ou de la Présence de Dieu." *Cahiers de Neuilly* 3 (April 1942) 25–39.
———. "La Signification des Actes des Apôtres." *Bulletin du Cercle Saint Jean-Baptiste* (October-November 1961) 7–14.

———. "La Signification Religieuse du Dimanche." *Cahiers de Neuilly* 18 (1948) 1–9.
———. "La Signification du Synode." *La Nouvelle Revue des Deux Mondes* 1 (1972) 5–14.
———. "Signification de Teilhard de Chardin." *Études* 312 (1962) 145–61.
———. "The Silence We do not Want." *L'Osservatore Romano* (June 29, 1972) 11.
———. "La Sincerite de l'Apotre: Compte-rendu de la Conférence du R. P. Daniélou." *Bulletin du Cercle Saint Jean-Baptiste* (April 1950) 4–5.
———. "The Situation of the Church after the Synod." *L'Osservatore Romano* (April 9, 1970) 6–7.
———. "Some Thoughts on the New Eve." *Our Lady's Digest* (March-April 1966) 318–20.
———. "Une Source de la Spiritualité Chrétienne dans les Manuscrits de la Mer Morte: La Doctrine des Deux Esprits." *Dieu Vivant* 25 (1955) 127–36.
———. "Les Sources Bibliques de la Mystique d'Origène." *Revue d'Ascetique et de Mystique* 23 (1947) 126–41.
———. "Le Source Juives de la Doctrine des Anges des Nations chez Origène." *Recherces de Science Religieuse* 38 (1951) 132–37.
———. "La Source du Temple." *Bulletin Saint Jean-Baptiste* (April 1965) 253–64.
———. "Soyez Saints comme Je Suis Saint." *Bulletin du Cercle Saint Jean-Baptiste* (April 1955) 1–2.
———. "The Specific Character of Religious Life." In *Religious Woman—Minister of Faith*, 17–41. Boston: St. Paul Editions, 1974.
———. "La Sphere et la Croix." *Bulletin du Cercle Saint Jean-Baptiste* (April 1946) 1–2.
———. "Spiritual Life in the Tradition of the Western Church." *Ecumenical Review* 15 (April 1963) 283–90.
———. "Spiritual and Political Values." *The Tablet* (June 20, 1959) 556–57.
———. "The Spiritual Roots of the Atlantic Community." *Freedom & Union* 15 (1960) 8–14.
———. "La Spiritualité Missionaire de Sainte Therese de Lisieux." *Bulletin du Cercle Saint Jean-Baptiste* (November 1947) 1.
———. "La Spiritualité des Pères Grecs." *Christus* 7 (1955) 424–27.
———. "Spiritualité de Ressuscités." *Bulletin Saint Jean-Baptiste* (July 1968) 400–408.
———. "La Spiritualité Trinitaire de Saint Ignace." *Christus* 11 (1956) 354–72.
———. "Strengthen Unity." *L'Osservatore Romano* (August 15, 1974) 8.
———. "La Structure Missionaire de l'Église." *Bulletin du Cercle Saint Jean-Baptiste* (July 1949) 5–8.
———. "La Structure Personnelle de l'Espérance." *Cahiers de Neuilly* (July 1949) 15–21.
———. "Le Sujet du Schéma XIII." *Études* 322 (1965) 5–18.
———. "Introduction" to *Sur l'Incompréhensibilité de Dieu*, by Jean Chrysostome. Paris: Éditions du Cerf, 1951.
———. "Sur l'Horizontalisme." *L'Osservatore Romano* (20 September 1968) 2.
———. "La Survie." *Bulletin Saint Jean-Baptiste* (October-November 1967) 8–19.
———. "La Survie dans la Perspective Chrétienne." *Les Cahiers de Neuilly* (July 1956) 104–12.
———. "Le Symbole de la Caverne chez Grégoire de Nysse." In *Mullus: Festchrift Theodor Klauser*, eds. Alfred Stuiber and Alfred Hermann, 43–51. Münster, Westfalen: Aschendorff, 1964.
———. "La Symbolique Cosmique au Temple de Jerusalem chez Philon et Josephe." In *Le Symbolisme Cosmique des Monuments Religieux*, 83–90. Roma: Is. M. E. O., 1957.

Bibliography

———. "Le Symbolisme Baptismal du Véhicule." *Sciences Ecclésiastiques* 10 (1958) 127–38.
———. "Le Symbolisme Cosmique de la Croix." *La Maison-Dieu* 75 (1963) 23–36.
———. "Le Symbolisme Eschatologique de la Fête des Tabernacles." *Irénikon* 31 (1958) 19–40.
———. "Le Symbolisme de l'Eau Vive." *Revue des Sciences Religieuses* 32 (1958) 335–46.
———. "Le Symbolisme du Jour de Paque." *Dieu Vivant* 18 (1950) 45–56.
———. "Le Symbolisme des Quarante Jours." *La Maison-Dieu* 31 (1952) 20–33.
———. "Le Symbolisme des Rites Baptismaux." *Dieu Vivant* 1 (1945) 17–43.
———. "Symbolisme et Théologie." In *Interpretation der Welt: Festschrift für Romano Guardini zum achtzigsten Gerburtstag*, ed. Helmut Kuhn, 663–74. Würzburg: Echter-Verlag, 1965.
———. "Les Tâches du Foyer Chrétien." *L'Anneau d'Or* 132 (1966) 402–16.
———. "Technical Civilization and Atheistic Humanism: Problems They Create for Our Apostolate." *Christ to the World* 4 (1959) 221–29.
———. "Témoignage Cathlolique." In *Protestantisme Français*, eds. Marc Boegner and André Siegfried, 431–44. Paris: Plon, 1945.
———. "Le Témoignage de Jean." *Bulletin du Cercle Saint Jean-Baptiste* (January 1964) 7–16.
———. "Temps et Mission." *Bulletin du Cercle Saint Jean-Baptiste* (June-July 1954) 4–9.
———. "Tendances Vivantes du Catholicisme Américain." *Esprit* 18 (1950) 689–93.
———. "Terre et Paradis chez les Pères de l'Église." *Eranos-Jahrbuch* 22 (1953) 433–72.
———. "Les 'Testimonia' de Commodien." In *Forma Futuri: Studi in Onore del Cardinale Michele Pellegrino*, ed. Michele Pellegrino, 59–69. Torino: Bottega d'Erasmo, 1975.
———. "Un Testimonium sur la Vigne dans Barnabé XII, 1." *Recherches de Science Religieuse* 50 (1962) 389–99.
———. "'That the Scriptures Might Be Fulfilled': Christianity as a Jewish Sect." In *The Crucible of Christianity*, ed. Arnold Toynbee, 262–82. New York: World Publishing Company, 1969.
———. "Le Thème du Paradis Perdu dans la Littérature Contemporaine." *Cahiers de Neuilly* 13 (1946) 1–17.
———. "Théodoret et le Dogmae d'Éphèse." *Recherches de Science Religieuse* 44 (1956) 243–48.
———. "La Théologie et l'Apologétique." In *Cinquante Ans de Pensée Catholique Française*, 105–15. Paris: Fayard, 1955.
———. "La Théologie Missionaire des Pères Grecs." *Bulletin du Cercle Saint Jean-Baptiste* (December 1955) 4–7.
———. "La Théologie du Salut dans le Christianisme Primitif: Le Livre de l'Agneau." *Bulletin du Cercle Saint Jean-Baptiste* (December 1956) 31–36.
———. "La θεωρια chez Grégoire de Nysse." In *Studia Patristica*, vol. XI, ed. F. L. Cross, 130–45. Berlin: Akademie-Verlag, 1972.
———. "The Timeliness of Teilhard de Chardin." *Philosophy Today* 6 (Fall 1962) 212–23.
———. "Tombeau Vide." *Bulletin Saint Jean-Baptiste* (January 1968) 104–13.
———. "Tout est Grace." *Axes* (June-July 1969) 40–41.
———. "Tout est Grace." *Bulletin du Cercle Saint Jean-Baptiste* (May 1955) 1–2.
———. "Toward a Theology of Hospitality." *The Catholic Worker* (June 1952) 4
———. "Les Traditions Secrétes des Apôtres." *Eranos-Jahrbuch* 31 (1962) 199–215.

———. "La Tradition selon Clément d'Alexandrie." In *Conferenze Patristiche, II: Aspettie della Tradizione*, ed. Jean Daniélou, 5–18. Roma: Institutum Patristicum Augustinianum, 1972.

———. "Le Traité de Centesima, Sexagesima, Tricesima et le Judéo-Christianisme Latin avant Tertullien." *Vigiliae Christianae* 25 (1971) 171–81.

———. "Le Traité 'sur les Enfants Morts Prématurément' de Grégoire de Nysse." *Vigiliae Christianae* 20 (1966) 159–82.

———. "Transcendance du Christianisme." *Études* 273 (1952) 289–303.

———. "The Transcendence of Christianity." In *Introduction to the Great Religions*, trans. Albert J. La Mothe, Jr., 133–42. Notre Dame, IN: Fides Publishers, 1964.

———. "Transcendence et Incarnation." *Dieu Vivant* 6 (1946) 91–96.

———. "Le Transfiguration de l'Âme par la Grâce." *Bulletin du Cercle Saint Jean-Baptiste* (May 1956) 5–7.

———. "Travaux Protestants sur l'Ecriture." *Bulletin du Cercle Saint Jean-Baptiste* (January 1949) 7–8.

———. "A Travers la Presse: La Mort de Gandhi ou la Mauvais Conscience de l'Occident Chrétien." *Études* 256 (1948) 402–4.

———. "A Travers les Revues: Christianisme et Progrés." *Études* 255 (1947) 399–402.

———. "Traversée de la Mer Rouge et Baptême aux Priemiers Siècles." *Recherches de Science Religieuse* 33 (1946) 402–30.

———. "Trinité et Angélologie dans la Théologie Judéo-Chrétienne." *Recherches de Science Religieuse* 45 (1957) 5–41.

———. "La Trinité dans l'Existence Humaine." *Bulletin du Cercle Saint Jean-Baptiste* (October-November 1964) 5–17.

———. "Trois Réponses Autorisées." *La Documentation Catholique* 64 (1967) 644–45.

———. "Trois Theologiens Anglicans." *Bulletin du Cercle Saint Jean-Baptiste* (January 1951) 6–9.

———. "The Truth about God." *L'Osservatore Romano* (January 13, 1972) 10.

———. "Truth and Error." *L'Osservatore Romano* (December 31, 1970) 11.

———. "Tu es Qui Venturus Es?." *Bulletin du Cercle Saint Jean-Baptiste* (January 1951) 1–3.

———. "Tu Solus Sanctus." *Bulletin du Cercle Saint Jean-Baptiste* (March 1950) 1–2.

———. "Les Tuniques de Peau chez Grégoire de Nysse." In *Glaube, Geist, Geschichte*, eds. Ernst Benz, Gerhard Müller and Winfred Zeller, 355–67. Leiden: Brill, 1967.

———. "Typologie et Allegorie chez Clément d'Alexandria." *Texte und Untersuchungen zur Geschichte der altchristlichen Literatur* 79 (1961) 50–57.

———. "La Typologie Biblique de Grégoire de Nysse." In *Studi in Onore di Alberto Pincherle*, ed. Alberto Pincherle, 185–96. Roma: Aterneo, 1967.

———. "La Typologie Biblique Traditionelle dans la Liturgie du Moyen-Age." *Settimane di Studio del Centro Italiano di Studi Sull'alto Medioevo* 10 (1963) 141–61.

———. "La Typologie de la Femme dans l'Ancien Testament." *La Vie Spirituelle* 80 (1949) 491–510.

———. "La Typologie D'Isaac dans le Christianisme Primitif." *Biblica* 28 (1947) 363–93.

———. "La Typologie Millenariste de la Semaine dans le Christianisme Primitif." *Vigiliae Christianae* 2 (January 1948) 1–16.

———. "La Typologie de la Semaine au IVe Siècle." *Recherches de Science Religieuse* 35 (1948) 382–411.

Bibliography

———. "D'Une Extrémité à l'Autre." *Bulletin du Cercle Saint Jean-Baptiste* (June-July 1964) 96–98.
———. "Unica Sponsa." *Bulletin du Cercle Saint Jean-Baptiste* (January 1952) 1–2.
———. "The Unique Church." *L'Osservatore Romano* (March 21, 1974) 11.
———. "Union des Chrétiens et Mission." *Bulletin du Cercle Saint Jean-Baptiste* (January 1952) 7–9.
———. "L'Union des Églises et l'Avenir du Monde." *La Documentation Catholique* 47 (1950) 219–20.
———. "L'Unité des Chrétiens et l'Avenir du Monde." In *Unité des Chrétiens et Conversión du Monde*, 9–24. Paris: Editions du Centurión, 1962.
———. "L'Unité des Chrétiens et l'Avenir du Monde." *Bulletin du Cercle Saint Jean-Baptiste* (June-July 1961) 64–73.
———. "L'Unité des Deux Testaments dans l'Œuvre d'Origéne." *Revue des Sciences Religieuses* 22 (1948) 27–56.
———. "Unité et Diversité Leçons de l'Âge Patristique." *Bulletin du Cercle Saint Jean-Baptiste* (October-November 1963) 18–26.
———. "Unité de l'Eglise et Diversité des Civilisations." *Bulletin du Cercle Saint Jean-Baptiste* (June-July 1957) 177–80.
———. "Unité et Pluralité en Matière de Théologie." In *Philosophies Chrétiennes*, 11–21. Paris: Fayard, 1955.
———. "Unité et Pluralité de la Pensée Chrétienne." *Études* 312 (1962) 3–16.
———. "The Universal Priesthood and the Ministerial Priesthood." *L'Osservatore Romano* (June 17, 1971) 6, 12.
———. "Ut Sint Unum." *Bulletin du Cercle Saint Jean-Baptiste* (January 1955) 1–2.
———. "Valeurs Spirituelles de la Communauté Atlantique." *Études* 302 (1959) 196–210.
———. "Le Ve Esdras et le Judéo-Christianisme Latin au Second Siècle." In *Ex Orbe Religionum*, edited by Geo Widengren, 162–71. Leiden: Brill, 1972.
———. "La Vérité de l'Homme." *Études* 310 (1961) 3–15.
———. "La Vie Intellectuelle en France." *Études* 246 (1945) 241–54.
———. "La Vie Monastique et ses Problèmes Actuels." *Dieu Vivant* 7 (1946) 59–60.
———. "La Vie et l'Œuvre de Mère Marie de la Providence." In *Le Purgatoire Mystére de Foi*, 109–123. Paris: Fayard, 1957.
———. "Vie d'Oraison et Presence au Monde Missionaire." *Documents UMC* 35 (November 1965) 50–57.
———. "La Vie Suspendue au Bois: Deut 28, 66 dans les Catéchèses archaïques." In *Eglise et Tradition*, edited by Johannes Betz, Heinrich Fries and Franz Xaver Arnold, 35–45. Le Puy: X. Mappus, 1963.
———. "Vigile sous les Armes." *Construire* 14 (1944) 114–34.
———. "La Vigne Eternelle." *Bulletin du Cercle Saint Jean-Baptiste* (March 1946) 3.
———. "La Vision Chrétienne de l'homme d'après le Concile." *Les Cahiers de Neuilly* (April 1966) 1–16.
———. "Une Vision Chretienne du Paradis." *Bulletin du Cercle Saint Jean-Baptiste* (May 1954) 11–13.
———. "La Vision de la Gloire." *Axes* (April-May 1975) 3–6.
———. "La Vision des Ossements Desséchés dans les Testimonia." *Recherches de sciences religieuse* 53 (1965) 220–33.
———. "Une Vision Nouvelle de la Littérature: Le XIXe Siècle d'Albert Thibaudet." *Études* 230 (1937) 484–93.

———. "Un Vision Nouvelle des Origines Chrétiennes, le Judéo-Christianisme." *Études* 327 (1967) 595–608.

———. "La Vision Totale chez Teilhard de Chardin." *Revue de Paris* 76 (1969) 1–9.

———. "The Vital Environment of the Sacraments." *L'Osservatore Romano* (May 11, 1972) 3, 12.

———. "Vocation des Cultures." *Axes* (October-November 1972) 5–7.

———. "La Vocation de Saint Jean-Baptiste." *Bulletin du Cercle Saint Jean-Baptiste* October-November 1962) 7–16.

———. "Vrais et Faux Prophetes." *Axes* (October-November 1973) 3–8.

———. "We are Still Living in Sacred History." *L'Osservatore Romano* (June 5, 1969) 12.

———. "Western Christianity and the Missions." *The Catholic Mind* 54 (1956) 18–26.

———. "What is Changing and What is Unchangeable in the Church." *Christ to the World* 18 (1973) 377–83.

———. "What the Dead Sea Scrolls Tell Us about Jesus." In *The Sources for the Life of Christ*, 22–32. New York: Hawthorn Books, 1962.

———. "What Good is Institutional Christianity." In *Christian Witness in the Secular City*, ed. Everett J. Morgan, 131–41. Chicago: Loyola University Press, 1970.

———. "'The Word Goes Forth': Christianity as a Missionary Religion." In *The Crucible of Christianity*, ed. Arnold Toynbee, 283–98. New York: World Publishing Company, 1969.

———. "XVIIIes Journées du Cercle." *Bulletin Saint Jean-Baptiste* (June-July 1965) 352–54.

———. "Y a-t-il une Nature Humaine?" In *De Homine: Studia Hodiernae Anthropologiae*, vol. II, 5–12. Romae: Officium Libri Catholici, 1972.

———. "Le Yogi et le Saint." *Études* 259 (1948) 289–305.

Reviews

———. *L'Ascèse Chrétienne*, by Dom Anselm Stolz. *Dieu Vivant* 11 (1948) 152–54.

———. *Le Culte dans l'Église Primitive*, by Oscar Cullman. *Dieu Vivant* 7 (1946) 135–38.

———. *De Resurrectione (Epistula ad Rheginum)*, by Ediderunt M. Malinine, H.-Ch. Puech, G. Quispel, W. Till, R. McL. Wilson and J. Zandee. *Vigiliae Christianae* 18 (1964) 187–88.

———. *Essai sur Moi-Même*, by Marcel Jouhandeau. *Études* 257 (1948) 127–28.

———. *Foi et Gnose*, by P. Th Camelot. *Dieu Vivant* 3 (1945) 135–38.

———. *Gnosis, La Connaissance Religieuse dans les Epîtres de Saint Paul*, by Paul Dupont. *Dieu Vivant* 18 (1951) 143–45.

———. *Gregorii Nysseni Contra Eunomium libri*, by Werner Jaeger. *Gnomon* 34 (1962) 557–59.

———. *Gregorii Nysseni: In inscriptiones Psalmorum; In sextum Psalmum; In Ecclesiasten Homilae*, ed. Jacobus McDonough and Paulus Alexander. *Gnomon* 36 (1964) 40–43.

———. *Gregorii Nysseni Opera dogmatica minora. I*, by Fridericus Müller. *Gnomon* 31 (1959) 612–15.

———. *Griechische Mythen in christlicher Deutung*, by Hugo Rahner. *Dieu Vivant* 10 (1948) 134–35.

———. *Les Harmonies des Deux Testaments*, by Joseph Coppens. *Dieu Vivant* 16 (1950) 149–53.

Bibliography

———. *Histoire d'Abraham ou les Premiers Âges de la Conscience Morale*, by Raïssa Maritain. *Études* 257 (1948) 132.
———. *Jésus Transfiguré*, by Harald Riesenfeld. *Dieu Vivant* 14 (1949) 143–45.
———. *Makarius, das Thomasevangelium und das Lied von der Perle*, G. Quispel. *Vigiliae Christianae* 22 (1968) 301–4.
———. *Origen's Doctrine of Tradition*, by R. P. C. Hanson. *Theologische Literaturzeitung* 84 (1959) 292–94.
———. *Les Origines de l'Église: Christianisme et Judaïsme aux Deux Premiers Siècles*, by Leonhard Goppelt. *Theologische Literaturzeitung* 89 (1964) 758–60.
———. *Philo: Foundation of Religious Philosophy in Judaism, Christianity and Islam*, by Harry Austryn Wolfson. *Revue de l'Histoire des Religions* 138 (1950) 230–32.
———. *The Philosophy of the Church Fathers, Vol. 1: Faith, Trinity, Incarnation*, by Harry Austryn Wolfson. *Theological Studies* 17 (1956) 594–98.
———. *Poèms (1910–1930)*, by T. S. Eliot. *Études* 257(1948) 131.
———. *Q. S. F. Tertulliani Adversus Iudeos*, by Hermann Tränkle. *Erasmus* 16 (1964) 653–57.
———. *Signum Crucis*, by Ercih Dinkler. *Erasmus* 20 (1968) 134–38.
———. *Sören Kierkegaard-Les Miettes Philosophiques*, by Paul Petit. *Études* 257 (1948) 116–17.
———. *The Terminology of the Holy Cross in Early Christian Literature as Based upon Old Testament Typology*, by Gerardus Quirinus Reijners. *Gnomon* 39 (1967) 256–58.
———. *Tractatus Tripertitus. Pars I: De Supernis*, by Ediderunt Rodolphe Kasser, Michel Malinine, Henri-Charles Puech, Gilles Quispel, Jan Zandee adiuvantibus Werner Vycichl and R. McL. Wilson. *Vigiliae Christianae* 29 (1975) 70–72.
———. *Traité d'Histoire des Religions*, by Mircéa Eliade. *La Maison-Dieu* 22 (1950) 170–72.
———. *Travaux Liturgiques de Doctrine et d'Histoire: II. Histoire: La Messe*, by B. Capelle. *La Maison-Dieu* 71 (1962) 202–3.
———. *Types of Religious Experiences Christian and Non-Christian*, by Joachim Wach. *Dieu Vivant* 23 (1953) 156–58.
———. *Zur typologie des Johannesevangeliums*, by Harald Sahlin. *Dieu Vivant* 18 (1951) 152–53.

Dictionary and Encyclopedia Entries

———. "Apostolic Church II. Apostolic Church." In *Sacramentum Mundi: An Encyclopedia of Theology*, 82–84. New York: Herder and Herder, 1968.
———. "Demon: II. Dans La Littérature Ecclésiastique jusqu'a Origène." In *Dictionnaire de Spiritualité Ascetique et Mystique: Doctrine et Histoire*, col. 152–89. Paris: Buchesne, 1932.
———. "Daniel." In *Reallexikon Für Antike und Christentum, Volume III*, 575–85. Stuttgart: Anton Hierseman, 1957.
———. "David." In *Reallexikon Für Antike und Christentum, Volume III*, 594–603. Stuttgart: Anton Hierseman, 1957.
———. "Exodus." In *Reallexikon Für Antike und Christentum, Volume VII*, 22–44. Stuttgart: Anton Hierseman, 1969.

Bibliography

———. "Exorcisme." In *Dictionnaire de Spiritualité Ascetique et Mystique: Doctrine et Histoire*, 1995–2004. Paris: Buchesne, 1932.

———. "Fels." In *Reallexikon Für Antike und Christentum, Volume VII*, 7723–32. Stuttgart: Anton Hierseman, 1969.

———. "Feuersäule." In *Reallexikon Für Antike und Christentum, Volume VII*, 786–90. Stuttgart: Anton Hierseman, 1969.

———. "Humanisme et Spiritualité." In *Dictionnaire de Spiritualité Ascetique et Mystique: Doctrine et Histoire*, 947–59. Paris: Buchesne, 1932.

———. "Judeo-Christianity." In *Sacramentum Mundi*, 210–13. New York: Herder & Herder, 1968.

———. "Mystique de la Ténèbre chez Grégoire de Nysse." In *Dictionnaire de Spiritualité Ascetique et Mystique: Doctrine et Histoire*, 1872–1885. Paris: Buchesne, 1932.

Interviews, Discussions, etc.

———. "Bercail Unique ou Petit Troupeau?" *Spiritus* 24 (August-September 1965) 278–88.

———. "A Cardinal Meets His Challengers." *U.S. Catholic/Jubilee* (October 1969) 6–13.

———. "The Central Idea of my Thought and of all my Life." *Christ to the World* 14 (1969) 322–25.

———. "Conférence de Presse du Cardinal Daniélou (1)." *La Documentation Catholique* (5 October 1969) 872–77.

———. "Confrontation." *Bulletin du Cercle Saint Jean-Baptiste* (June-July 1964) 47–55.

———. "Dialogue et Annonce de Jésus Christ." *Spiritus* 24 (August-September 1965) 240–53.

———. "Discours de Réception du Cardinal Daniélou a l'Académie Française." *La Documentation Catholique* (20 January 1974) 84–90.

———. "Écriture et Tradition." In *L'Ère des Ordinateurs*, 153–74. Paris: Desclée de Brouwer, 1966.

———. "In Connection with the Crisis of Religious Life." *Christ to the World* 18 (1973) 53–58.

———. "L'Idée Centrale de toute ma Pensée et de toute ma Vie." *Le Christ au Monde* 16 (1969) 348–51.

———. "Interview du Cardinal Daniélou." *La Documentation Catholique* (5 October 1969) 882.

———. "La Parole et le Salut du Monde." *Spiritus* 24 (August-September 1965) 254–77.

———. "Perspectives d'Avenir sur la Dialogue Méditerranéen." *Bulletin Saint Jean-Baptiste* (June-July 1966) 439–44.

———. "Présence de Claudel: Débat." in *La Pensée Religieuse de Claudel*. Paris: Desclee de Brouwer, 1969: 191–223.

———. "Réhabilitation de la Chrétienté?" *Ecclesia* 198 (1965) 75–80.

———. "Variations in Perspective on Secularization and Unbelief: Discussion by Harvey Cox, Jean Daniélou and Milan Machovec, under the Chairmanship of Peter Berger." In *The Culture of Unbelief*, 91–105. Berkeley: University of California Press, 1971.

———. "Y a-t-il une Crise de la Vie Religieuse?." *La Documentation Catholique* 69 (1972) 1029–31.

Secondary Sources

Auricchio, John. *The Future of Theology*. Staten Island, NY: Alba House, 1970.
Benedict XVI. *Deus Caritas Est*. Libereria Editrice Vaticana, 2005.
———. "Letter of His Holiness Benedict XVI to Cardinal Renato Raffaele Martino on the Occasion of the International Seminar organized by the Pontifical Council For Justice and Peace on 'Disarmament, Development and Peace: Prospects for Integral Disarmament.'" Libereria Editrice Vaticana, 2008.
Bianchi, Ugo. "L'Origène de J. Daniélou, Reconsidée." In *Origeniana Tertia: The Third Internacional Colloquium for Origen Studies*, 159–65. Roma: Edizioni dell'Ateneo, 1985.
Bloy, Léon. *Le Femme Pauvre*. Paris: Mercure de France, 1897.
Boersma, Hans. *Nouvelle Théologie and Sacramental Ontology: A Return to Mystery*. Oxford, 2009.
Bouillard, Henri. *Conversion et grâce chez. S. Thomas d'Aquin: Étude historique*. Paris: Aubier, 1944.
Boussard, Léon. "A l'académie Française: Le cardinal Daniélou sous la Coupole." *La Nouvelle Revue des Deux Mondes* (Decembre 1973) 564–68.
Bouyer, Louis. "Christianisme et Eschatologie." *La Vie Intellectuelle* (October 1948) 6–38.
———. *La Décompostion du Catholisme*. Paris: Aubier-Montagne, 1968.
———. "Mysticism/ An Essay on the History of the Word." In *Understanding Mysticism*, ed. Richard Woods: 42–55.
Boyancé, Pierre. "Philon d'Alexandria selon le P. Daniélou." *Revue des Études Grecques* 72 (1959) 377–84.
Boyle, Nicholas. *Who Are We Now?: Christian Humanism and the Global Market from Hegel to Heaney*. Notre Dame, IN: University of Notre Dame Press, 1998.
———. "Understanding Thatcherism." *New Blackfriars* 69 (1988) 307–24.
Burrell, David. "Christians, Muslims (and Jews) before the One God: Jean Daniélou on Mission Revisited." *Interpretation* 61 (2007) 34–41.
Candler, Peter M., Jr. "The Logic of Christian Humanism." *Communio* 36.1 (2009) 69–91
———. "The New Scholasticism: Where is it Going?" in *Thomism: A Very Critical Introduction*. Grand Rapids: Eerdmans, forthcoming.
Carré, A.-M. "Jean Daniélou." *The Tablet* 17 (April 24, 1976) 398–99.
———. *Parole et Culture: Le Cardinal Jean Daniélou*. Paris: Cerf, 1976.
Celsus. *On the True Doctrine: A Discourse against the Christians*. Translated by R. Joseph Hoffmann. Oxford: Oxford University Press, 1987.
Cessario, Romanus. "An Observation on Robert Lauder's Review of G. A. McCool, S.J." *The Thomist* 56 (October 1992) 701–10.
Chaney, Charles L. "An Introduction to the Missionary Thought of Jean Daniélou." *Occasional Bulletin* 17 (May 1966) 1–10.
Chenu, M. D. *La Théologie est-elle une Science?* Paris: Fayard, 1957.
Coffey, David. "Some Resources for the Students of *La nouvelle théologie*." *Philosophy & Theology* 11 (1999) 367–402.
Congar, Yves. *Le Mystère du Temple ou l'Économie de la Présence de Dieu à sa Créature de la Genèse à l'Apocalypse*. Paris: Cerf, 1958.
Connolly, James M. *The Voices of France: A Survey of Contemporary Theology in France*. New York: MacMillan, 1961.
Cullmann, Oscar. *Christ and Time*. Translated by Floyd Filson. London: SCM, 1951.

Bibliography

Daley, Brian. "The *Nouvelle Théologie* and the Patristic Revival: Sources, Symbols and the Science of Theology." *International Journal of Systematic Theology* 7 (October 2005) 362–82.

D'Ambrosio, Marcellino. "*Ressourcement* Theology, *Aggiornamento*, and the Hermeneutics of Tradition." *Communio* 18 (Winter 1991):530–55.

Davies, W. D. "Paul and Jewish Christianity according to Cardinal Daniélou: A Suggestion." *Recherches Science Religieuse* 60 (1972) 69–79.

Dawson, John David. *Christian Figural Reading and the Fashioning of Identity*. Berkeley: Unversity of California Press, 2002.

———. "Figural Reading and the Fashioning of Christian Identity in Boyarin, Auerbach and Frei." *Modern Theology* 14 (April 1998) 181–96.

De Boisdeffre, Pierre. "Le Père Daniélou." *La Nouvelle Revue des Deux Mondes* (March 1977) 534–43.

De Guibert, Joseph. *The Theology of the Spiritual Life*. Translated by Paul Barrett. New York: Sheed & Ward, 1953.

Delaney, John J. "Michael." In *Dictionary of Saints*, 2nd ed., 435. New York: Doubleday, 2003.

De Lange, Maurice. "L'Ecclesiologie de Jean Daniélou." Ph.D. diss., Université Laval, 1990.

De Lubac, Henri. "Cardinal Daniélou: an Evangelical Man." *L'Osservatore Romano* (August 8, 1974) 7.

———. *Catholicisme: les Apsects Sociaux du Dogme*. Paris: Cerf, 1938.

———. *Le Drame de l'Humanisme Athée*. Paris: Éditions Spes, 1944.

———. *Mémoire sur l'occasion des mes écrits*. Belgium: Culture et Verité. 1989.

———. "On the Death of Cardinal Daniélou." *Communio* 2 (1975) 93–95.

———. "La recherché d'un homme nouveau." In *Affrontements mystiques*. Paris: Éditions du Témoignage chrétien, 1949) 2–92.

Donnelley, Philip J. "Current Theology: On the Development of the Dogma of the Supernatural." *Theological Studies* 8 (September 1947) 471–91.

Dupuy, Michel. "Présence de Dieu." in *Dictionairre de Spiritualité, Ascétique et Mystique, Doctrine et Histoire, Tome XII*. Paris: Beauchesne, 1986.

Escobar, Julio Roque de. "The Death of Cardinal Daniélou." *Communio* 2 (1975) 317–19.

———. "Reflections on the Death of Cardinal Daniélou." *Communio* 3 (1975) 318–19.

Fontaine, Jacques. *Actualité de Jean Daniélou*. Paris: Cerf, 2006.

———. "In Memoriam: Jean Daniélou." *Revue des Études Latines* 51 (1974) 526–27.

Foster, Edgar G. "Daniélou and the Angelomorphic Christology of Tertullian." In *Angelomorphic Christology and the Exegesis of Psalm 8:5 in Tertullian's Adversus Praxean: An Examination of Tertullian's Reluctance to Attribute Angelic Properties to the Son of God*, 1–18. New York: University Press of America: 2006.

Frei, Fritz. *Médiation Unique et Transfiguration Univerelle: Thèmes christologiques et leurs perspectives missionaries dans la pensée de J. Daniélou*. Berne: Peter Lang, 1981.

Geffré, Claude. "Nouvelle théologie." In *The Encyclopedia of Christianity, vol. 3*. Grand Rapids: Eerdrmans, 1999.

Garrigou-Lagrange, Réginald. *Perfection chrétienne et contemplation*. Paris: Desclee, 1923.

Gilson, Étienne. *Letters of Étienne Gilson to Henri de Lubac*, trans. Mary Emily Hamilton. San Francisco: Ignatius Press, 1988.

Greenstock, David L. "Thomism and the New Theology." *Thomist* 13 (1950) 567–96.

Guggenheim, Antoine. "La Théologie de l'Accomplissement de Jean Daniélou." *Nouvelle Revue Théologique* 128 (2006) 240–57.

Bibliography

Hanby, Michael. "Desire: Augustine beyond Western Subjectivity." In *Radical Orthodoxy: A New Theology*, edited by John Milbank, Catherine Pickstock, and Graham Ward. London: Routledge, 1999.

Henry, P. "The Christian Philosophy of History." *Theological Studies* 13 (1952) 419–32.

International Theological Commission. *Communion and Stewardship: Human Persons Created in the Image of God*. Rome: 2000–2002.

Jacquin, Françoise. *Histoire du Cercle Saint Jean-Baptiste: L'Enseignement du Père Daniélou*. Paris: Beauchesne, 1987.

———. "Le Père Daniélou: Le Particulier et l'Universel." In *Histoire Religieuse: Histoire Globale, Histoire Ouverte: Mélanges Offerts à Jacques Gadille*, 433–49. Paris: Beauchesne, 1992.

Jeffords, Clayton N. *Reading the Apostolic Fathers: An Introduction*. Peabody, MA: Hendrickson, 1996.

John, Eric. "Daniélou on History." *The Downside Review* 72 (1953) 2–15.

Johnston, William. *The Inner Eye of Love*. London: Harper Collins, 1990.

Julian, John. "Veni Creator Spiritus." In *Dictionary of Hymnology*, 2 vols., edited by John Julian. Grand Rapids: Kregel, 1985.

Kerr, Fergus. *Twentieth-Century Catholic Theologians: From Neoscholasticism to Nuptial Mysticism*. Oxford: Blackwell, 2007.

Kraft, R. A. "In Search of 'Jewish Christianity' and its 'Theology': Problems of Definition and Methodology." *Recherches Science Religieuse* 60 (1972) 81–92.

Laboudette, M., M-J. Nicolas, and R. L. Bruckberger. *Dialogue Théologique*. Saint-Maximin: Les Arcades, 1947.

Lauder, Robert E. "On Being or Not Being a Thomist." *The Thomist* 55 (April 1991) 301–19.

Lebeau, Paul. *Jean Daniélou*. Paris: Fleurs, 1967.

LeClercq, Jean. "Action and Contemplation: Two Ways Toward the Ultimate Reality." In E. Glenn Hinson, *Spirituality in an Ecumenical Perspective*. Louisville: Westminster John Knox, 1993.

———. *The Love and Learning and the Desire for God: A Study of Monastic Culture*. Translated by Catherine Misrahi. New York: Fordham University Press, 2001.

Leprince-Ringuet, Louis. "Le cardinal Jean Daniélou." *La Nouvelle Revue des Deux Mondes* (July 1974) 3–5.

Louth, Andrew. *Theology and Spirituality*. Oxford: SLG, 1978.

———. *Discerning the Mystery: An Essay on the Nature of Theology*. Oxford: Clarendon Press, 1983.

Löwith, Karl. *Meaning in History: The Theological Implications of the Philosophy of History*. Chicago: University of Chicago Press, 1949.

Mahue, René. "Le Cardinal Daniélou et l'Unesco." *Nouvelle Revue des Deux Mondes* (1974) 6–10.

Maritain, Jacques. *Humanisme Intégral: Problèmes Temporels et Spirituels d'une Nouvelle Chrétienté*. Paris: Aubier, 1936.

———. *Scholasticism and Politics*, trans. Mortimer J. Adler. Garden City, NY: Image, 1960.

Marshner, W. H. "Cardinal Daniélou on Liturgy." *Sacred Music* 101 (1974) 10–15

Mauriac, *Le Mystère Frontenac*. Paris: Grasset, 1933.

Mayeski, Marie Anne. "Catholic Theology and the History of Exegesis." *Theological Studies* 62 (March 2001) 140–53.

Bibliography

Mayeur, Jean-Marie. "Des Clercs devant la Religion Populaire: Aux Origines d'un Débat." In *La Religion Populaire*, 341–46. Paris: Centre National de la Recherche Scientifique, 1979.

McCool, Gerald A. *Catholic Theology in the Nineteenth Century: The Quest for a Unitary Method*. New York: Seabury, 1977.

———. *From Unity to Pluralism: The Internal Evolution of Thomism*. New York: University of Fordham Press, 1989.

McGinn, Bernard. *The Foundations of Mysticism: Origins to the Fifth Century*. New York: Crossroad, 1991.

———. "The Letter and the Spirit: Spirituality as an Academic Discipline." *Christian Spirituality Bulletin* 1 (Fall 1993) 2–10.

McGinn, Bernard, and Patricia Ferris McGinn. *Early Christian Mystics: The Divine Vision of the Spiritual Masters*. New York: Crossroad, 2003.

McIntosh, Mark. *Mystical Theology: The Integrity of Spirituality and Theology*. Oxford: Blackwell, 1998.

Merton, Thomas. *Contemplation in a World of Action*. Notre Dame, IN: University of Notre Dame Press, 1998.

Mettepenninggen, Jürgen. *Nouvelle Théologie New Theology" Inheritor of Modernism, Precursor of Vatican II*. New York: T. & T. Clark, 2010.

Milbank, John. *Theology and Social Theory: Beyond Secular Reason*. 2nd ed. Oxford: Blackwell, 2006.

Mimouni, Simon C. "Le Judéo-Christianisme Ancien dans l'Historiographie du XIX éme et du XXéme Siècle." *Revue des Études Juives* 151 (1992) 419–28.

Murray, John Courtney. "Current Theology: *Sources Chrétiennes*." *Theological Studies*, 9 (1948) 250–89.

Nichols, Aidan. *Catholic Thought Since the Enlightenment*. Pretoria: University of South Africa, 1998.

———. *The Service of Glory: The Catechism of the Catholic Church on Worship, Ethics and Spirituality*. Stuebenville, OH: Franciscan University Press, 1997.

———. *The Shape of Catholic: An Introduction to Its Sources, Principles, and History*. Collegeville, MN: Liturgical, 1991

———. "The Theology of Jean Daniélou: Epochs, Correspondences, and the Orders of the Real." *New Blackfriars* 91 (January, 2010) 46–65.

———. "Thomism and the Nouvelle Théologie." *The Thomist* 64 (January 2000) 1–19.

Nygren, Anders. *Den kristna kärlekstanken genom tiderna: Eros and Agape*. Stockholm, 1930.

O'Grady, Desmond. "Jean Daniélou." *U.S. Catholic* 33 (1967) 28–30.

Peddicord, Richard. *The Sacred Monster of Thomism: An Introduction to the Life and Legacy of Reginald Garrigou-Lagrange*. South Bend, IN: St. Augustine's, 2004.

Pierce, Joanne M. and Michael Downey. *Source and Summit: Commemorating Josef A. Jungmann, S. J.* Collegeville, MN: Liturgical, 1999.

Pottier, Bernard. "Le Grégoire de Nysse de Jean Daniélou." *Nouvelle Revue Théologique* 128 (2006) 258–73.

Prunieres, Jérôme G. "L'itinéraire du P. Daniélou au delà des distinctions." *Études Franciscaines* 18 (1968) 32–53.

Purcell, Michael. "The Natural Desire for the Beatific Vision: Desiring the other in Levinas and 'La Nouvelle Théologie.'" *Philosophy & Theology* 9 (1995) 29–48.

Rahner, Hugo. "La Théologie Catholique de l'Histoire." *Dieu Vivant* 10 (1948) 93–115.

Bibliography

Rondeau, Marie-Joséphe. *Jean Daniélou, 1905–1974*. Paris: Cerf, 1975.

———. "Jean Daniélou, Henri-Irénée Marrou et le Renouveau des Études Patristiques." In *Les Pères de l'Église au XXe Siècles: Histoire, Littérature, Théologie: L'Aventure des Sources Chrétiennes*, 351–78. Paris: Cerf, 1997.

———. "Le Père Daniélou au Concile." In *Le Deuxième Concile du Vatican (1959–1965)*, 333–37. Rome: Ecole Française de Rome, 1989.

Rondeau, Marie-Joséphe and Brian Van Hove. "Cardinal Jean Daniélou, S.J." *Fellowship of Catholic Scholars Quarterly* 28 (Summer 2005) 26–29.

Schoof, Mark. *A Survey of Catholic Theology, 1800–1970*. Translated by N. D. Smith. Glen Rock, NJ: Newman, 1970.

Scully, Eileen. *Grace and Human Freedom in the Theology of Henri Bouillard*. Bethesda, MD: Academic, 2007.

———. "Henri Bouillard and the 'Nouvelle Théologie.'" *Grail* 7 (Summer 1991) 73–86.

Sheldrake, Philip. *Spirituality & History: Questions of Interpretation and Method*, rev. ed. Maryknoll, NY: Orbis, 1995.

Simon, Marcel. "Réflexions sur le Judéo-Christianisme." In *Christianity, Judaism and other Greco-Roman Sects*, 53–76. Leiden: Brill, 1975.

Smits, Brendan. "Epiphany of Love: The Thought of J. Daniélou on Poverty." *Round Table* 29 (1964) 127–37.

Stolz, Anselm. *The Doctrine of Spiritual Perfection*. New York: Crossroad, 2001.

Tanquerey, Adolphe. *Précis de théologie ascétique et mystique*. Paris: Société de s. Jean l'évangéliste, Desclée et Cie, 1923.

Turner, Denis. *The Darkness of God: Negativity in Christian Mysticism*. Cambridge: Cambridge University Press, 1995.

Turner, H. E. W. *The Pattern of Christian Truth: A Study in the Relations between Orthodoxy and Heresy in the Early Church*. London: A. R. Mowbray, 1954.

Vallquist, Gunnel. "Jean Cardinal Daniélou." *The Month* (October 1974) 741–43.

Von Balthasar, Hans Urs. *Man in History: A Theological Study*. London: Sheed & Ward, 1968.

———. *Prayer*. Translated by Graham Harrison. San Francisco: Ignatius, 1986.

———. "Theology and Sanctity." In *Explorations in Theology, I: The Word Made Flesh*, translated by A. V. Littledale and Alexander Dru, 181–210. San Francisco: Ignatius, 1989.

———. *A Theology of History*. San Francisco: Ignatius, 1994.

———. "Toward a Theology of Christian Prayer." *Communio* 12 (Fall 1985) 245–57.

Wainwright, Geoffrey. "'Bible et Liturgie': Daniélou's Work Revisited." *Studia Liturgica* 22 (1992) 154–62.

———. "«Bible et Liturgie» Quarante ans après Daniélou." *La Maison-Dieu* 189 (1992) 41–53.

Ward. Maisie. *France Pagan? The Mission of Abbé Godin*. London: Sheed & Ward, 1949.

Weigel, George. "John Paul II and the Crisis of Humanism." *First Things* 98 (December 1999) 31–36.

Williams, A. N. "The Future of the Past: The Contemporary Significance of the *Nouvelle Théologie*." *International Journal of Systematic Theology* 7 (October 2005) 347–61.

Williams, Rowan. *Christian Spirituality: A Theological Journey from the New Testament to Luther and St. John of the Cross*. Atlanta.: John Knox, 1979.

———. *The Dwelling of the Light: Praying with the Icons of Christ*. Grand Rapids: Eerdmans, 2003.

Wood, Susan K. *Spiritual Exegesis and the Church in the Theology of Henri de Lubac.* Grand Rapids: Eerdmans, 1998.